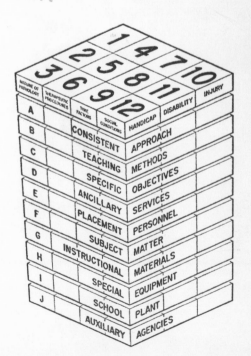

PRESCRIPTIVE TEACHING

PRESCRIPTIVE TEACHING

LAURENCE J. PETER
University of British Columbia

McGRAW-HILL BOOK COMPANY

New York · St. Louis · San Francisco
Toronto · London · Sydney

PRESCRIPTIVE TEACHING

FOREWORD

Teaching, evaluating, and guiding the atypical child have served as challenges for some of the greatest minds of the greatest educators of all time. Names such as Montessori, Sequin, Itard, Witmer, Grace Fernald, and Anne Sullivan are immediately recalled. Many of the educational methods first developed for handicapped children have been found useful in the education of all children.

The advent of psychological evaluation, the refinement of medical diagnostic techniques, and the social welfare and rehabilitation movement have all contributed greatly to our understanding of individual children. Because of the contributions of various fields, we now take the interdisciplinary team concept for granted in our planning for handicapped children. Unfortunately, with such a team of specialists with diverse viewpoints helping the handicapped child, we have all too often seen fractionalized, uncoordinated efforts. Almost all professional persons in a pupil personnel service program or a special education program in almost any school system have, at times, been discouraged by the lack of a unified approach or by failures in the breakdown of communication among members of the clinic team, or by the lack of adequate follow-through.

The most egregious breach in professional effort in school psychological services, in my opinion, has been the failure to extrapolate psychological and sociological findings into day-to-day classroom practices for the individual child studied. The interdisciplinary team has all too often only been a convenient euphemism when specific educational recommendations were needed.

Professor Laurence J. Peter has provided a rationale as a basis for efforts to coordinate and operationalize psychological test findings and case-history data regarding children referred for special services so that these children can be more adequately helped in the context of the school. He has appropriately termed his approach Prescriptive Teaching.

Dr. Peter has developed a theoretical model for a *rapprochement* among the various specialists who work with the handicapped. This multidimensional model provides a structure for medical, psychological, and social-work diagnoses to be converted into relevant educational terms and, furthermore, provides for adequate follow-through on specific recommendations. Dr. Peter's approach emphasizes frequent consultation by the pupil personnel specialist with the child's classroom teacher. In this book the reader will find a systematic, direct approach for meeting the needs of the child who is having educational difficulties in the regular or special class.

The approach Dr. Peter outlines is based on careful planning for each individual child before an educational prescription is agreed upon. Consequently, this approach does not suffer from "hardening of the categories," an endemic disorder in special education and guidance programs all too frequently found in the planning for exceptional children.

As we survey some of the outstanding centers for educating exceptional children throughout the United States and Canada, we find many dedicated psychologists and teachers already applying many of the techniques described in this book. Dr. Peter, however, has gone beyond the specific techniques to a theoretical rationale and thus provides a sound underpinning for educational methodology.

Most readers are probably familiar with a number of skillful, perceptive special educators in their locale. However, the reader will want to examine especially the work of Elizabeth Freidus at the Lexington School for the Deaf and of Elsa Haeusserman at the Brooklyn Jewish Hospital. In Los Angeles, there are several settings where outstanding prescriptive teaching is now going on, notably the Clinic School at UCLA, the Marianne Frostig School, and the Belle Dubnoff School. In the Midwest, the Coleman School in Detroit for the neurologically handicapped and the Orthogenic School at the University of Chicago for emotionally disturbed children should be mentioned. The Devereaux Schools on both the East and West Coasts have pioneered in many aspects of prescriptive teaching.

The late Grace Fernald's book *Remedial Techniques in Basic School Subjects,* published by the McGraw-Hill Book

Company in 1943, has remained in print unchanged for over twenty years and is now approaching the level of a classic in educational literature. The methods presented in this earlier book have helped thousands of children. Dr. Peter has utilized the methods of Dr. Fernald in his work in the British Columbia schools, as well as some of the methods of those specialists mentioned in the preceding paragraph.

I feel that Professor Peter in this volume has been able to synthesize much knowledge concerning exceptional children and normal children. His book represents the first attempt to develop a complete circuit with feedback, methodology, and general principle for translating interdisciplinary diagnosis of the problems of a wide range of exceptional and normal children into educational modification and/or remediation. He also provides a theoretical rationale for a systematic approach to educating and guiding a large segment of our school population, and in this way he has made a significant contribution to the fields of school psychology, guidance, and special education.

JAMES F. MAGARY, Ph.D.

Formerly Psychological Coordinator,
Devereux Schools, and later
Coordinator of Special Education
at the University of Southern California

PREFACE

Prescriptive teaching deals with the means of achieving sound educational goals for disturbed or handicapped children. It is based on an interdisciplinary approach which accomplishes therapeutic aims by educational means. Prescriptive teaching provides a methodology for dealing with a wide range of problems in the regular classroom or in special education.

There has been a long-standing need for a systematic approach to link medical, psychological, and social diagnoses to educational practices. Prescriptive teaching provides the missing link for translating interdisciplinary diagnosis into educational implementation.

This book is addressed to school psychologists, school counselors, and others responsible for converting diagnostic findings into recommendations for teachers and other school personnel. As a textbook it is intended to be used for courses in school psychology and counseling. It will be of particular interest to those in the field of special education and should prove to be worthwhile supplementary reading for courses in administration, guidance, pupil personnel practices, mental health, introduction to exceptional children, psychological foundations of education, and rehabilitation counseling.

The author has also kept in mind that students and professional workers in such fields as medicine, psychiatry, social work, nursing, and speech therapy may want to investigate their contribution to the educational program. Therefore, the information is presented in such a way that it will be comprehensible and informative to readers who are not specialists in psychology.

Necessarily, in so vast a field, the analysis of some topics will not include the amount of detail that a reader may want. References are provided which deal more comprehensively with each topic, so that the reader can pursue his interests in a more intensive manner. This allows the present volume to deal more fully with the unique contributions of prescriptive teaching.

An ultimate application of the study of human psychology is the alteration of a person's behavior into more constructive channels. Prescriptive teaching is a practical program for achieving that purpose. It achieves this by focusing attention on the interaction of the child with his environment and on the environmental changes associated with improved learning.

LAURENCE J. PETER

CONTENTS

xi

1

INTRODUCTION

Prescriptive teaching is a method of utilizing diagnostic information for the modification of educational programs for children with problems. It accomplishes this purpose by determining the educational relevance of the child's disability, and devising teaching procedures to yield desirable changes in the child's academic progress, emotional condition, and social adjustment.

DEFINITION OF PRESCRIPTIVE TEACHING

The word "prescribe" means literally to "write beforehand" and "prescriptive," to "set down the direction." If teaching is based upon sound learning principles, these principles prescribe teaching. If modifications of teaching are made for the handicapped child and these modifications are based upon a diagnosis of the child's difficulty, the diagnosis prescribes the modification of teaching. If diagnosis does not help determine the direction of teaching, it has little value educationally. In this context, teaching includes any school function which facilitates learning, the most important of which is instruction in the classroom. Prescriptive teaching for the handicapped child consists of those modifications of instruction and other school variables which are based upon individual diagnosis in the direction of assisting the child's learning. On the basis of all available facts regarding the child with problems, the required individual educational program is prescribed This prescrip-

tion is based on a scientific rationale which relates the specific elements
of the educational program to diagnostic information.

Prescriptive teaching is implemented through the modification of
the variable factors in the school such as the teacher's attitude or
approach, his teaching methods, the specific educational objectives for
the child, special services, placement and personnel, curriculum, instructional materials, and equipment.

With certain special education problems this approach is not new.
Educators working with handicapped children have developed techniques which result in improved learning for the mentally retarded,
blind, deaf, and orthopedically disabled. These techniques are a trib-
ute to the devotion and ingenuity of teachers. The story is well known
of a teacher, Anne Sullivan, who went to Alabama many years ago
and established communication with the mind of a blind and deaf
child named Helen Keller.

Those of us who work in schools are familiar with less well-known
examples of teachers who have accomplished outstanding results with
handicapped children. We have seen the seriously handicapped child
who, given a skilled teacher with an effective approach, makes significant progress in his learning. Teachers working with withdrawn, hostile, or insecure children have helped them find appropriate activities,
acceptable expressions of feelings, and opportunities to learn their
real strengths and adequacies. Children from extremely deprived social situations, or with severe physical and emotional disabilities, have
learned to overcome these disabilities or their handicapping consequences. Through the use of the organized structure of prescriptive
teaching, effective programs can be devised for children and favorable
results achieved with greater frequency than formerly.

Prescriptive teaching starts with the regular contact between child
and teacher in the classroom. The modification of this contact in a
manner consistent with the child's special needs, along with other
modifications, achieves improved interaction within the classroom and
more effective learning.

UTILIZATION OF DIAGNOSTIC RESOURCES

In most communities a child can be referred by the school to
a variety of diagnostic and treatment resources, such as hospitals,
mental-hygiene and child-guidance clinics, social agencies, and school

psychological and other services (Andrew and Willey, 1958). It is appropriate that the schools have become more aware of these services and that children are being referred with increasing frequency, but these services are essentially roads away from education and into other fields. In practice the progression from teacher to other resources varies from one school system to another, but the direction is usually the same. The child presenting problems is referred by the teacher to the school administration or school counselor, then to the school psychologist, school social worker, school nurse, child-guidance clinic, social agency, or psychiatric clinic. The resources vary, but the movement is always out or away from the classroom. It is not uncommon to see a problem originally defined as a learning problem redefined as a health problem or as personality deviation, and thus the road away from the classroom is established. Prescriptive teaching is essentially a road back. To establish the road back so that medical, psychological, and social-work recommendations are implemented in the classroom requires that the handicapping consequences to the learning of each disabled child be determined and that diagnostic findings be converted into pedagogical terms.

As a method, prescriptive teaching follows a procedure which involves moving both out of and back into education. In moving out, the method follows the generally accepted practices of referral to psychologists, psychiatrists, social workers, speech therapists, medical practitioners, and others. In moving back into education, it establishes what is educationally relevant in terms of the handicapping consequence to learning. The process then converts this into a prescription for teaching which is communicated to the teacher and to others who are responsible for action, so that implementation can take place. Follow-up and evaluation of results and, where desirable, further diagnosis, modification, and follow-up are included. By moving back into education this process brings the resources of the school to bear on the problems in a way which achieves positive results.

It is important that a more effective link be established between the area of diagnosis and the area of action within the school for the following reasons:

1. The school is the one institution where nearly all children have social contact which can be positively used if therapeutic concepts are converted into learning terms.

2. Overcoming handicaps and most changes in behavior involve learning. Improvement in emotional state involves

learning new emotional responses and the school has responsibility for the promotion of appropriate learning.

3. The educator's area of competency is in teaching and learning. If the relevant aspects of medical, psychiatric, psychological, and social-work diagnostic findings are converted into pedagogical terms, the teacher can bring his skills to bear on the problem.

4. Coordination and integration of services in the interest of the handicapped child are most effective when areas of responsibility are defined. Differentiation of areas of competency and responsibility must be accomplished before effective integration of services can take place. Educators, then, make their contribution toward the relief of suffering of the maladjusted child through teaching, while other professions make their contributions through their special competencies.

5. Some maladjusted children come from homes that cannot be reached by existing clinical and psychiatric services. Some parents seem to be unable to cooperate with these attempts to help their child. But the school is an important influence in the child's life, and this influence can be exercised on the child's behalf, consistent with clinical findings, whether the parents become involved in the treatment or not. In school he is in close contact with the teacher. This contact in the classroom and the total school situation can be modified so that each child's needs are met, and the reduction of underachievement, improvement of interaction within the classroom, and modification of emotional problems are realized more fully although limited by the lack of parental involvement in treatment.

The advances made in psychological measurement, social work, psychiatry, and educational psychology have all assisted in providing various types of information which can help teachers assist the child in learning. The comprehensive diagnostic procedures of the child-guidance clinic and the clinic conferences have provided for greater understanding of the child and improved communication between the different professions involved (Gilbert, 1957).

The full benefit to the handicapped child of this combination of specialists is yet to be realized. A greater realization of the therapeutic potential of the school through a more systematic methodology for implementing diagnostic findings is within our professional grasp. Prescriptive teaching has been developed to focus information from all available resources on the full utilization of the potentialities of the school to meet the needs of the child. This individualization of education is frequently stated as an aim of guidance in the school. Although the emphasis in this book is on education of the disturbed or handicapped child, the same principles apply to all children.

PRINCIPLES OF GUIDANCE

Guidance is a part of the individualization of education to assist each pupil in developing to his highest possible fulfillment through the actualization of his potentialities (Miller, 1961). The school psychologist helping place a child effectively in relation to educational and vocational opportunities, the counselor working with an individual or group, the principal in making provision for an individual, the teacher in promoting the optimal development of the unique individuality of a child, are all fulfilling a guidance function. Guidance is a point of view that recognizes the worth of the individual and affects the total school program (Woodbury, 1958).

There are two aspects to this total concept of guidance: process and service. The guidance process in education refers to activities which assist pupils in adjustment and the attainment of educational objectives such as self-realization, human relationships, and civic responsibility. This process is part of instruction, curriculum, and the total school program. The organized program of services which is primarily the responsibility of guidance specialists includes counseling, testing, individual inventory, and occupational information and placement and is referred to as guidance services.

Guidance as process is particularly concerned with assisting individual students to discover their needs, assess their potentialities, develop their life purposes, formulate plans, and implement procedures toward self-actualization (Willey and Andrew, 1955). Teaching involves both instruction and guidance as inseparable functions. Because counselors, school psychologists, school social workers, speech therapists, mental hygienists, and school principals are all involved in guidance along with the teacher, it cannot be delegated in a discrete manner to separate functionaries. Guidance as process is continuous assistance to the developing individual as a part of the total process of education. Some objectives of guidance are the same as the objectives of instruction. Good instruction will always include some guidance, but good guidance includes more than teaching. Guidance includes such services as counseling, testing, and placement.

A major consideration is how guidance services can best support the guidance process. The problems involved are numerous; major problems result from the large number of ideas about guidance, including the organization and administration of services, the question of who should provide and who should receive services, the qualification of specialists and their relationships to nonspecialists, and a lack of research evidence to determine which ideas have greatest validity. Studies of guidance services are predominantly surveys and descriptions (Dugan, 1960), and few deal with outcomes. Other problems such as budget, staff, and qualifications could be resolved in time if this major difficulty were removed. As long as we have this abundance of ideas about guidance with a comparative paucity of adequate research regarding the outcome of these ideas, any proposals for the organization of guidance services should include proposals for research.

The recommendations for guidance services in a prescriptive teaching program are based upon the following assumptions:

1. Guidance services are justified to the extent that they facilitate the guidance process as outlined above.

2. Guidance services should fulfill functions not being served by the guidance process in other divisions of the educational program.

3. Guidance services concerned with developmental tasks or problems of normal children or adjustment problems of handicapped or disturbed children are serving the same objective of promoting individual growth and development.

4. Guidance services may need to vary for different groups of children, such as the kindergarten pupil and the high school senior as well as the mentally retarded, normal, gifted, and maladjusted.

5. Guidance services should be appropriate to the school or school system and to the educational and general developmental level of the child. These assumptions apply equally at various levels in the school.

Elementary School Guidance Services

Guidance services are relatively new to elementary schools and are generally not provided in quantity sufficient for all children. Services are usually provided only for children who are considered to be maladjusted. This practice may be missing some of the guidance potential for prevention of problems and for promotion of wholesome development in nonpathological cases. It is, therefore, recommended that services be provided which are available to all children rather than to handicapped children only (Detjen and Detjen, 1963).

There are children whose impairment of ability to learn is a result of serious neurotic conflicts. These children should receive psychiatric as well as psychological evaluation. There are many children who have learning problems that are not embedded deeply in their psychic structure. Their underachievement or behavior problem is more an expressive symptom and may be helped by school programs that take their problems into account. For example, a child may be underachieving as a result of expression of derogatory self-regard stemming from sibling rivalry. When he is given recognition for achievement in an area where his sibling has not demonstrated success, he may improve his responses in other areas. A child with visual-motor difficulties may respond to perceptual training and overcome his learning problem. These children are not seriously disturbed or ill and can overcome their problems through relatively minor educational modifications. It appears that the majority of learning problems are not of the deeply embedded type and that most will respond to school programs if appropriate modifications are made for the individual. The intensive study and treatment of a few sick children will make only a small contribution to the understanding of minor but numerous learning problems.

Counseling

Children entering primary school are not able to derive the same benefits from counseling as are more mature students. This is due in part to their inability to deal adequately with their behavior symbolically or plan their future behavior meaningfully, and in part to the nature of their ongoing relationships with adults. Young children, coming to school to learn to read and write, see teachers and school personnel as people in authority or parental surrogates directing them

toward this objective. Because of the preponderance of directive treatment by adults, the immaturity of the child, and very limited contact
with a counselor, the child may have difficulty in perceiving the counselor as other than another directing person. He may be confused or
disappointed by an authority who does not have answers to his problems. This problem may be overcome by modification of counseling
techniques to meet the developmental level of the child, by increasing
counselor time with elementary children, or by the teacher providing
the ongoing guidance and counseling.

When behavior problems arise involving primary children, it is
usually most effective to counsel them near the time and place of the
incident. A child who is upset and who cannot verbalize will frequently become quite coherent and explain the essence of what happened when taken to the scene of the upsetting incident. From a
practical standpoint, this kind of counseling is best performed by the
teacher. Heffernan (1951) discusses the advantage of counseling children singly and in groups at the time of their difficulty or disputes.
Young children can often express feelings in drawings and paintings
as well as in play therapy. If the guidance worker is competent to use
these techniques, useful insights regarding primary pupils can be obtained along with early treatment and prevention.

It is important to consider the appropriateness of the counseling
techniques employed with young children. As children grow and
mature, they develop ability to deal symbolically with behavior and
can therefore derive insight from interviews with the counselor in an
office. Although this is a developmental continuum with a gradual
change of counseling technique indicated, there are some general suggestions that the change in direction toward specialist counseling
should occur around the time the child is nine years old. There are
many variables such as mental age and social and emotional immaturities and superiorities which account for individual differences, but
generally around the time children move from primary to intermediate divisions of elementary schools they are capable of developing
useful insights about their behavior. They have also developed logical
thinking (Inhelder and Piaget, 1958) to an appropriate level. This is
only a general guide and the individual response should always be the
determining factor in providing the kind of counseling to meet individual needs.

Counseling is effective in gaining understandings of the individual
child which are important to guidance as process. Because the teacher
will give guidance of one kind or another, regardless of the special-

ist's opinion regarding his qualifications, it is essential that any effective guidance program in the elementary school be teacher-centered. Prescriptive teaching is a teacher-centered guidance program with the responsibility of making teacher guidance good guidance. The teacher has the best opportunity to learn about the child, and when he is helped to make effective use of this opportunity, he makes a superior contribution to the guidance process (Hiesner, 1959). This approach also supports the professional status of the teacher. If the teacher is not included, there is an implication that he is not a good teacher. Carey (1957) found that with the hiring of pupil personnel specialists, those guidance responsibilities previously performed by teachers and administrators had been too frequently shifted to these specialists. She found much confusion concerning specific roles of staff members in the guidance of individual pupils and conducted a study which compared specialist-centered with teacher-centered guidance programs. She found that the teacher-centered approach, where the guidance specialist had the role of an aid to the teacher, contributed more to the guidance process. The nature of requests for additional help showed greater understanding of child growth and development on the part of teachers and principals. Requests for help contained more complete and usable information. The achievement of appropriate guidance roles by school staff enabled the guidance specialists to fulfill a more effective role in tasks which required training beyond that ordinarily expected of teachers; through in-service education they worked with the teachers and administrators to strengthen their guidance skills and knowledge.

In-service Responsibility

Much of teaching is dependent upon the teacher-pupil relationship, but teacher training and practice teaching seldom provide opportunities for working through this relationship. Emphasis is placed on preparing lessons and working with children in classes or groups. Child development becomes meaningful when the teacher's understanding of a child is developed through a relationship over an extended period of time. Understanding through this relationship is encouraged when consultation and interpretation are provided for the teacher.

Many of our teachers have not worked through their own basic attitudinal problems which block implementation of the principles of child psychology and learning to which they think they are committed at the time they receive their credentials. Teachers, therefore, need an opportunity for the kind of systematic consultation which is characteristic of the clinical professions. In this teacher-centered program the in-service aspect is an appropriate function of prescriptive teaching.

In-service responsibility of the program not only helps teachers overcome their attitudinal problems but also extends and develops the guidance process among all faculty members. All feel an involvement in the program when their opinions are requested in individual evaluations of students. This program is a cooperative undertaking by all staff members, and it utilizes resources of the community and coordinates them with the work of the school. Neither the teacher, counselor, school psychologist, social worker, nor psychiatrist knows who can best help a child with problems, but by using an interdisciplinary approach they can improve the quality of their decisions.

In summary the greatest opportunity for guidance in the elementary school is found in daily teacher-pupil interactions. Guidance services should be adapted to meet needs at various developmental levels. The central emphasis of prescriptive teaching is the improvement of the quality of teacher-pupil interaction, but improvement does not mean only adjusting the child; it means assisting the teacher with his attitudinal problems on an in-service basis. A major portion of the time of the school psychologist or guidance specialist coordinating the prescriptive teaching program is devoted to individual and group consultation with teachers. Emphasis of the program is on improvement of the quality of educational experience at school, a function which only the school performs. In the school district where the author developed this program, clinical and social services, available through community agencies, were obtained for the client rather than provided by the school. This allowed the school to direct its resources toward the area of its major function. In affluent school districts the school might provide psychotherapy and other direct treatment services for individual children.

Guidance services are well established as an integral part of the secondary school system. Mathewson (1962), Miller (1961), and others listed in the references have described secondary school guidance services and these descriptions will not be repeated here. Experience shows that the prescriptive teaching approach can be implemented through the facilities of traditional secondary school guidance services.

PRESCRIPTIVE TEACHING METHOD

Guidance as process and guidance as organized services place the individual at the center of the learning, developing, actualizing, and adjusting continuum. Prescriptive teaching contributes to this objective through the individualization of education.

Prescriptive teaching, a process which employs an interdisciplinary approach to diagnosis, determines the educational relevance of the child's disability and devises teaching procedures to yield positive results. It achieves this through a methodology based on a scientific formulation which relates the specific elements of the educational program to the diagnostic information.

An adequate educational program is based on evaluation of the child and his total dynamics, not simply in relation to his problems but also in relation to whatever conflict-free areas of response he has. They include every interest, desire, or need which can motivate a positive, active response in the educational setting.

Prescriptive teaching emphasizes development of the areas of major deficits found in the child's diagnostic profile. Although the child may have a biological, developmental, or emotional factor inhibiting some functions, a part of the deficit is the result of psychological withdrawal from the activities requiring use of the deficient skills. During growing stages the child avoids activities in which he faces failure and later shows marked deficits.

The method employed in overcoming these deficits is milieu therapy. This is defined as the scientific manipulation of the environment aimed at inducing changes in behavior, learning, and personality. Cumming and Cumming (1962) show that a controlled environment can bring about changes in behavior and personality. Behavior is controlled by its environmental consequences. An effective procedure for producing behavioral change is the manipulation of the environment to create consequences that produce the desired responses. When it is desired to create, maintain, strengthen, alter, or eliminate a particular set of behaviors, attention is directed toward the operational environmental determiners. The essence of prescriptive teaching is that the environment is manipulated to allow reinforcing consequences to become attached to the learning that is desired.

PLAN OF THE BOOK

This book presents the rationale of prescriptive teaching as well as the methodology for establishing and operating the program and is, therefore, both a textbook and a practical handbook. It attempts to explain the program in a logical sequence starting with a child's having problems in the classroom and progressing through stages of diagnosis, treatment, and evaluation of outcomes. Chapter 2 explains the theoretical basis of the structure employed. Because prescriptive teaching is a dynamic system, it cannot be understood without knowledge of each phase and its interaction with other phases of the program.

The Prescriptive Teaching Circuit

The program is based on the concept of a communication circuit in which each phase prescribes the succeeding phase. The four phases of the circuit are illustrated on page 13.

PHASE 1, REFERRAL.   The circuit starts with the child in the classroom. The teacher, observing the child underachieving, withdrawing, becoming hyperactive, aggressive, delinquent, or having inadequate social relationships, decides that he wants assistance, and a referral is made to the school psychologist or coordinator of diagnostic services.

A case study is conducted, and the diagnostic findings are translated into a prescription for teaching. Chapter 3 reviews the diagnostic considerations involved in determining the educational relevance of handicaps. In many ways Chapter 4 is the core of the book. It presents a model for converting diagnostic findings into a prescription for teaching, and it relates diagnostic variables to school variables so that educational implementation is appropriate to individual needs. Chapter 5 applies the method to the education of exceptional children. Chapter 6 presents three case studies which illustrate the methods embodied in the model.

PHASE 2, REPORTING.   The recommendations regarding modifications of instruction and other aspects of the school program are reported to the teacher and to others responsible for the child's education. This phase is achieved through translating the diagnostic findings into educational terms which communicate meaningfully to those responsible for educational implementation. The methods employed to communicate from the area of diagnosis to the area of implementation are described in Chapter 7.

PHASE 3, IMPLEMENTATION. The teacher and other school personnel implement the prescription through modifying certain variables in the educational program. The appropriate modification of teaching methods, special services, curriculum, objectives, and materials, based upon diagnostic findings, provides the educational milieu in which the child can improve his learning. This is discussed in Chapter 8 and illustrated by examples presented throughout the book.

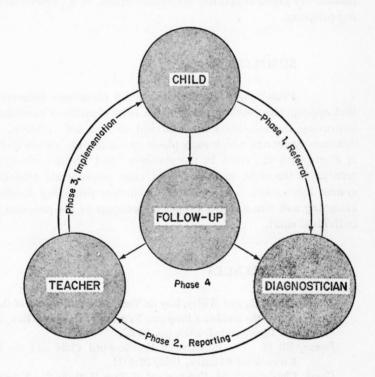

The Prescriptive Teaching Circuit

PHASE 4, FOLLOW-UP. The feedback mechanism in this circuit is provided by follow-up. After implementation, the child's behavior is observed to determine the outcomes of the educational modifications. If the desired learning is occurring, the follow-up directs the feedback to the area of implementation. This supports the modifications that are operating. If the desired learning is not occurring, follow-up directs the feedback to the area of diagnosis, and the process continues through the phases leading to further modification. This system of feedback determines when educational provisions are effective and when it is time for further modification. With this phase the circuit is complete, and the dynamic function becomes a reality. This follow-up system is described in Chapter 9.

Some of the outcomes are discussed in Chapter 10, and recommendations are given regarding the establishment of a prescriptive teaching program.

SUMMARY

Prescriptive teaching assembles diagnostic information so that appropriate teaching can make a more significant contribution to improving the education of disturbed or disabled children. It is a dynamic system in which each phase prescribes the succeeding phase. It starts with the child in the classroom and forms a circuit which returns to the child in the form of more appropriate teaching. The system has within it a regulatory structure providing feedback for achieving and maintaining proper adjustment of the program for the individual child.

REFERENCES

Andrew, Dean C., and Willey, Roy de Verl. *Administration and Organization of the Guidance Program.* New York: Harper & Row, Publishers, Incorporated, 1958, pp. 36–57.

Bower, Eli M. "The Emotionally Handicapped Child and the School," *Exceptional Children,* 1959, 26:6–11.

Carey, Charlotte C. "A Comparison of Two Methods for Effective Use of Guidance Personnel," *Dissertation Abstracts,* 1957, 17(9): 1948–1949.

Cumming, J., and Cumming, Elaine. *Ego and Milieu.* New York: Atherton Press, 1962.

Detjen, Ervin W., and Detjen, Mary F. *Elementary School Guidance* (2d ed.). New York: McGraw-Hill Book Company, 1963.

Dugan, Willis E. "The Organization and Administration of Guidance Services," *Review of Educational Research,* April, 1960, 30:105–114.

Gilbert, Louis Jay. "Team Guidance: A Dimension of Education," *The Journal of Educational Sociology,* April, 1957, 30:363–366.

Heffernan, Helen. *Guiding the Young Child.* Boston: D. C. Heath and Company, 1951.

Heisner, H. Fred. "10 Point Program for Guidance," *The School Executive,* May, 1959, 78:66–67.

Henney, Nella Braddy. *Anne Sullivan Macy: The Story behind Helen Keller.* Garden City, N.Y.: Doubleday & Company, Inc., 1933.

Inhelder, Barbel, and Piaget, Jean. *The Growth of Logical Thinking from Childhood to Adolescence.* New York: Basic Books, Inc., Publishers, 1958.

Lerch, Albert M. "The Role of the Elementary Teacher in Guidance," *Grade Teacher,* May, 1959, 76:99–100.

Loughary, John W. *Counseling in Secondary Schools.* New York: Harper & Row, Publishers, Incorporated, 1961.

Mathewson, Robert Hendry. *Guidance Policy and Practice.* New York: Harper & Row, Publishers, Incorporated, 1962.

Miller, Carroll H. *Foundations of Guidance.* New York: Harper & Row, Publishers, Incorporated, 1961.

Peter, Laurence J. "Prescriptive Teaching for the Emotionally Disturbed Child," *The B.C. Teacher,* March, 1962, 41:218–221.

Rehage, Kenneth J. "Guidance in Elementary School," *The Elementary School Journal,* November, 1959, 60:61.

Rothney, John W. M., and Farwell, Gail F. "Evaluation of Guidance and Personnel Services," *Review of Educational Research,* April, 1960, 30:168–175.

Tallman, Irving, and Levine, Samuel. "The Emotionally Disturbed Child in the Classroom Situation," *Exceptional Children,* 1960, 27:114–126.

Willey, Roy de Verl, and Andrew, Dean C. *Modern Methods and Techniques in Guidance.* New York: Harper & Row, Publishers, Incorporated, 1955.

Woodbury, Roger M. "Team Action Makes Guidance Work," *The School Executive,* December, 1958, 78:50–51.

Wrenn, Gilbert C. *The Counselor in a Changing World.* Washington, D.C.: American Personnel and Guidance Association, 1962.

2

THE PRINCIPLE OF STRUCTURE IN THE LEARNING PROCESS

Learning is a broad concept which influences virtually every type of alteration in behavior which occurs as a result of experience or practice. Maturation and learning apply to all new behavior including the whole spectrum from simple motor learning to acquisition of attitudes and cognitive approaches.

Throughout this book the author treats child development as the basis for the principle of structure in the learning process. This principle of structure is the basis for all the educational modifications in the prescriptive teaching program.

The development of the modes of learning will be explained in relation to the stages of growth in normal child development. Learning difficulties and personality problems will be discussed in terms of inefficiencies in this development. Stages in the growth and development of children have been identified, and their sequence has been revealed by numerous elaborate normative studies. Of particular importance to the learning process are four aspects of development: (1) the motor system, (2) the perceptual processes, (3) the associative system, and (4) personality development. The first neurological system to develop is the motor system. It develops and becomes functional before the perceptual system is operative. The cognitive or associative system is the last to become functional and is a product of the two earlier systems which are operating.

The child's first learnings are motor learnings which play an important role in establishing later intellectual development. The motor system is the basis for elaborations and expansions which produce the more advanced associative system. The motor, perceptual, and associative systems will be discussed together, but for purposes of explanation the personality aspects are discussed separately.

DIFFERENTIATION

The dynamics of physical growth, according to the information from genetics, embryology, and physical anthropology, demonstrate that there is a pattern of development through which all children must pass. Established at conception, this pattern is partially fulfilled before birth. Although the organism grows as a unitary whole, extremely early in the prenatal period of development the neuromuscular system takes on design and primitive patterns of behavior are laid down. Much of the genetic unfolding of the human body comes during fifteen or twenty years following birth. During the time a child is going to school his physical development is inexorably following his innate pattern of growth. Each physical development gives rise to new behavioral potentialities. Each new development of his body offers new possibilities of knowing and of acting. The pattern of growth is similar for all, but the rate of fulfillment varies from child to child. Physical development is a significant kind of individual variation which is related to school problems, such as the child being physically not mature enough for the perceptual-motor tasks of schoolwork.

The body differentiation that occurs between birth and pubescence is about the same for all children, but some accomplish this maturation in as little as ten years while others take eighteen years. Bodies matured to pubescence in ten years are as perfect sexually as those taking eighteen years. Both are considered normal, and no organic superiority is evidenced by early, average, or late development. But children are classified, and the demands made upon them are gauged by how many times the earth has traveled around the sun since their birth, rather than by their own progress toward maturity.

Children are sent to school at age six rather than on the basis of how much their bodies have grown. Girls are more mature than boys at the age of six. On the average it takes girls 13½ years to grow from birth to pubescence and boys about 15 years to accomplish this development. Physical maturity is only one of the factors that contributes to the readiness of children for learning to read in the first grade.

The human organism is required to make more complex, more rapid, and more complicated adjustments than other organisms. Demands are made in terms of the response which the organism is required to make to the environment which surrounds it. The ever-changing demands of the constantly changing human environment require flexibility in the organism. The developmental or learning period establishes perceptual constancies so that what is learned is retained and shapes successive perceptions while allowing for flexibility or flux in the perceptual field.

In the human organism, perception is an important psychological function linking the organism with its environment in a unique manner. Perception is man's ability to recognize stimuli through the reception of sensory impressions and the ability to identify and interpret sense data by correlating them with previous experience. This identification and integration of stimuli is a process occurring in the brain and not in the peripheral organs, such as the ear and the eye.

Visual, auditory, kinesthetic, and tactual perceptual modes of learning are related to the academic and intellectual pursuits of the school. Gustatory and olfactory perceptual modes are of less importance to the learning of school subjects and to general orientation in a social and spatial world. Inefficiencies in one or more of the four main perceptual modes of learning result in underachievement at school as well as in other symptoms. The relationship of one processing mode to another can be studied and used as the basis for effective remedial teaching.

The behavior under study is triply determined: by the external stimuli, by the activity of the receptor and effector organs at the periphery, and by the activity of the central nervous system. The events taking place in the periphery of the body are modified by manipulation of the external stimuli. This activity by the receptor and effector organs is related to concomitant activity in the central nervous system. Activity in the higher centers is expressed in behavior taking place in an effector organ. Therefore external events play an important part in determining behavior, but the central functions play an important part in the organization of behavior or learning. The centralization of activity taking place in the periphery is a role of brain function. Color contrast and color constancy, for example, are phenomena due to brain activity. Light of certain wavelengths entering the eye stimulates a specific activity in the retina. In the brain, this activity in the retina resulting from different light rays or wavelengths is differentiated as color. In time these experiences result in centralized color constancy so that the color concept can be employed without the activity in the eye. When color contrast and constancy are well developed, an individual may be capable of blending colors to reproduce in paint a quite accurate color reproduction of a scene observed at some previous time. Similarly, constancy and contrast of form and size are developed centrally from experience with objects of varying form and size, through visual and kinesthetic processing modes. In the brain-injured or seriously disturbed child, who may have adequate eyesight, the centralizing function may be impaired. In this case, the child is hyperactive because a lack of centralization leaves him no alternative but to respond actively to stimuli. The response cannot be delayed because contrast or constancy is lacking for the control of behavior.

Developmentally, motor activity progresses from the central nervous system toward the periphery. First the infant develops control of head movements, moving his head from side to side, then raising it, before he develops control of parts further from the brain. He flexes his upper torso and moves his arms from the shoulders. The development of motor control moves down the body and out toward the periphery following a regular sequential pattern. In the normal infant visual perception is the preeminent sense modality. He sees objects before he has the motor development to move toward them or reach out and take them. His vision directs much of his motor control.

Visual perception and visual-motor coordination are the bases of much that the growing child learns. He learns to recognize the objects he looks at and integrate the visual perception with stimuli experienced by other sense modalities. Hearing is next in importance to sight in the perceptual hierarchy. It is so close to sight in the development of control within the organism that it can take over the dominant position if the child has inefficiencies in his visual processing mode. This condition is seen in many children who speak well, have a good vocabulary, and even have superior comprehension but have great difficulty in learning to read. Kinesthetic and tactual perception in the normal-sighted child with this type of reading problem are still largely directed by visual and auditory modalities. The senses of smell and taste are subordinate. This hierarchy of sense modalities with vision and hearing at the top, with vision usually the more important, followed by kinesthetic and tactual modes, and with smell and taste of least importance, provides a basis for diagnosis of learning difficulties.

DEVELOPMENT OF THE
PROCESSING MODES OF LEARNING

When the composite functions within one processing mode are at the expected level, then coordination is achieved within that mode. When the coordinated perceptual processes are at the expected level, then perceptual organization is adequate. When an area is not adequate or commensurate with the other three, it is regarded as a perceptual deficit. A functional area that is inadequately developed will result in a learning problem.

The organism moving through a spatial-temporal environment, responding to many stimuli, discriminating and adapting, is in a process of developmental progression. The child is becoming more complex in his motor skills, social mobility, and intellectual achievements. He moves, looks, listens, touches, grasps, manipulates, and learns. He processes the messages from his environment through visual, auditory, kinesthetic, and tactual modes. He may also employ olfactory and gustatory modes. These functions are the means for identifying stimuli and eventually integrating them into an organized system for purposive behavior. Purposeful behavior, in a progressively responsive manner, is derived from a sequence of stimuli perceived, identified, symbolized, and categorized. This complexity of integration is progressively enacted over the first few years of a child's life. A series of crucial problems must be solved in the formation of sensorimotor schemata and mechanisms of mental assimilation (Piaget, 1952). The child has to learn to overcome the force of gravity, to balance, to sit, to crawl, to walk, and to explore independently before he develops verbal or cognitive intelligence. Practical or sensorimotor intelligence must be developed beforehand and is the basis of cognitive intelligence. How does he employ these perceptual modalities in this process of development?

He guides his movements by visual steering through a series of fixations on objectives. His conquest of space increases as he raises his head higher. He pulls himself up and stands while supporting himself with his hands. He scans visually and integrates the new perspective. He lowers himself to a sitting position and scans again, thus organizing his perception of space. When he finds the correct amount of muscle tension, through standing and shifting, to maintain erect posture and balance, he takes a step which changes these relationships. When he integrates these changes he starts walking. Balancing while walking involves shifting his weight from side to side which develops laterality or the internalized left-right concept. Maintaining balance in all directions while moving becomes centralized so that only the goal of movement is consciously determined. He explores other means of moving and checks these against crawling and walking. Eventually he hops, jumps, runs, rolls, and slides. He now has alternative goal-in-space achievement methods.

He notices that some methods result in achievement of his goal in less time than another. He varies his speed in relation to space. He discovers that distant goals are smaller but that the closer he moves to them the larger they appear. He perceives perspective and size constancy so that he symbolizes the true size of objects at a distance. He perceives the three dimensions of objects at a distance when he can only see one side. He steps forward, visually guided toward a goal, as his internal laterality maintains his balance and corrects deviations from his visualized route. The line is visualized as a straight course from the child to the goal or a series of straight-line fixations or intermediary goals. If equalization of all forces in relation to the visual guide is not achieved, he will fall or veer off course. The organization of sideness within the organism allows him to orient himself in space. He learns the significance of space above and below as well as in front of and behind him. He learns that there is a world behind him even without looking around to see. He is the center of his unique world and all direction in space is a projection of his centralized explorations.

Normally vision guides his explorations and organizes the spatial coordinates. His hands are directed by his eyes in purposeful actions or manipulations. Speed and distance, size and form, position in space are checked visually to orient his body movements. His competency in the spatial world is the result of a processing problem of which he lacks conscious awareness. It is a complex system of visual-auditory-kinesthetic-tactual feedbacks that help him make the adjustments necessary for efficiency and comfort.

Centering results visually as he looks about and places himself spatially in relation to what he sees. Auditorially, centering results as he learns sound constancy, sound discrimination, and differences in pitch and volume, and as he learns to use two ears in centering one auditory image to detect direction. He centers the differential tactual sensations in his two hands into a single image.

When he identifies himself as a person in space making organized meanings out of his environmental stimulation, he is ready to attach symbolic meaning to his world. The people around him name objects and actions, and they react in ways giving him more control of his environment when he names them correctly. He becomes gradually skillful in identifying what he sees, hears, touches, and feels. He usually achieves this skill at about two years of age (Piaget, 1952).

With these abilities he is able to learn to communicate and share his experiences with others. He can symbolize his world and understand another's symbolization of theirs. Having expanded his perception beyond the limits of direct experience, he can now venture forward, expanding his visual-spatial world at progressively higher levels.

PERCEPTUAL PROBLEMS

Not all children achieve centralized organization of these modes of learning. Many children are handicapped by a lag in their visual-perceptual development. They have difficulty in recognizing objects and their relationships one to another. Space is distorted and unstable, so the child is clumsy and prone to accidents. When he arrives at school, his distortion and confusion of visual symbols make reading, writing, and arithmetic difficult or impossible even if he has high intelligence. His inability to cope with the academic learning situation can lead to emotional disturbance with repercussions in the home and in his relationships with his peers and teachers.

The causes of visual-perceptual lag can be traumatic experiences in the child's early relationships, defective visual mechanism, brain injury or dysfunction, or an unexplained developmental difficulty. Developmental failures resulting in inadequacies in any of these four areas can result from sensory deprivation, lack of experience or opportunity in one area, undue emphasis on specific features of development to the detriment of others, overprotection, limitations on explorations, or experiences in dealing with an external world which were so painful that he turns his attention to an inner world of fantasy.

The deaf child by organizing and centering the adequate modes of seeing, motion, and feeling can progress well, but the early organizations take longer so that he is usually slower in his development of symbolisms.

The blind child eventually learns to guide himself by auditory cues and tactual stimuli. This takes longer, but eventually he organizes a system of coordinates and achieves centering.

DIAGNOSIS

In the past, some famous teachers—Pestalozzi, Froebel, Montessori, and Fernald—were very successful in teaching children who could not be taught by the traditional methods of their time. These eminent teachers recognized that the key to learning was perception. They all, in different ways, developed teaching methods based upon perceptual modes of learning. Although their methods were spectacularly successful, they had only limited influence on teaching generally for two reasons. They did not establish a scientific theory or rationale upon which research could be based. Secondly, their diagnosis was usually intuitive, and intuitive methods cannot be communicated. Without adequate methods of evaluation or testing for diagnosing perception, the implementation of their successful teaching methods by others lacked rational organization. There are remedial programs based upon the methods of these eminent teachers, and these programs have a degree of success. A child having difficulty learning to read in a regular class, where visual perception is the dominant mode employed, may be handicapped by visual-perceptual inefficiencies. Without diagnosis of his perceptual modes, he is placed in a remedial program employing kinesthetic methods. With this method he has a fair chance of improving his perception of words. There is also a fair chance that a real solution of his reading disability has been missed. He still may make temporary gains because of the novelty of the technique or the Hawthorne effect. Today, with the addition of new tests and research, we should be able to do a better job of assessing perceptual abilities and effecting a genuine solution.

The following is an approach to diagnosing or analyzing learning disorders through evaluation of the processing modes of learning. Studies of perceptual difficulties and their relationship to underachievement have been conducted by many investigators. The relationship of perceptual deficits to remediation received particular attention in remedial education (Kephart, 1960), and the results achieved show the advisability of studying underachievers in this way.

An underachieving child referred for diagnosis should receive a thorough evaluation including a review of the family and medical history and his school record. This is essential even though the diagnosis of educational problems is to be in terms of the processing modes of learning, and the remediation in school is to be through the learning of perceptual skills and organization. Although the etiology is not of prime importance in determining the educational therapy, it has a bearing on outcomes as will be explained more fully in the problems dealt with later in Chapter 5. If the child has a chronic or permanent physical condition which will not respond to medical treatment, he may have greater difficulty in overcoming the handicapping consequences to his learning than will the child whose physical disability responds to treatment. In both cases educational therapy will deal with the handicapping consequences, but understanding the physical health problems improves the educational diagnosis, and in some cases the educational or psychological diagnosis assists with the medical diagnosis. The family history may reveal a chronic situation within the home that has resisted treatment over a long period of time. In this case the child is in a similar situation to the one with chronic physical disability. For example, he may have to go on living with his alcoholic parents, and the educational therapy will deal with the handicapping consequences of this chronic social situation. In this case the perceptual inefficiencies probably are related to emotional disturbance. The study of the family may indicate that social work or a psychiatric referral would help the parents and reduce the child's difficulties. Therefore, all the pertinent information should be included when evaluating the learning problem.

Evaluation of the perceptual modalities may be a complex process. First there is evaluation of the child's physical condition starting with the medical examination and health record. A number of health problems can be related to learning problems. Impaired eyesight, hearing, and neurological defects have a direct bearing on underachievement, but it should not be assumed, for example, that poor eyesight is the cause of the problem. It may be the prime cause or it may be only a contributing factor. There are many superior scholars who have defective eyesight. So far, the relationship between reading disability and eye defects has not been reliably established.

Samples of the child's schoolwork, when studied by the teacher and psychologist, may reveal his perceptual difficulties and frustrations. His drawings may show his unique perceptual distortions but may also reflect inadequacies in his visual-motor development; that is, he may recognize objects adequately but not be able to reproduce them. His writing should be studied for reversals and transpositions. All his work should be observed for spatial relationships, kinds of errors, number of erasures, perseveration, and incompletions. In observing him at work his dominant perceptual mode can frequently be detected. If he copies words letter by letter, rather than by holding a visual image and writing a syllable at a time or the whole word, visual-perceptual difficulties are indicated. If he cannot reproduce a word after looking at it, his visual imagery is defective. If he is shown a word in the dictionary, copies it, then cannot reproduce it when the word is removed from view, there is indication of visual-perceptual deficits. If he can write words phonetically from dictation when they are spelled phonetically, his auditory perception would seem to be adequate. If this child is asked to write opposites of well-known words and he has considerably more trouble, it appears that his auditory perception is better than his visual. In using this technique, it is necessary to use a list of common words and to illustrate first with examples of what you mean by opposites. Ask him to write the opposite of "good," "black," "girl," "night," etc. If he does significantly better with the words he hears, this is an indication that he relies more on auditory than visual cues. If he recognizes words but has difficulty in writing, his difficulty may be more kinesthetic than visual, or he may have poor visual-motor coordination. In studying the results of reading-readiness tests and other group or individual tests, the concern should be more with how the score was achieved rather than with the score itself. Careful scrutiny of the child's written and graphic work along with observations of the child in action will usually provide some clues to his perceptual inefficiencies.

Individual psychological testing can provide further information or validate the observations that were made of the child's schoolwork. The Stanford-Binet and Wechsler intelligence tests provide significant data for the case study. The administration of these tests provides the psychologist with an opportunity to observe firsthand how an individual solves problems and adjusts to new situations. Both tests are administered similarly in that the examiner presents each item in a precise, standardized manner and each response is scored objectively. The Stanford-Binet test presents verbal, object, and picture stimuli with verbal stimuli outnumbering the others. Verbal responses predominate although drawings and motor responses, such as pointing to the answer, are used. The variety of tasks provides opportunities for observing the child's perceptual modes. In this test the performance items are few in number compared with verbal performance. The most important performance tests are those included in the Wechsler Intelligence Scales. Separate IQs for verbal and performance tests measure different abilities. The verbal scale is appropriate for those who can communicate their ideas by speech, and the quality of their responses serves to show whether their verbalization is really communicative. The performance scale gives a profile of motor performance as well as aiding in determining the extent of possible organic damage with, for example, a subtest of block designs.

A child who does much better on performance tests than on verbal tests is suspected of having a language handicap. Deafness, social deprivation, excessive mobility, and bilingual background may cause poor performance on tests of word knowledge and verbal reasoning. Similar poor performances may also reflect auditory-perceptual inefficiencies in the child who tests adequately in an audiometric examination, or pure-tone test. Since performance tasks depend very little on schooling and because instructions are very simple, verbal handicaps reduce the score only slightly. Low scores on the performance scale are indicative of visual, perceptual, and visual-motor inefficiencies. These may be the result of developmental problems, brain injury, or emotional disturbance. A child whose verbal and performance scales differ by 15 points or so should be regarded as in need of complete evaluation. The performance subscores should not be used as a basis for diagnosis without the support of other data.

The Bender-Gestalt test examines how the child takes in, rearranges, and reports visual information. This test, which is the most popular visual-motor test, evaluates perception in terms of the child's drawings of figures with different patterns of organization. Projective tests, such as the Rorschach Ink Blot Test, Thematic Apperception Test, Children's Apperception Test, and Machover Figure Drawing Test, may also reveal some visual-perceptual difficulties. As most evaluations will include an intelligence test, it is well to keep in mind the how of the child's responses. How did he solve the assembly of this object? How did he handle the blocks? Did he perceive the concept of the design? The qualitative aspects of the test items may provide direction to further evaluation.

New tests are being devised and some recent additions seem to be more appropriate for evaluating perceptual difficulties than the traditional intelligence and personality tests mentioned above. Two new tests of perceptual development which are of particular interest in educational therapy are the Kephart Perceptual Survey Rating Scale (Kephart, 1960) and the Frostig Developmental Test of Visual Perception (Frostig, 1961). Both these tests provide diagnostic profiles which are directly related to remediation of perceptual deficits.

The Kephart Perceptual Survey Rating Scale consists of a series of graded physical activities such as balancing while on a walking board and tests of directionality. The author provides scoring criteria for each subtest and the total scale gives a diagnostic profile. The remediation uses the same equipment as the testing. This scale is of particular importance because of the thoroughness of the test items. It samples perceptual-motor skills involving the whole body using large muscle groups and fine coordination. The remedial aspects of this approach hold considerable promise for many handicapped children and particularly for the underachiever and the emotionally disturbed child.

The Frostig Developmental Test of Visual Perception has some commendable, unique features. It is based on the idea that visual perception inefficiencies are the principle causes of underachievement in primary grades. It is a paper-and-pencil test which can be used as an individual or group screening device in kindergarten or primary grades. The test measures certain operationally defined perceptual functions and contains five subtests: eye-motor coordination, perception of figure-ground relationships, constancy of space, position in space, and spatial relationships. The raw score for each subtest is converted into a perceptual age equivalent and a perceptual quotient is derived in a manner similar to IQ scoring. The test has been useful as a screening tool with kindergarten and first-grade children by identifying those who would benefit by perceptual training. By indicating the areas of visual-perceptual disability, it provides the basis for instituting remedial treatment.

The objectives in perceptual diagnosis are to (1) determine the efficiency of the various information-getting modes, (2) evaluate the functional areas within the processing mode, (3) establish the present rank order of the perceptual modalities, and (4) relate the perceptual profile to the specific learning situations of the child. A student may have a specific area within a processing mode which is causing underachievement. Inefficiencies within the visual perception in the functional area of constancy of shape would result in spelling and writing handicaps. If the child cannot hold a stable visual image of a word, he will have great difficulty in trying to reproduce the word in writing. Remediation is frequently achieved through a program of motor training oriented to providing opportunities for the child to achieve visual-auditory-kinesthetic-tactual efficiencies in the processing of information, emphasizing single- or combined-mode activities.

PERSONALITY DEVELOPMENT

We have seen how the child's perceptual development links him with his environment and how differentiation of form, space, sound, etc., precedes speech development and his symbolic world. Along with perception of the external world is the development of perception of self. The self consists of the accumulated perceptual experience of the individual child. It started when his life began and developed through his unique experience. The self-concept is constructed in the field of relationships to others, largely through the perceptual processes discussed earlier. Language development occurs as a result of social relationships and is part of the self. There are aspects of the self which are not readily available to conscious memory. These are experiences which seem to be forgotten and are referred to as the unconscious self. Important as unconscious memory is to personality, our interest educationally is focused on conscious relationships of the child with his environment. For our purposes, in the school setting, we shall direct our attention to the conscious self because the unconscious self is difficult to deal with for the very reason that it is below the level of consciousness. Therefore, in this perceptual approach we refer to personality in terms of the conscious self.

The self is the organization of experience over the child's lifetime, centralized in how he sees himself. This self-concept is inexorably linked with his concept of the external world.

The child has a very adaptable nervous system. This allows him to interact with his environment and attain through prolonged feats of learning an adequate self-concept. The child's competence is his capacity to interact effectively with his environment. He is motivated to be competent in his interaction with his environment. When the child's behavior is disturbed and his environment does not appear to contain the forces or stimuli appropriate to the behavior, the distortion of his perceptual field may be the cause. The child who perceives all behaviors as threatening may tend to withdraw. This withdrawal is his means of dealing competently with his perception. The child who perceives everyone as untrustworthy will respond with behavior characterized by his paranoid projection, and he will be unable to differentiate realistically between those behaviors which are threatening to him and those which are not. These perceptual distortions limit the available responses that the child can make. This limitation, by definition, is a disability or inability to respond in a particular way. If the child perceives one person, one situation, one school subject, or one thing as threatening, the result is a disability of limited handicapping significance. The child who perceives himself as inadequate in one subject or one skill may compensate in other areas and be able to function quite well in all areas except the one. The child with an impaired self-image who feels that he is unwanted, unworthy, inadequate, insignificant, or guilty will have disabilities in many areas. Handicapping consequences of this kind of disturbance have relevance in many areas of the child's existence.

Justice cannot be done to an explanation of the perceptual approach to behavior and personality in the present volume. Combs and Snygg (1959) in their book *Individual Behavior* have developed and explained lucidly this approach to understanding behavior. It is recommended that the reader who intends to apply the perceptual approach should read this book. Perceptual psychology views behavior as a product of the perceptual field of the individual at the moment of action. Individual behavior is a response to how things appear to the behaver. To understand behavior we must understand the nature of the perceptual field of the individual. The perceptual field includes his view of himself and his world. His perceptual field is influenced by his perceptual modes which are his unique means of relating self to his phenomenal world. To modify behavior in a desired direction requires first that we understand the nature of the individual's perceptual field. Knowing the meanings that exist for the individual child makes it possible to create appropriate conditions which will facilitate desirable changes in his behavior, personality, and learning. Knowing some general characteristics of a field makes planning these conditions more meaningful.

THE PERCEPTUAL FIELD

In psychology the term field is used to indicate the complex totality of interdependent influences or forces within which an organism functions. The perceptual or phenomenal field consists of those influences or forces of which the organism is aware. The boundaries of the field are, therefore, determined by the organism's perception. A child's perceptual field is therefore all that he hears, sees, smells, tastes, or feels, including his concept of self and its relationship to that which he is experiencing. His perceptual field is continually changing through the dynamic interaction between self and the perceived external world. In other words, perception of the external world, including how the child sees others and how he views their treatment of him, shapes his perception of himself which in turn shapes his perception of the external world; and so the field is in flux. It is this fluidity that makes change of behavior possible so that adjustment and need satisfaction are achieved in changing circumstances. Reasoning, remembering, forgetting, and learning are functions of the capacity for change in the perceptual field.

Development of form constancy described earlier indicated that constancy was not static, but was rather a centralized organization of experience which made possible the differentiation and matching of form. Similarly, experience with sound, color, heat, and cold is organized so that finer and finer discriminations are possible. Therefore, there is constancy and there is also change. In the total field the self-concept is organized and has some level of stability. Without stability in the perceptual field successful living and learning would be an impossibility. Relating new experience to past happenings, remembering, and learning skills are all dependent on field stability. Excessive inconsistency or ambivalence on the part of the important persons relating to the child result in an unorganized, unpredictable, and unstable field. An example is the overprotective but rejecting mother whose child is unstable and unpredictable. His overt behavior is so inconsistent in relation to the teacher's treatment of him that the teacher has difficulty understanding him. Understanding the meaning of the child's behavior involves understanding his perceptual field. One approach to exploration of his phenomenal field is through projective testing. His responses to the pictures in the Thematic Apperception Test may indicate that he perceives the people who are most giving to him as also the most threatening to his security, and he perceives that he is unworthy of real acceptance. This small sample of his perception increases our understanding of why he reacts unfavorably to the teacher's attempts to treat him in a friendly manner. We have seen that inefficiencies in the perceptual modes of learning, resulting in lack of form, size, color, and sound constancies, are related to certain learning and developmental problems. Disturbances in the child's social relationships result in distortions and instability in the perceptual field which in turn produce disturbed behavior and relationships. Later chapters deal with teaching techniques designed to facilitate stability in the child's phenomenological or perceptual field.

Organization of the field was first studied by gestalt psychologists. They pointed out that perception was always organized into a configuration and demonstrated closure—the phenomena that incomplete figures are perceived as complete configurations even with awareness that part is missing. They believed that perception was not a mass of meaningless unrelated stimuli, but that human understanding and creativity were much more than the sum of unrelated stimuli. As the child develops sound discrimination, he hears notes in music as different or distinct sounds but organizes the separate notes in the music he is hearing into a configuration of sounds or a melody. He accomplishes this partly through listening to the distance between the notes or the interval. That is to say, his organization of perception is dependent upon his establishment of the relationship between one stimulus and another. As we observe an artist draw, his first few lines may seem meaningless, but configuration appears and we feel that now we know what he wants those lines to mean. If we watch him long enough, we may have to change our configuration several times as more lines are added, and we come closer, by a series of approximations, to the artist's perception. Our original organization of the first few lines remains so that we can alternate between it and our perception of the artist's finished work. A child in school may consciously be trying to do an arithmetic problem, but another configuration may be alternating with his arithmetic assignment. If the intruding activity has not been brought to a conclusion or closure, it will continue and may remain as figure or alternate with the arithmetic assignment. His mother is ill, causing him to speculate regarding whether she will recover or not. This is important to him because her continued illness or death will drastically alter his life. This kind of figure-ground alternation can seriously interfere with the educational assignment in which a child is formally engaged.

The perceptual field is only a small fraction of the potential. If we move rapidly through our environment, we develop one organization, and if we sit and study one square foot of earth we develop another. The child examining a fallen leaf, turning it over in his hands, noting first the main structure and successively the finer vein patterns, perceives the form, texture, color, smell, structure, and maybe even the taste of this leaf which has become to him an important part of his perceptual field. His perceptual development may be quite different from that of his brother who is climbing the tree, and for each the same tree is taking on unique meanings.

Organization of the perceptual field, although the content and structure vary from one situation to another, is always in the direction of meaningful configuration. This characteristic applies to the child's meaningful configuration of social relationships as well as to his perceptions of sounds or objects. He perceives and differentiates between people, but he organizes these more discrete data in terms of his perceived relationships. How he sees himself, how he sees others, the relationships between others and between others and self are the basis of this configuration. This is a particularly important configuration because on this depends the adequate or inadequate concept of self. An inadequate self-concept is crippling to the individual because it limits or narrows his repertoire of available responses in any given situation. An adequate self-concept facilitates the actualization of the individual's potentialities, thus increasing or broadening his available repertoire of responses. This does not mean that the child with an adequate self-concept will avoid human problems and not feel conflict, anxiety, frustration, sadness, pain, and guilt, but he will be in a growth process moving toward becoming a fully functioning person. The adequate self-concept views self realistically and accepts self including liabilities of genetic or social origin while maintaining essentially a positive perception of self. This positive view of self is also the realistic view that facilitates self-actualization through perception of what the individual can do in any situation. A child with an essentially positive view of self and a feeling of being acceptable is able to deal effectively with life.

In the earlier discussion of perceptual development the process of differentiation was explained. Considering differentiation in a perceptual field, we see this process as the emergence of figure from ground. Meaning is derived from any object, person, or event as a result of differentiation of the item from the ground or all other items and as a result of the relationship of the item to the totality observed.

This emergence of the part from the whole while still being part of the whole is known to psychologists as the figure-ground relationship.

An example of the figure-ground relationship in the visual field will illustrate its effect on behavior. I entered the living room, which appeared as ground. My son was the first figure differentiation I made. My presence in his perceptual field changed the relationship for him. The room was ground, and the picture on the television screen was figure. I became figure, and the television became ground. He got out of my chair and moved to the sofa. His figure-ground relationship resumed its former characteristics, and I became ground and "Gunsmoke" became figure. My chair is figure and my son, living room, and television are ground until I make myself comfortable in my favorite chair. I then become more precisely aware of "Gunsmoke." Two events cannot appear in figure simultaneously. This manuscript intrudes as figure between gunfights and during commercials. The door to my den becomes figure. After a series of changing figure-ground relationships I am at my desk, pen in hand, and a piece of paper before me is figure. I begin to write, and the words become figure and the paper becomes ground.

Most illustrations use visual aspects of the field. We can all recall experiences to illustrate figure differentiation in the other senses or combinations of perceptual modes. A minor rattle or squeak in an automobile may be differentiated as figure. A faint smell of smoke at first vaguely perceived changes relationship from ground to figure. A very subtle flavoring of food or drink becomes figure as we consciously explore its delicacy. Pain and awareness of bodily functions as well as symbolism and abstract ideas can become figure.

This characteristic of the field is also of importance in our educational treatment. We look at a puzzle and are instructed to find the hidden faces in the picture. We scan the trees and clouds looking for details that might be an eye, ear, or other recognizable part. A face appears. Once this figure-ground relationship is differentiated the whole field shifts because of the dynamic flux characteristic. Now we start seeing faces everywhere in the picture.

A child's record shows problems in every area of human relations. His behavior at any moment is a function of his total perception in existence at the time of behaving. He perceives people as untrustworthy and himself as undeserving. He behaves in a manner which is consistent with this perception. His behavior results in social disapproval which supports his derogatory concept of self and of others. To modify the distortion in his field, someone has to take the place of the first face differentiated as figure in the puzzle mentioned above. If this someone relates to him in a unique way consistently demonstrating interest, concern, and acceptance toward him and his ideas and accomplishments, he eventually differentiates this someone as tentatively trustworthy. He may respond by testing behavior. He perceives his behavior as establishing the reliability of his relationship with this figure. If he finds that he is not rejected and that interest in his accomplishment is maintained, when his testing behavior is socially undesirable or even threatening, he validates his tentative differentiation of the figure-ground relationship. In other psychological terms the figure becomes more dominant and develops constancy. In the child's terms he sees that one person accepts him as he is, that this person is reliable, and that the child himself is worthwhile to at least one person. The field is now in flux and other figures may be differentiated and new figure-ground relationships established. Without this differentiation there existed a severe restriction in his available responses as a consequence of rigidity or lack of flux in his perceptual field. In the foregoing illustration we see modification through what is frequently called a therapeutic relationship. This will be fundamental to understanding the role of counseling which will be discussed later.

Development or growth of the psychological self is dependent upon perceptual processes established early in life and upon social configurations in the perceptual field. Much of the balance of this book will deal with closure and modification of stimuli which will allow children to establish configurations which expand their repertoire of available responses for movement toward more fully functioning, self-actualizing personalities.

We have seen how the self-concept is developed in relation to the total perceptual field and how an adequate self-concept is essential to the actualization of potential and achievement of a fully functioning personality. Our investigation of the perceptual field showed that fluidity of the field was related to personal adjustment while rigidity was related to disability. We also saw that structure and stability in the field were essential to learning. The organization of the field had meaningful direction in its characteristics called closure and configuration. Finally we looked at differentiation and figure-ground relationships and saw their relevance to the counseling relationship. This frame of reference for understanding personality grows out of, and is dependent on, the motor and perceptual modes of learning discussed earlier.

THE LEARNING PROCESS
AND ENVIRONMENTAL STRUCTURE

The human organism with its highly plastic nervous system attains its capacity to interact effectively with its environment through prolonged feats of learning. This capacity to learn varies up and down the phylogenic scale with the human child having the most adaptable nervous system. In normal development the child interacts so as to organize his perceptions adequately for further exploration of his environment. Because so much of his competency depends upon interaction over a long period, there are many opportunities for interference with the process. Sensory deprivation resulting from physical abnormalities within the organism or from stimulus deprivation or extreme disorganization in the environment interferes with the learning process. When this interference is extensive, developmental processes are impaired, and the child's learning capacity is impeded generally or in some specific aspect.

In order to restore the child's learning capacity and mental health through the educational processes we must know what educational modifications to make. Prescriptive teaching makes educational modifications upon the principle that where a child has been unable to organize his perceptions or centralize his concepts, the solution lies in organization of the environmental stimuli. The only way we change a child's thought processes, values, and behavior is by changing the stimuli. The more disturbed the child is, the more order or structure is needed in his environment. The more his perception is distorted, the more he needs structuring of his stimuli.

Normal children interact with their environment and make reasonable order out of their experience. The disturbed child is a disturbing influence in his home and school and is frequently subjected to more disorder in his environment than is the normal child. The mother of such a child will say that she had no trouble with her other children but that she has tried everything she could think of with this child and he still misbehaves. At school the situation may not be much better. The author has had many referrals of children who had been subjected to extreme disorder by well-intentioned school personnel. In attempting to find a means of making a disturbed or disturbing child settle down, he was seated in various places in the classroom, placed with groups and isolated from groups, encouraged and punished, sent out of the room and made to stay in, and was seen by various consultants and diagnosticians. Advice from various sources included suggestions that (1) he should be made to behave, (2) he should be treated permissively, (3) he is expressing hostility and that this is good for him, (4) the parents need casework so that their better adjustment will eventually be reflected in the child's behavior, and (5) the child needs psychotherapy so that he can become adjusted and in turn be able to learn in the regular school setting.

The prescriptive teaching approach regards diagnosis of disturbed children which does not lead to more structure in the child's environmental stimuli as of little practical value and in some cases as harmful. The diagnostic procedures themselves are merely additional stimuli. Prescriptive teaching suggests that the underachieving or disturbed child needs modification of his learning environment and that this modification should have structure based on the principles of development outlined earlier.

THE PRINCIPLE OF STRUCTURE

The child interacts with his environment. As he perceives, so he behaves. Environment operates on his behavior to reinforce or shape future behavior. This dynamic interaction between the child and his environment is the part of learning we can control. The concomitant activity in the child's central nervous system is dependent on this interaction.

Most of the learning we are concerned with in school bears little relation to basic drives or tissue needs, such as hunger or thirst. School learning is seldom related to need reduction in terms of basic drives.

Rather, the goal of the school is to develop the child's competence. Motivation and competence are inextricably woven together. The child is motivated to seek effective relationships or transactions with his environment. He interacts with his environment through visual, auditory, kinesthetic, tactual, gustatory, and olfactory perceptual modes. He develops language and thinking, explores novel objects and places, and manipulates surroundings producing effective changes in his environment. The purpose of these activities is to develop competence in interacting with environment, and the child actively seeks competence as a necessary part of survival. This need to interact with his environment and the need for competency in this interaction are basic to most school learning.

The child's motivation is to be competent in his interaction with his environment. He is motivated to read if reading increases his feeling of competence. Where interference with the interaction is persistent, the child may appear to lack motivation, whereas he has merely changed his perception of what promotes competence. He is still motivated, but his motivation has been deflected because he cannot interact in a particular way. If interference with his interaction is extensive, he may appear to lack any motivation to interact with his environment.

Since the child is motivated to interact competently with his environment, he will grow and learn if his stimuli are structured appropriately. In structuring the environmental stimuli the following considerations of basic developmental principles should be kept in mind.

SEQUENCE. The structure must be built on a normal developmental sequence. For example, the first neurological system to develop is the motor system. It becomes functional before the perceptual system. The association system develops later and depends upon the other two. A child who is slow in his academic learning may have motor or perceptual inefficiencies which can be alleviated by certain physical activities. His inadequate sense of direction causes him to have great difficulty in learning to read. Practicing reading avails him little until he centralizes directional concepts. At the motor level he can learn this through balancing activities or at the perceptual level through visual and kinesthetic activities. The progression is from gross to specific control, or from general to specific action. Reading which required the specific action is dependent upon development of the gross action first. Similarly form constancy and form discrimination are established for simple shapes before complex ones. Prescriptive teaching starts at the visual-motor level at which the child is competent and builds through a sequence to the higher level of learning.

FREQUENCY. The frequency with which a child interacts with stimuli is structured in relation to the child's learning capacity or specific disability. A retarded child will need many more repetitions than a brighter child before he can retain a concept. He will have to read a word frequently before he will remember it. A child with a perceptual problem of form differentiation will benefit from many repetitions of form sorting activities.

SIMPLICITY AND COMPLEXITY. A child having difficulty in coping with a normal environment rich in stimuli can benefit from a simplified environment. He may not be able to learn because he reacts to all perceived stimuli. He does not differentiate figure from ground and retain the relationship. He is assisted in accomplishing differentiation by having all extraneous stimuli removed. He then perceives what is figure and what is ground and develops differentiation.

The cultural-familial retarded child who has lacked intellectual stimulation will improve his intellectual development in a stimulus-rich environment where there are many interesting things to see, touch, manipulate, and experience through his various perceptual modalities.

For the culturally deprived child, the number of stimuli is increased. For the disturbed child who does not deal adequately with stimuli in complexity, the number of stimuli is reduced. In the extreme case of the hyperactive child, the number is reduced to the one stimulus associated with the particular learning desired. Thus the number of stimuli presented at one time is part of structure in the learning process.

CLOSURE. For a child to interact competently with his learning situation, the questions he must answer, or the closures he must make, have to consist of gaps that he is intellectually capable of filling. When a youngster cannot perceive the gestalt because the stimuli are arranged so that the gap we expect him to bridge mentally is too wide, the solution lies in rearranging the stimuli so that the gap is narrower. For example, a child has a learning problem and cannot draw simple geometrical shapes. To start with he is given a stencil of a square which he uses for a number of drawings. He progresses to a stencil with one side missing where he fills in the missing side freehand. He then works with a two-sided or L-shaped stencil and fills in the other two sides freehand. The final stencil is for one side only, leaving three sides to be done freehand before he tries to draw all four unaided. In the beginning the gap was narrowed and then widened progressively until he could complete the closure desired. Later in this book, methods of increasing closure for auditory, kinesthetic, and tactual learning will be discussed. Stimuli are structured so that configuration or closure takes place, and then stimuli are rearranged to require progressively greater closure.

REINFORCEMENT. Behavior which is followed by reinforcement is more likely to occur again in the same or similar situation. The organization of the child's behavior is a consequence of the structure of the reinforcements in his environment. When he started to talk, those sounds he made which approximated language were reinforced.

Mother smiled and picked him up when he made an "mmm" sound which was the beginning of shaping his behavior so that he would learn to say "mama." Reinforcement shapes behavior by a series of approximations approaching the specific behavior desired. The schedules of reinforcement for the child learning to speak are intermittent. Mother does not reinforce his every vocal utterance. When he first learns to ask for food, he is reinforced frequently, and he starts asking for food all his waking hours. Mother stops giving the frequent reinforcement and eventually the excessive asking ceases. He still knows how to ask for food and probably has learned something about when to ask. Continuous reinforcement helps establish behavior, but intermittent reinforcement is sufficient to maintain it. Reinforcements which occur on a ratio basis increase the rate of responses. If reinforcement is related to the number of responses, the child will work faster and longer in order to be reinforced more frequently. One type of teaching machine requires that the answer be dialed for each question presented. When the answer is correct, the dial can be pushed down easily and occasionally a token is dispensed for a correct response. Ten tokens are exchanged for a candy or a marble. The child works at top speed and improves his ratio of correct responses. When the incorrect response is selected, the knob jams and a new question is presented. This delays positive reinforcement and is therefore avoided as the child progresses. In employing this device the author has observed the reinforcing effect of the ratio principle in the almost feverish rate at which the child responds and in the reluctance to stop at the close of a session. He has also observed the aversive control of the incorrect response. It becomes mildly punishing as it deprives him of, or delays, the reinforcement.

The types of reinforcement, the frequency, whether immediate or delayed reinforcement is employed, and whether the schedule of reinforcement consistently shapes desirable behavior, or whether, as sometimes happens, the reinforcement is of behavior we are trying to eliminate are all part of the structure of the learning process.

CONSISTENCY OF APPROACH. A youngster's social interaction may indicate perceptual distortion or disorganization. Perhaps he is irresponsible and unpredictable, or suspicious and untrusting, or his competency in his interaction with his social environment may be his ability to put things over on someone. He needs a wider repertoire of responses and thus an improved differentiation in his perception of human relationships. A person who has considerable contact with him and who can adopt a consistent approach which has potentially positive outcomes can provide the structure most likely to effect this improvement. As this person becomes figure or is differentiated, the field is in flux and opportunities for modification of social relationships occur. The adoption of a consistent approach to use in working with a disturbed child is not a permanent modification but is used until the therapeutic relationship has established differentiation and the child is forming normal social relationships. When the child has developed sufficient organization to deal with normal inconsistencies, the specific therapeutic relationship can be gradually withdrawn or be modified to approximate a normal approach. In the application of this principle of structure in the classroom with the teacher adopting the consistent approach, the problem of termination of the relationship or of reduced contact is usually resolved when the child is promoted.

Consistency of approach as a concept of structure will be dealt with again in succeeding chapters. Both research and experience indicate the practicality of the idea that emotional and social learning can be based on the same principles as motor and perceptual learning. While some teachers have had difficulty in accepting this principle, its application has met with enthusiastic support by those who have observed the results.

The principle of structure applied to social learning is parallel to that used with other problems of differentiation. If a child has problems with form constancy and discrimination, we give him constant forms to deal with until differentiation is established and then gradually add variety to the forms presented. Similarly the child with problems of social relationships is presented with a consistent approach from his social environment until differentiation is established and then variety is added gradually.

SUBJECT MATTER. The structure of subject matter is related to the learning process. If basic concepts or underlying principles of a subject area are learned early, subsequent learning is more meaningful. Traditional arithmetic teaching emphasized learning a vast number of unrelated number facts or combinations. Somehow years later when the child studied algebra, he was supposed to understand the principle underlying all his number combinations. The problem was further complicated by the use in earlier stages of inadequate or incorrect explanations which had to be abandoned later. Emphasis in modern curriculum development is on early understanding of principles with successive experience enhancing the structure.

SUMMARY

All educational remediation of personality and learning problems is dependent upon modification of environmental stimuli. Prescriptive teaching is based upon the principle of structure in the organization of variables under the control of the school.

REFERENCES

Breckenridge, Marian E., and Murphy, Margaret N. *Growth and Development of the Young Child.* Philadelphia: W. B. Saunders Company, 1958.

Combs, Arthur W., and Snygg, Donald. *Individual Behavior.* New York: Harper & Row, Publishers, Incorporated, 1959.

Frostig, Marianne. *Developmental Test of Visual Perception.* 1961. Available from the author, 7257 Melrose Ave., Los Angeles, Calif.

Gallagher, James J. *The Tutoring of Brain-injured Mentally Retarded Children.* Springfield, Ill.: Charles C Thomas, Publisher, 1960.

Gesell, Arnold. *The Embryology of Behavior.* New York: Harper & Row, Publishers, Incorporated, 1945.

Gesell, Arnold. *Studies in Child Development.* New York: Harper & Row, Publishers, Incorporated, 1948.

Gesell, Arnold, and Ilg, Francis. *Infant and Child in the Culture of Today.* New York: Harper & Row, Publishers, Incorporated, 1943.

Gesell, Arnold, Ilg, Francis L., and Bullis, Glenna E. *Vision: Its Development in Infant and Child.* New York: Harper & Row, Publishers, Incorporated, 1949.

Hebb, Donald O. *The Organization of Behavior: A Neurological Theory.* New York: John Wiley & Sons, Inc., 1949.

Hurlock, Elizabeth B. *Child Development.* New York: McGraw-Hill Book Company, 1956.

Kephart, Newell. *The Slow Learner in the Classroom.* Columbus, Ohio: Charles E. Merrill Books, Inc., 1960.

Machover, Karen. *Personality Projection in the Drawing of the Human Figure.* Springfield, Ill.: Charles C Thomas, Publisher, 1957.

Martin, William E., and Stendler, Celia B. *Child Behavior and Development.* New York: Harcourt, Brace & World, Inc., 1959.

Merry, Frieda K., and Merry, Ralph V. *The First Two Decades of Life.* New York: Harper & Row, Publishers, Incorporated, 1950.

Piaget, Jean. *The Origins of Intelligence in Children.* New York: International Universities Press, Inc., 1952.

Templin, Mildred C. *Certain Language Skills in Children.* Minneapolis: The University of Minnesota Press, 1957.

3

DIAGNOSIS

It is the purpose of diagnosis to determine the educational relevance of handicaps. Prescriptive teaching is based upon diagnostic findings arrived at through the use of standard evaluation techniques. Data, gathered by the case-study method using an interdisciplinary approach, are integrated and focused on the educational relevance of the disabilities.

Diagnostic, predictive, and therapeutic activities are bound together in a dynamic interrelationship. Evaluation of the therapeutic relationship is an aspect of diagnosis as is the follow-up study conducted to validate the prediction. In some situations, diagnosis and therapy are carried on conjointly, and in others diagnostic procedures dominate first contacts and are followed by activities which are mainly therapeutic. Frequently members of the diagnostic team are also members of the treatment team. Diagnosis is differentiated from prediction and treatment in this chapter for purposes of explanation, whereas in practice diagnosis is a part of planning and continues as that part of treatment which continually evaluates progress.

Simple cause-and-effect relationships are established for certain specific diseases, but for emotional disturbance and learning problems multiple causation is usual. Our exact knowledge of causality is insufficient to form the only basis for treatment. Knowing the cause or even part of the cause is helpful, but to be of benefit to a large number of children with problems our treatment has to be based on symptomatology rather than etiology. Frequently the cause is in the past, but the symptom has become autonomous. Our decision must be to treat the symptom when we cannot treat the underlying condition.

In medicine, application of this principle has relieved much suffering and has lead to greater understanding of disease. After the Spaniards conquered Peru and Bolivia, Spanish Jesuits discovered that bark from cinchona trees was an effective remedy for treatment of malaria. It was 200 years before pure quinine was separated from the bark and identified as the effective ingredient. Still later it was discovered that mosquito bites caused the disease, and eventually the organism carried by the mosquito was found. One of the most widespread of all diseases would have gone unchecked for hundreds of years if treatment had been postponed until the cause was understood. When we arrive at a hypothesis that is validated in terms of reduction of the principal symptoms, we should not assume that we now know the cause of the problem. When one hypothesis is supported by evidence, there still may be other contributing factors.

CASE–STUDY METHOD

The clinical or case-study method is a process by which we collect all available evidence—social, psychological, educational, biographical, and medical—that promises to help us understand an individual child.

Every child who is referred for evaluation should receive careful diagnosis before recommendations are made. The case study begins by obtaining a description of the symptoms which bring the child to the attention of the diagnostic team. For example, a child referred as a poor reader may have one or more kinds of reading disability. The first step in this case is to request that the teacher evaluate the child's reading rate, comprehension, word attack, sight vocabulary, phonics, and attitude toward reading. Through his initial evaluation, the process of differential diagnosis is started. We are beginning to discover which kind of disability is represented in this particular case. In other cases our first step is to discover other symptoms associated with the one particular symptom for which referral was made.

Structure of the case study is provided by the problem-solving technique employed. The hypotheses are derived from generalizations or knowledge of behavior principles and child development. In the case of our poor reader a hypothesis that his intelligence is less than required for reading competency could be tested. If this individual intelligence test score indicates normal intellectual ability, we test hypotheses about visual and auditory defects, emotional disturbance, and inadequate previous instruction. Because multiple causation is frequently responsible for learning problems, each possibility should receive consideration and investigation. Even when evidence supports a course of action, this does not absolve us of responsibility for investigating other possibilities. Our child with the reading problem appears to have poor visual discrimination of form and suffers from emotional tension. If we hypothesize that he is disturbed because he is unable to read and be competent like his age-mates, we provide him with remedial teaching to develop his form discrimination and form constancy in an adapted reading program. If his reading improves and his emotional tension subsides, the hypothesis is validated. Following the special instruction if he is still tense and reading difficulty persists, it is hypothesized that his perceptual difficulty is supported by his emotional tension. Treatment is then directed toward reducing tension created by pressures in the home or other areas. One of these hypotheses need not exclude the other. If the evidence, collected earlier in the case study, showed that he had emotional problems before he started school and that his perceptual development was seriously impaired, then both modified parental treatment and remedial teaching would be advisable, and with the parents' cooperation, the two modifications would be employed concurrently. In this example we have not proved whether the perceptual difficulty was caused by emotional disturbance or emotional disturbance by perceptual difficulties. We have not determined whether reading improved more as a result of the home or school modification. What we have found is an effective way to teach this child.

The case study is used to organize diagnostic data and relate them to the things school can do. In prescriptive teaching the hypothesis is valid if the treatment based on it is accompanied by reduction or removal of the undesirable symptom. This does not prove that causation of the symptom is really understood or that treatment caused the cure. Many other variables exist which are not controlled by the school, and they could be the important factors. This is a particularly important point to consider in terms of research, but in the operation of a program it is of less importance. In prescriptive teaching the validation of diagnostic findings places emphasis on outcomes rather than etiology. Understanding the background as accurately as possible improves discrimination and the quality of our hypotheses, but the criteria for validation depend on evidence that the prescribed treatment is accompanied by problem reduction.

The more complete our picture of the child's total life situation, the more congruent are our predictions. Because the behavior we are trying to understand is a response to some aspect of environment, the contemporary life situation of the child is investigated, which includes studying the home and family influences, social activities, school progress, sources of conflicts, and sources of support. The child's characteristics, including intellectual potential, special aptitudes, and individual perceptions, are equally important because the behavior being investigated is a product of interaction between the individual and his environment.

Each of the diagnostic techniques used in the total case study lacks the validity that we desire. As diagnostic tools are refined and their power to differentiate and predict improves, we may be able to rely less on follow-up studies to validate our procedures. In using current techniques we should know their predictive validity and its relationship to the situation. The situation provides limitations to action. For example, usually the placement of a child is limited to the special and regular classes available in the school. Our diagnostic techniques are worthwhile if they improve our choice of class for the child even if this is not a very fine discrimination.

The techniques of each profession, when brought together in the interdisciplinary team conference, result in better quality decisions. The effectiveness of this approach relies on the skill of the team in coordinating the contributions of the professions represented and upon the statistical validity and scientific methodology of the medical, psychological, and social-work techniques used in diagnosis.

Information for the beginning phase of the case study is mainly gleaned from school, medical, and family areas.

School

The school usually has a wealth of information about the child, distributed among a number of people and a number of records (Hunt, 1956). Teacher reports, anecdotal records, reports of parent-teacher interviews, and principal's records of the child's conduct provide information for the study. The cumulative school record provides information regarding intelligence tests and other standardized tests, school grades, attendance, number of schools attended, referrals to special services, and so forth. If the teacher fills out a referral form stating the present problem, the psychologist's time in collecting some of this information is considerably reduced. It is important to bear in mind that records and forms serve to facilitate collection of data but will not take the place of personal interviews with teachers.

In interviewing the teacher, it is advisable to ask some questions of a structured nature in order to determine the teacher's evaluation of certain characteristic attitudes of the child. Questions which ask if the child is tired or energetic, restless or relaxed, quarrelsome or friendly, lazy or industrious, dependent or independent, quiet or noisy, popular or unpopular, aggressive or withdrawn, will help to sort out the teacher's opinions of the child. Questions about the child's first reactions to school may contribute a great deal. Kindergarten teachers and first grade teachers see much evidence of the degree of a child's disturbance at school entry in his crying, vomiting, incontinence, anxieties, refusal to permit mother to leave the classroom, and refusal to attend school. The transition of the young child from his family into school is one of the first important role changes in the growing-up process. This event includes rapid role change or redistribution of relationships among family members and represents potential problems for the child. School entry is an emotionally hazardous circumstance. It represents a time-limited transition, marked by increased tension within the family. The transition period is characterized by a regular sequence of adaptation phases as shown by the child's emotional reactions. During the first weeks of school, children express tension by physical reactions such as loss of appetite, fatigue, stomach upsets, intensification or resumption of previous behaviors, bed-wetting, thumb-sucking, increased irritability, hitting out at siblings or other children, uncooperativeness, increased dependence on mother, increased talkativeness, and reluctance to go to school. This phase is usually followed by increased independence including assertiveness, acting-out, not wanting to have a baby-sitter, playing farther from home, and visiting other homes more often. The next phase includes more grown-up behavior such as acceptance of more responsibility or self-help, increased cooperativeness, and imitation of older children. This is followed by new attitudes and interests including more interest in other children, and decreased shyness.

For most mothers school represents a problem of divided loyalty. The mothers express some sense of loss during the first days of school. Parents also fear criticism aimed against their child or themselves because of the child's inadequate preparation for school. School entry is accompanied by specific tensions related to redistribution of family roles. These tensions are normal and usually are resolved without special treatment. When they are not resolved, serious consequences follow for the child. The teacher is almost always the first professional person aware of the existence of this problem. It is important for him to know the usual developmental phases of school entry, when to try to provide extra help for parent or child, and when to procure additional services.

If the child has attended a number of schools, the reasons given for the moves are often indications of the stability or instability of the family. Contacting schools attended has several advantages, since they may give information about subject difficulties which can be traced to gaps in teaching due to these changes. Also of importance is the effect on the child's personality of breaking up his friendships. Information about his adjustments to new situations in new schools is also valuable.

A careful study of the attendance record of the student is often revealing. Poor attendance and unsatisfactory reasons given for absences are indicative of certain kinds of problems. The interviewer should also obtain the teacher's estimate of the parents' means of control of children, insight of the parents, amount of pressure at home, and stability of the parents.

The classroom is a laboratory of human relations where children can be observed in a variety of social situations. Teachers have an opportunity to make observations of an objective nature although they vary considerably in their ability to do this. The school psychologist can encourage and assist the teacher in this function by helping establish criteria for more objective evaluation of children. The child may have had several teachers in one school, and it is important to receive reports from each of these teachers.

It must not be assumed that all information gathered from the teacher's comments can be used directly. Much of this information must be interpreted in the context of information from other sources. He may become too personally involved to make objective observations of the child's behavior. However the teacher will probably be more objective in his observations than will parents.

The amount of observation time varies greatly from child to child. The child whose behavior interferes with the learning of other children or of the whole group probably will be observed more often than will the child whose behavior problem affects only himself. A number of factors in the teacher's own personality and background affects his interest in certain kinds of children. Some teachers will have more interest in academic remedial problems, while others will have more interest in the personal-social adjustment of the child. The interviewer can, with practice, learn to give meaningful ratings on the basis of the teacher's comments.

Another way of interpreting these comments is to compare them with information gathered from other sources. In the case method, it is important to get information from more than one area and to try to understand the client on the basis of more than just historical information. Educational information is particularly valuable as a record of past ability and in comparing present with past performance. A child's schooling is such an important part of his life that it is necessary to study his behavior in the educational setting in order to make a realistic evaluation.

Medical Record

In schools where comprehensive medical records are available, we have an up-to-date picture of the overall physical development of the child. This picture is quite objective and helps us to understand the child's physical growth as well as his mental and emotional development. Where public health records are available to the school health service and where communication between school nurses, public health personnel, and private physicians is conducted in an atmosphere of mutual trust and respect, the school health record will be of great value. It will be quite complete and will indicate where further information is obtainable regarding hospitalization or special treatment of the child.

The prescriptive teaching program was developed in the Vancouver, British Columbia, school system where school health services were provided by the city's public health department. The integration of mental-health services provided by the Vancouver Metropolitan Health Association and the school health service has aroused the interest of teachers for many years (American Public Health Association, 1953). This integration provided the school with the services of extensive diagnostic resources. In most cases the child's health record contained considerable information, but a medical examination was frequently requested as an additional source of up-to-date information. Contact with the family physician was usually made through the public health services. The school health nurse made a home visit when the case study required more information regarding home conditions, particularly those pertaining to the physical or mental health of the child or other family members. The author not only read the medical history of each child and interviewed the school nurse but also had a conference with the school physician concerning each child.

The school psychologist is confronted with problems which cannot be readily answered by merely looking at the medical record. Physical impairment or functional disability may produce handicaps which are relevant to the child's learning. The loss of sensation as a result of visual or auditory disability has obvious consequences to learning. Other physiological dysfunctions may result in loss of motion, memory, or ability to communicate. These in turn may effect the child's self-concept, his social interaction, and his ability to reason.

Where the child's condition has a known identity, the medical doctor can often provide information about the nature of the problem, the treatment prescribed, and the length of time usually required for recovery. Whether treatment is required or not, it is valuable to know the probable duration of the condition.

Coordination and integration of educational and health services will function well where the areas of competency of the school nurse, psychologist, and medical doctor are understood. In this program the school medical doctors took an active part in improving communication and establishing cooperative diagnostic procedures which made use of their extensive knowledge. They participated with the author in the development of the diagnostic aspect of the prescriptive teaching method.

Family History

The social history can be regarded as a description of the family life situation. In this program the family history was usually provided by the school nurse. In cases where the family had been referred to social agencies or to a clinic, a full social history was written by the caseworker. From certain families, it was not possible to obtain accurate or complete family histories. This was particularly noticeable in cases of alcoholic parents, broken homes, and excessively hostile or suspicious parents. With children whose parents were too disturbed to become involved constructively, the case method was carried out and the recommendations made which would improve the situation for the child in the school even if the parents would not accept advice or casework help.

PERSONNEL

The personnel of the diagnostic team varies from case to case. A typical school-centered team includes the teacher or teachers, the principal, school nurse, and school psychologist. In secondary schools or elementary schools with counselors, they are members of the basic team also. To this team are added the school physician, speech therapist, hearing specialist, representatives from agencies dealing with the child or his family, and others as warranted by the nature of the case. The clinic-centered team, outside of the school, may include any or all of the school team. Children requiring diagnosis or treatment beyond the scope of the school team are referred to clinics or agencies, and the school is represented on the clinic team to determine the educational relevance of the problem.

Vital to the function of the school-centered team are contributions of the teacher, principal, school nurse, school counselor, school psychologist, and in some cases the social worker and speech therapist. A brief description of their contributions to diagnosis follows.

Teacher

The idea that the teacher is the important person in a school guidance program and that he should work in close cooperation and harmony with the guidance specialist has received fairly wide acceptance, further attesting to the fact that guidance and psychological services for children cannot be the function and prerogative of one group of professional specialists. Every teacher will encounter students with whom he is not equipped to deal competently unless he has the assistance of guidance or psychological services. This is not because of a lack of competence but because his background of training and experience emphasized development of instruction whereas the background of the psychologist emphasized individual diagnosis.

Prescriptive teaching is based on the assumption that the school's function is to educate and the teacher's function is to teach, and that the teacher's greatest contribution is through his competency as a teacher. Therefore he need not try to become more like a psychologist, social worker, psychoanalyst, or medical practitioner. To be effective in bringing the teacher's competency to bear on the problem, the educational significance of the handicap must be established and the prescribed procedures stated in learning terms. Changes in behavior involve learning new behavior, and therefore, the educational approach to problems is through learning.

Teaching is not only the school's major contribution to treatment but is also an important part of diagnosis. Diagnostic teaching is achieved through knowing the child for a long period of time, through testing, and through follow-up study. These three aspects of diagnostic teaching as employed in the prescriptive teaching program are explained below.

LONGITUDINAL RELATIONSHIP. The teacher has an opportunity to make observations over a considerable length of time and of a continuous nature. He also has the opportunity to work through a relationship with the child. This makes possible a diagnosis on the basis of the child's responses to his relationships with the teacher and with his peers. This opportunity is not usually possible at the clinic or with the guidance specialist. Misleading evaluations of the child's responses can be made when observation time is short, as is the case in most clinical evaluations. It is not uncommon to find a child who responds with enthusiasm to new situations and the opposite problem of the child who responds poorly to new situations but develops more security in the routine situation. The longitudinal relationship makes possible the cumulative observations of the child. The teacher is able to observe how the child responds to support and clarification (Driscoll, 1954). The longitudinal aspect of diagnosis affords opportunities to see how the child responds to instruction, peer relationships, limits, and the teacher's interest over a considerable length of time.

TESTING. A teacher can carry out many testing procedures as part of his regular teaching responsibility, and this testing can also be used in the diagnostic process. Achievement tests, whether teacher-made or standardized, provide useful information for evaluating the individual child. Sociometric studies, which show the child's relationship within the class group, are useful indicators of the child's social adjustment and acceptance. The observations made by teachers of children in standard situations provide additional data. Observation of the way in which a child responds to the rules of a game, while not intended as a test, provides opportunities to make objective evaluations of behavior.

A goal of testing is to obtain measurements which lead to more objective evaluations. The goal of measurement is to give quantitative evaluation to formerly qualitative observation. The importance of this process is that it makes possible better prediction of behavior and evaluation of progress. A major purpose of testing is to provide a basis for predicting a child's success in the succeeding grade. Tests of personal-social adjustment, sociometric studies, and observations in standard situations are also useful, within the limits of their validity and reliability, in prediction and in evaluation of progress.

FOLLOW-UP. In diagnosis through follow-up the emphasis is shifted from the pretest to the outcomes. Because the teacher is usually not an expert in individual diagnostic techniques, he has to rely more on his personal and professional knowledge in deciding on a course of action to follow for a particular child. On the basis of his experience a hypothetical prediction is made. Appropriate treatment is decided upon and the child is treated consistently for a period of time on the basis of this tentative evaluation. The diagnosis is based primarily on the follow-up of the results achieved. In determining the validity of the tentative evaluation and consistent treatment, four criteria are used:

1. Was there a remission of the symptom?
2. Did the symptom return?
3. Did a substitute symptom appear?
4. Was there an increase in anxiety?

Adequate follow-up is frequently lacking in the school approach to behavior problems. A set routine is developed, and this becomes the standard procedure to follow with a lack of regard for the consequences to the individual. The school psychologist can provide help by assisting the teacher in establishing the criteria for improvement. The author has found that when the teacher knows what to look for, he will do a more adequate job of objective follow-up.

In diagnostic teaching the emphasis is more on follow-up, whereas in clinical procedures the emphasis is more on diagnostic case-study procedures. Teachers can achieve some valuable diagnostic results by following the steps in this procedure.

Principal

The principal is the main administrative officer who has a direct authority relationship to the staff of a school. Since he has responsibility for what goes on in the school building, it is important that he be involved in the prescriptive teaching process. If the school is not too large and he knows the children, he may be able to contribute information regarding the child to the diagnostic study. The principal or his assistant has records of offenses against school rules as well as complaints received from the community. These facts and the principal's impression of the child are important data for a case study.

School Nurse

The school nurse is the person in the school representing the school health service. Wilson (1953) lists the responsibilities of school health services as: health appraisal, health counseling and follow-up, emergency-care procedures, communicable-disease control, school sanitation, and health of school personnel. Although there is great variety in the means of provision of health services there are two general structures: (1) school health services rendered through educational agencies, and (2) school health services provided by public health agencies. Either structure can be effective as long as the school nurse has available to her the resources of the public health agency so that, when needed, the services of psychiatric or child-guidance clinics, sight-and-hearing diagnostic and treatment centers, rehabilitation clinics, neurological departments, and others can be coordinated with those of the school health services.

The school nurse is professionally prepared to recognize deviation from normal in physical, mental, and emotional health of pupils and to interpret health needs of pupils to parents, school personnel, and community groups. The importance of the school nurse's participation in individual evaluations of children cannot be overemphasized because of the relationship of physical and mental health to behavior and learning problems. The psychologist's evaluation of intellectual potential, perceptual development, and personal-social adjustment along with the nurse's evaluation of physical health factors such as eyesight, hearing, growth and development, and physical disorders complement each other in creating a diagnosis of greater value. Either without the other could be misleading.

In most school health services the nurse makes home visits and counsels parents on health problems. She frequently is the only school representative who can provide accurate information about the home, and in many instances her effective working relationships with parents provide the basis for parental cooperation. She has opportunities to observe children in ways different from those of teacher, counselor, or psychologist. She is alert to children who use illness or minor aches and pains to avoid difficulties or to gain attention and sympathy. The unique function of the school nurse and school physician is in diagnosis and evaluation of physical health and concern for the physical well-being of children. Evaluation of emotional, mental, and educational well-being of the child is a responsibility she shares with the teacher, the psychologist, and others. Therefore, coordination of efforts is required for effective implementation of the case-study method.

In the employment of the case-study method, the social history is frequently provided by the school nurse in school districts without school social workers. The school nurse's knowledge of the home and her relationship with the parents provide a basis for her writing the social history.

School Counselor

The major contribution of the school counselor to the public school guidance program should be that of working intensively with individual pupils. The counselor's responsibility is to assist individuals in their decision making. The decisions may be about placement, developmental tasks, or adjustment problems.

The counselor's basic professional preparation is in education, with additional graduate work in guidance and personnel services. He is in a strategic position to know the child well and to evaluate the child's reaction to a one-to-one relationship. The counselor also administers group tests and maintains individual records. He is a valuable member of the diagnostic team because of this special knowledge and because in many cases he will be carrying out part of the treatment program.

Social Worker

The newest member on the guidance team is the school social worker, who acts as liaison between school and family and school and community agencies. For some time schools have had attendance officers and visiting teachers who performed some of the duties now assigned to school social workers. Now that we have arrived at the point in history where school contacts practically every child, the quantitative goal of democratic education is almost achieved. The present interest in the qualitative aspects seems to be a logical next step. School social work is an aspect of individualization of education that may contribute significantly to this movement.

In the development and operation of prescriptive teaching, the author worked with a number of social workers as consultants to the program, but none was assigned specifically to the role of school social worker. Where families required social casework, referrals were made to appropriate agencies, and it appeared that coordination of services was adequate in most cases. In school systems where services of school social workers are available, the social histories as well as much of the liaison work could be their responsibility.

Speech Therapist

The speech correctionist contributes to diagnosis by identifying pupils who have one or more of the following speech characteristics: (1) deficiency, (2) significant deviation from that of the normal child, (3) interference with communication, and (4) a source of significant stress for the child. On the basis of this evaluation along with the rest of the case study a decision is made regarding a therapeutic program of speech correction. In many cases the decision is against direct treatment of the speech problem; with other youngsters the teacher carries out the recommended practices. The speech correctionist, therefore, is involved on the team as a diagnostician, as a consultant, and as a therapist.

✔ School Psychologist

A school psychologist is professionally prepared in the study of human behavior, intelligence, motivation, learning, aptitudes, and conduct and should be qualified to work in a school setting because of his special knowledge regarding classroom organization, curriculum, teaching, conduct control, and special education. The great diversity of school districts requires at present that school psychologists do a wide variety of jobs utilizing a variety of methods. They may super-

vise general testing programs, supervise classes for mentally retarded
pupils, do educational and vocational counseling, and supervise or
conduct research projects (Bower, 1955).

Many school psychologists were public school teachers who had
completed graduate work in psychology in preparation for this role.
Others were clinical psychologists who had studied education in order
to qualify as school psychologists. Whichever background the school
psychologist has, to be truly effective in this role he must have competencies in both fields and be able to relate one to the other (Cutts,
1955).

Here we shall deal briefly with the school psychologist's functions
relating to the individual child. He accepts referrals of children presumed to be exceptional or in need of extra help. This may present
problems because of staff shortages and the amount of time that must
be devoted to appraisal, remediation, and follow-up. The recommended ratio of one school psychologist per one thousand schoolchildren (Cutts, 1955, p. 80) is seldom achieved. It may be advisable to
work out a priority system with the principal of the school so that
those cases of greatest concern to the school are dealt with first.

Professional preparation and certification of school psychologists in
the United States varies from state to state (Hodges, 1960), but considerable progress has been made in the development of effective training programs (Ferguson, 1963). The growth of this profession in
recent years provides more opportunities for diagnosis and remediation of learning problems in children. The school psychologist studies
the child in relation to the child's school progress and adjustment. It
is not within the scope of this book to present the theory and methodology of individual examinations. Individual psychological appraisal
is a skill that must be arduously acquired through years of professional coursework and in practical experience examining children
(Wall, 1956).

The school psychologist's evaluation is accomplished through three
main techniques: the interview, intelligence tests, and personality
evaluation. All interview information obtained from the child, even
though doubtful as to accuracy, does represent the child's point of
view and in this way is valuable. In interviewing, not only the words
must vary with the age level of the child but the form of questions
will depend on the mental and chronological age of the child, the
education level, and his general understanding. Setting the right tone
and getting off to a good start are very important with the small child,

because an interview is a new experience and he has little understanding of the situation. We should not overlook the possibility of receiving meaningful information through the child's direct report. Most elementary school children can give a useful direct report. In reply to questions such as "What kind of person are you?" or "How does it look to you?" the child will describe himself and his situation in such a way that the school psychologist can picture the child's perception of self and of his world. The emphasis of the psychologist as a tester has sometimes resulted in depending too much on test data. One purpose of projective testing is to discover how the child perceives himself, but it is not always necessary or desirable to use these projective techniques or to rely on them too heavily to understand the child's perception of self.

The accumulation of biographical and personal information facilitates our understanding of the child, his problems, how his handicap developed, and why he shows this behavior which is characteristic of him. This information can be augmented by test results.

Psychologists use two types of tests, psychometric and projective. The psychometric test is used to measure some characteristic of the child, and the projective test is used to reveal the quality of the child's personality.

Intelligence testing has been a major function of the school psychologist from the beginning of the profession. The quantification or measurement of aptitudes such as mental ability and motor or mechanical ability is used by the school psychologist in the educational planning and placement of the child. Because psychological evaluation is used for prediction, it must provide insight into what the child is capable of becoming. Intelligence testing is one of the means of estimating the child's potentialities and resources or capacity for development and accomplishment. This testing is achieved by presenting standard stimulus situations to which predetermined values have been assigned. The two most widely used individual intelligence tests are the Stanford-Binet Tests of Intelligence and the Wechsler Intelligence Scale for Children.

Projective tests are not really instruments of measurements but rather provide a method for the study of personality. This testing is accomplished by presenting to the child a stimulus situation in which he can give his own interpretation. The child's responses do not result in measurement but are interpreted to reveal personality characteristics. Projective tests, such as the Rorschach Ink Blot Test, Thematic Apperception Test, and Children's Apperception Test, provide the psychologist with a means of exploring the child's perceptual field or of gaining some understanding of how the child perceives himself and how he perceives his world. Using these tests along with special aptitude tests and interviews, the school psychologist makes his unique contribution to the case study.

The school psychologist interprets and communicates these findings and makes recommendations. In this role he is an adapter and translator of diagnostic information. He should be uniquely qualified to do this job because this communication is from the area of psychological diagnosis to the area of educational action and he should have competencies in both areas. He is still confronted with many problems. He must use caution in extrapolating to school situations the learning theories supported by carefully contrived laboratory experiments. Necessary though this caution is, it can become a habit which interferes with communication.

There remain many unanswered questions in psychology, and many answers that we do use are tentative. Still there is a wealth of studies of learning and a great deal can be tried out in school learning situations. If what we have seems better than having nothing, it is wise to use it, but with an open mind and withholding final acceptance until outcomes are evaluated. An informed speculation based on a learning theory is a better basis for direction than the alternative of guessing or doing nothing.

Without communication which adapts research findings to the classroom situation in learning terms, the teacher must make his own attempts to translate research findings and psychological theory into educational practice. He is much less equipped professionally to do this than is the school psychologist.

The psychologist who attempts to explain diagnostic findings in layman's terms and adapt them to everyday situations may be criticized for inaccuracies in his technical language, but from a communications point of view, language which does not communicate is inaccurate. If the psychologist has been a teacher and can communicate to teachers, he can learn how to show them the relevance of psychological findings to school practices. Most of the balance of this book deals essentially with this problem of translation, communication, and implementation of diagnostic findings.

Coordinator

Someone must be responsible for the coordination and integration of diagnosis and translation, communication, and follow-up studies. If the school psychologist has the background recommended, he will be prepared to work in this interdisciplinary setting and fulfill this function. The author is a school psychologist who has had many years of experience in teaching and psychology, and therefore this book is written from the point of view of his functioning as psychologist and coordinator of a prescriptive teaching program. In other school districts coordination would be the responsibility of the director of guidance or special services. It is essential that the coordinator be a competent educator and that he understand the language of psychology, medicine, and social work adequately to communicate within the interdisciplinary team approach to diagnosis.

SUMMARY

The case study is achieved by first gathering information from the school and then moving out for the medical, social, and psychological information. The team approach is standard practice in many school districts, but coordination has not been easily achieved. Where the school psychologist has a background of experience in education and can communicate well with the various professions involved, he can develop a coordinated team approach to diagnosis. Having moved out in order to gather information, we must, if the school is to aid in the rehabilitation process, move back with this knowledge. Some diagnostic procedures deal adequately with etiology but fall short of determining the educational relevance in terms of the child's present functioning and fail to specify appropriate educational modifications.

Prescriptive teaching resolves this problem by determining the educational significance of disabilities and by recommending an integrated program of educational modifications to meet the needs of the individual child. A diagnosis which is profound in its explanation of why a child has a problem at school is of limited value to a teacher. A diagnosis which suggests that, if the parents were less maladjusted or would become involved in treatment, the child's problem might be alleviated, is encouraging but of little value in deciding how best to teach the child. Recommendations regarding psychotherapy for the child, while of value, ignore the considerable potential of the school. These recommendations do not define the situational relevance of the handicap, nor do they answer many questions which have a bearing on what should happen to the child in school. Elaborate diagnostic procedures fall short of achieving desired results when clinical personnel are not willing or are not able to determine the educational relevance of the handicap and make appropriate recommendations about teaching. The potential of the school, with its ability to make a unique contribution to rehabilitation through learning, is not fully realized by this type of diagnosis. The school psychologist or school counselor with responsibility for coordinating school efforts on behalf of the exceptional child should be, by virtue of his training and position, the key person in converting diagnostic concepts into pedagogical terms so that they can be implemented in the school. The conversion of diagnosis into learning terms is the important contribution of prescriptive teaching discussed in the next chapter.

REFERENCES

Ahmann, J. Stanley, and Glock, Marvin D. *Evaluating Pupil Growth.* Boston: Allyn and Bacon, Inc., 1959.

American Public Health Association. "The Integration of Mental Hygiene and School Health Programs," *American Journal of Public Health,* June, 1953, 464–465.

Anderson, Harold H., and Anderson, Gladys L. *An Introduction to Projective Techniques.* Englewood Cliffs, N.J.: Prentice-Hall, Inc., 1951.

Bardon, Jack J. "School Psychologists," *The Clearing House,* May, 1960, 34:528–530.

Bower, Eli Michael. *The School Psychologist.* Sacramento: California State Department of Education, 1955.

Bradfield, James M., and Moudock, Steward H. *Measurement and Evaluation in Education.* New York: The Macmillan Company, 1957.

Cronbach, Lee J. *Essentials of Psychological Testing.* New York: Harper & Row, Publishers, Incorporated, 1960.

Cutts, Norma (ed.). *School Psychologists at Mid-century.* Washington, D.C.: American Psychological Association, Inc., 1955.

Driscoll, Gertrude. *How to Study the Behavior of Children.* New York: Bureau of Publications, Teachers College, Columbia University, 1954.

Eiserer, Paul. *The School Psychologist*. Washington, D.C.: The Center for Applied Research in Education, Inc., 1963.

Ferguson, Donald G. "Training Programs in School Psychology." In Gottsegen, Monroe G., and Gottsegen, Gloria B. (eds.). *Professional School Psychology*. Vol. II. New York: Grune & Stratton, Inc., 1963.

Gottsegen, Monroe G., and Gottsegen, Gloria B. (eds.). *Professional School Psychology*. New York: Grune & Stratton, Inc., 1960.

Gray, Susan W. *The Psychologist in the Schools*. New York: Holt, Rinehart and Winston, Inc., 1963.

Hadley, John M. *Clinical and Counseling Psychology*. New York: Alfred A. Knopf, Inc., 1958.

Hodges, Walter L. "State Certification for School Psychologists," *The American Psychologist*, 1960, 15:346–349.

Hunt, J. T. "School Personnel and Mental Health," *Review of Educational Research*, December, 1956, 26:502–536.

Lindgren, Henry Clay. *Mental Health in Education*. New York: Holt, Rinehart and Winston, Inc., 1954.

Marzolf, Stanley S. *Psychological Diagnosis and Counseling in the Schools*. New York: Holt, Rinehart and Winston, Inc., 1956.

Wall, W. D. (ed.). *Psychological Services for Schools*. New York: UNESCO Institute of Education, 1956.

White, Mary Alice, and Harris, Myron W. *The School Psychologist*. New York: Harper & Row, Publishers, Incorporated, 1961.

Wilson, C. C. *School Health Services*. Washington, D.C.: National Education Association, 1953.

4

TRANSLATING
DIAGNOSTIC FINDINGS

The model on page 63 is the key to prescriptive teaching. Within the structure of the model, medical, psychological, and social-work diagnoses are converted into educational terms. It provides for determination of what is educationally significant in the interdisciplinary diagnosis, which is a complex process requiring that a number of interrelated factors be dealt with simultaneously. This multidimensional model has been constructed to aid in relating factors in the child's total life situation to those which are relevant for educational planning.

The model has three main dimensions: (1) problem variables, (2) situation variables, and (3) school variables. Within these three dimensions the cells are arranged, in relation to each other, on a continuum of modifiability which facilitates arriving at a profile of educational modifications. This chapter describes the diagnostic variables and gives examples of the school variables. The reader is urged to refer to the illustration inside the covers of the book for reference when the various structures are mentioned in this and later chapters. Mainly the model serves to establish the link between diagnosis and the area of action within the school. The upper horizontal section of the model represents diagnosis and consists of twelve cells. All the cells are dealt with separately in the paragraphs following.

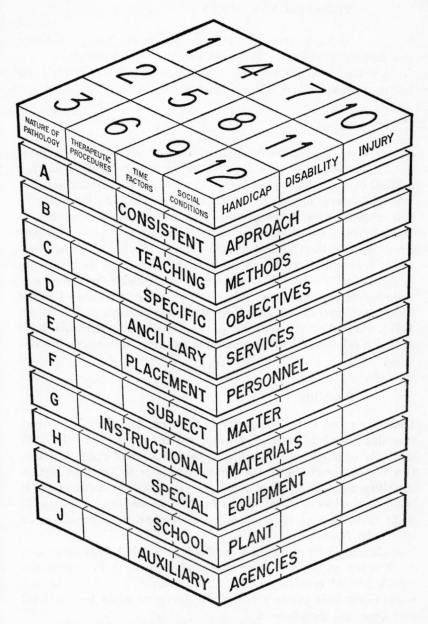

Model for Translating Diagnostic Findings into a Prescription for Teaching

63

PROBLEM VARIABLES

Impairment is dealt with at three levels: injury, disability, and handicap. These are arranged horizontally in the model from front to back with the most modifiable factor, handicap, at the front and the least modifiable factor, injury, at the back.

Injury

Injury is physical harm or damage. In only some cases is organic damage or cellular impairment a factor requiring investigation. The medical doctor is responsible for the diagnosis of the cellular, somatic, or organic loss or damage. A careful study of the child's health record and consultation with the school health services, school nurse, or private physician are necessary in determining whether physical injury does exist. Further medical examination or referral to a diagnostic center is required for some cases before the existence of injury can be established with certainty. It is not easy to determine the existence of neurological damage. Some behavior can be symptomatic of either emotional disturbance or neurological damage (Strauss and Lehtinen, 1947). Similarly many apparent physical ills have an emotional basis so that it is important to determine the nature of the organic involvement.

Disability

Disability refers to the incapacity to function. As injury is to structure, disability is to function. An injury to the eye might result in the disability of blindness or the loss of the sensation of sight. A limitation in the repertoire of the child's responses is his disability. A disability could be a loss of sensation called sensory deprivation. It could be the loss of physiological function or the loss of motion. It could be the loss of communication, or perception, or cognition, or integrative functions.

A disability may or may not involve injury. Disabilities occur as a result of injury, inheritance, or emotional disturbance. For instance, a child's lack of cognitive ability might accompany a brain injury, might result from primary mental deficiency, or might be associated with emotional disturbances.

Considering disability in this way is helpful in determining whether a child needs special help. A child with an injury to his visual mechanism might be unable to respond to visual stimuli. This limitation would be his disability. In terms of emotional disturbance, if a child has a phobia it will result in a limitation of his available responses.

A child with paranoid projection will tend to respond to all human contact with distrust. His disability is his inability to discriminate between those people he should trust and those he should not. The child with hostility toward adult authority will tend to be hostile toward all adults in authority. He will tend to have grave learning difficulties because he is not motivated to please his teacher.

This definition of disability differentiates between the child whose behavior is disturbed because of a disturbing situation, and a child whose behavior is disturbed because of a distortion in his perceptual field. The child whose disturbed behavior is provoked by a situation which is abnormal has available to him other responses when the stimulus situation is appropriate. The child who has an emotional disability will respond in accordance with his distorted perception even though the stimulus would tend to produce normal behavior in a less disabled child.

This concept of disability is useful in establishing criteria for improvement. The more disturbed the child is, the more limited his repertoire of responses. The neurotic child with severe anxiety will tend to be anxious about nearly everything. The extreme case is the psychotic child who reacts to every situation in his limited psychotic way. The fearful child, the aggressive child, the suspicious child, are all limited in their responses. This concept of disability allows us to see improvement in terms of increased repertoire of responses.

Disability is sometimes directly responsible for a learning difficulty. A child with paralysis may not be able to learn to run. His disability may be significant only in certain learning situations such as physical education. Some disabilities, as color blindness, have very limited handicapping consequence to the child's education.

Handicap

Handicap refers to that which impedes, hinders, or hampers some kind of action. A handicap to educational progress may be directly related to the disability or somewhat removed. A disability such as blindness is a considerable handicap in art but is much less of a handicap in music. An orthopedic handicap might be of great consequence in physical education but be of little significance in learning to read.

The term handicap is used here in regard to its significance to the learning process. The following illustrations contain three examples where the handicap varied, although the disability was classified as the same.

Grant was blind from birth and was classified medically as blind. This child with the disability of blindness had a severe handicap because he had no visual imagery or color sense with which to understand many of the things he could not see.

Walter lost his sight at four years of age as a result of an injury. He had developed color sense and visual imagery and could understand much that he could not now see.

Joan had a congenital defect which resulted in her having 20/400 vision and color blindness. She had a percentage of sight so small that she was classified as blind. Her visual disability resulted in her only being able to see things clearly a few inches from her eyes; in difficulty in finding her way around; and in needing assistance in coming to school. She went into a regular grade 1 class and at the end of the first year could read. Although she could not see the blackboard, she could read large type when it was held about 3 inches from her eyes.

Here are three children classified as blind: two because they have no sight at this time, the third classified as blind because of severe impairment. The handicapping consequence in each case was quite different.

A child with a physical disability may find it significant only in subjects where motor skills are of primary importance, such as physical education or industrial arts. The child with an emotional disturbance may have difficulty only in certain learning situations. A disability which affects social interaction will have more significance in group activities than when the child can work by himself.

A handicap must be evaluated in terms of the demands of the situation in which a person finds himself (Wright, 1960). Even a severe disability need not represent a major handicap. The inability to walk has handicapping consequences when the child's goal is to move about quickly. Being in a wheelchair is not a handicap when he is not going anywhere. The converse is also true. The child may have no disability and have a serious handicap. Disability implies deviation from a normal standard, and therefore, a child with normal intellectual potential is not considered to be mentally disabled. He may be seriously handicapped if his ambition is to become a nuclear physicist.

A disabled child is usually not one who is unable to do anything. He is also an able child. There are things he can do and things he cannot do. He is handicapped when the things he cannot do impede his progress toward a goal set for him by his or others' expectations. Since omnipotence is not a characteristic of anyone on this earth, all must function within limits. Those who function within the normal limits may be handicapped when the situation, the expectation, or the aspiration of the individual exceeds the normal limits. Those who function below the normal range in some ability may be handicapped when the situation, the expectation, or the aspiration of the individual requires that ability for attainment of a specific objective.

Emotional difficulties constitute the greatest number of problems among schoolchildren. The exceptional emotionally disturbed child is one whose emotional condition seriously interferes with his own school progress, or with the atmosphere conducive to the progress of the group of which he is a part (Cruickshank, 1958). The handicapping consequence of emotional disability is frequently in the altered or impaired self-concept of the child. The handicap resulting from the disability is often in the child's perception of the handicapping condition. A child with a slight physical disability may be severely handicapped educationally because he sees himself as ill, crippled, unfit, unacceptable, or incompetent. A large number of disturbed children are disabled primarily in their emotional responses. These children suffer from functional disorders which do not involve injury. Their handicap impedes communication, impairs their self-concept, interferes with their social interaction, limits their mobility, or results in distortions in their perceptions of their environment.

SITUATION VARIABLES

The levels of injury, disability, and handicap are important considerations, but the handicap is the educationally significant factor. Four areas of investigation which relate to injury, disability, and handicap are (1) the nature of the pathology, (2) the therapeutic procedures, (3) the time factors, and (4) the social conditions. These variables are arranged from front to back in our model from most modifiable to least modifiable.

Nature of the Pathology

The nature of the condition includes the description of the disturbance. In some conditions where the pathology is well-known, labeling is a kind of shorthand which helps communicate the nature of the condition. In some cases of mental retardation, common illnesses, and other well-known defects when the appropriate diagnostic classification is given, the nature of the condition will be adequately understood. In cases of emotional disturbance and in cases where the pathology is not readily classifiable, a description which elaborates the condition is more meaningful. It is essential to know whether the disease is infectious, contagious, epidemic, or psychosomatic. The school has little direct effect on the nature of the pathology, and therefore its placement level in the model is at the back.

Therapeutic Procedures

What is to be done for the child through therapy to alleviate his condition has educational relevance. Whether the therapeutic procedures include hospitalization, institutionalization, medication, psychotherapy, physiotherapy, or referral to a guidance clinic or a social agency has a bearing on the handicap. It is obvious that if the child will be hospitalized for some time, his education may suffer unless some modification is made to overcome this loss of time. If the child's condition is contagious, so that he is isolated, this results in a considerable handicap. The effect of medication over a long period of time may result in a change in the cellular structure and therefore be a remedy to the injury. But it may at the same time produce a handicap as a side effect. This handicap may be in the child's self-concept, altered as a result of his long-term use of medicine. Because of the necessity to take insulin, the diabetic child may see himself as more severely handicapped both generally and in the learning situation than his disability would warrant. If the child sees himself as chronically ill or severely handicapped, it may affect everything he does. It is not uncommon to see a child who starts going regularly to the clinic become more aware of his disability. Whatever is done as therapy has bearing on the handicap and must be considered in determining what educational procedures should be used. The school may be involved in carrying out some aspects of therapy, but the major responsibility for therapy rests with medical, psychological, and social-work personnel. This variable is quite modifiable but not on the basis of the usual school responsibility. The responsibility for procuring or accepting this help is most frequently that of the child's parents.

Time Factors

This variable consists of a number of factors which have a bearing on the handicap. One group of these time factors is included in the study of the stage of development of the child and the other is involved in the study of the development and probable duration or recurrence of the condition. The earlier brain injury occurs, the more profound the handicapping consequence. The stage of development when injury, or the onset of disease, occurs is related to the nature of the disability. Also the stage of development at which educational therapy begins is related to outcomes. The culturally deprived child who receives help in a nursery school or kindergarten can overcome more of the result-ant handicap than can the child who receives no special help until later. Mental retardation of the cultural-familial type responds to early treatment but is difficult to modify significantly in an older child (Kirk, 1962).

An emotional or physical disability may have increased or altered handicapping results according to the stage of development of the child. The child from a home where the social customs or the cultural values are at variance with those of the community may be somewhat unaware of this until adolescence. During adolescence the child is more concerned about his place in the world and the kind of person he is becoming. This increased concern is a result of the stage of develop-ment rather than any change in his home situation. The child with a deformity or scar may feel particularly conscious of this during ado-lescence. Problems which had little handicapping effect in the accept-ing home environment may become apparent when a child starts school.

The duration of a handicap has important implications in determin-ing the kind of teaching that will be prescribed for the child. Many illnesses, both physical and emotional, which are quite severe but of short duration will only result in the child missing a short time from school, and it is unnecessary to make any changes in educational programs. The child may be very disturbed by the loss of a parent or by some other tragedy. These situations do not imply that anything should be done in the way of diagnosis and planning. A child may seem much less disturbed by long-term emotional deprivation, but the nature of the disturbance is such that prescriptive teaching is advisable. A child with a permanent disability of a physical nature may require special equipment, special methods, special material, and in some cases modification of the school building throughout his entire school life. A child with a broken arm may manage using standard writing equipment. The child with an amputated arm may be well advised to use different writing equipment, and he may find that certain kinds of coil-bound notebooks are easier to use. The child with flu and the child with tuberculosis need different teaching prescriptions on the basis of duration of the illness.

Emotionally disturbed children can modify their response through appropriate learning, and therefore the time factor should be considered in terms of the length of time required to bring about some positive modification of their emotional responses.

The amount of follow-up is also dependent to some extent on the time factor. The child with a progressive condition, such as muscular dystrophy or arthritis, must be followed up over a long period of time in order to make modifications in the prescription to meet the changing needs. The child with a disability may need no special modification of the elementary school curriculum, but later in the secondary school, when curriculum planning leading to a vocation is involved, his disability should receive special attention.

Injury refers to cellular loss or damage which is permanent. Disability resulting from inherent conditions is usually regarded as permanent. A handicap accompanying an emotional disturbance may vary a great deal in duration. The condition which has existed for a long period of time usually results in chronic behavior problems because patterns of response tend to become habitual. The duration of the handicap has a bearing on treatment.

In one frame of reference functional disturbance can be viewed as a result of a certain type of undesirable learning. Because the child has a need to grow and achieve emotional maturity, and because functional disturbance occurs when events interfere with normal development, growth and improvement can be facilitated by the modification of these events. The school is effective in modifying the duration of the child's disturbance to the degree that the modification of school variables achieves desirable learning.

Social Conditions

There is a great diversity of elements to consider in our efforts to understand the social and cultural conditions of the child. All the pertinent child and family history must be considered. Socially and emotionally maladjusted parents tend to have children who are vulnerable to disturbance. Some children with behavior problems show little or no emotional disturbance. They reflect the values of their homes or social groups and engage in activities which are not within the range of the culturally permissible in terms of the standards of the middle-class school (Riessman, 1962). Not only the emotional conditions in the home and the cultural values of the family but also the social situation in which the child is to be treated need consideration.

The protection of society, in the case of communicable disease or in the case of the delinquent whose behavior is destructive and antisocial, is also a relevant factor. In some cases the attitude of the parents toward the child's condition or toward the therapeutic procedures has a real bearing on the handicapping consequence. Conditions where the child needs acceptance and society is not willing to accept the child must be seen from the points of view of both the child and society. Both the child who has tuberculosis and the child who has been in juvenile detention may experience rejection when returning to school. There are still taboos and prejudices about certain illnesses, and there are still moralistic attitudes toward people with emotional problems, particularly the child with destructive, aggressive behavior. We must be aware of society's needs in considering what to do with the child. If we are aware of the nature of the social and cultural considerations, both the needs of society and those of the individual, recommendations can be made which have promise of fulfillment.

Because the school is a part of the social situation of the child, it shares responsibility for modification of the social condition. It also can be influential in the modification of home and community conditions. Therefore the social condition is considered to be the most modifiable situation variable in terms of the school's responsibility.

COMPLETING THE DIAGNOSTIC STRUCTURE

The nature of the pathology, therapeutic procedures, time factors, and social conditions are considered in determining the importance of the injury, disability, and handicap. The teaching prescription is arrived at after all these factors have been explored.

When the situation variables and the problem variables are determined, the cells of the diagnostic structure will be completed. All twelve cells will be considered, but they may not all be utilized. If no injury is determined, only the disability level and its handicapping consequence are completed. This reduces the diagnostic structure to eight cells. Similarly, if the condition is to receive no therapy, the number of occupied cells would be reduced. Sometimes the information is inadequate, and it is not possible to fill some cells. Where parents are uncooperative, it is difficult to get an accurate picture of the nature of the social situation. This is particularly true where the parents are superficially cooperative but are actually defensive and give misleading information. In these cases, some questions remain unanswered or are answered tentatively until more complete information is available.

SCHOOL VARIABLES

The educational program is composed of elements which may be modified in relation to the pedagogically significant attributes of the handicap. Where permanent injury has handicapping consequences, this modification of the educational program improves the child's opportunity to accomplish and move toward the general educational objectives. In the case of the blind child, the auditory and tactile senses rather than vision are used in teaching reading. This modification assists the child to achieve intellectual and other educational objectives.

Where disability accompanies weak ego strength, modification of the educational program improves the child's opportunity to learn more appropriate emotional responses and therefore to overcome the disability and its handicapping consequences. The neurotic child with an inadequate self-concept is taught in a manner which helps him identify his efforts as valuable and himself as worthwhile.

The descriptions of exceptional children and remedial teaching are intended to be primarily illustrations of principles and not complete instructions.

The school variables are arranged from the top to the bottom of the model in order from the most modifiable to the least modifiable. Each school variable is a duplicate of the diagnostic structure. Thus it is possible to move the diagnostic structure down through the school variables modifying each in a manner consistent with the educational relevance of the handicap.

Consistent Approach (A)

An approach is a way of coming toward or reaching a person. In prescriptive teaching the approach is the teacher's contribution to improvement of the teacher-child relationship in a manner which promotes the child's social and educational growth. As explained in Chapter 2, the principle of structure in this kind of social learning requires that someone be initially differentiated, that this someone have stability, and that the relationship with this person have positive value for the child's development.

The concept of using a consistent approach as part of therapy in working with disturbed children is not new. The influence of psychoanalysis changed much of the rigid and punitive approach, employed with problem children, to a permissive approach. Today we have a variety of opinions regarding the amount of permissiveness and the amount of structure that should be employed in working with disturbed children. Bettelheim (1949) based his approach and procedures for treatment of emotionally disturbed children on orthodox psychoanalytic principles. The use of free expression and free play in the psychoanalytical situation has contributed a great deal to our understanding of children and to the etiology of emotional disturbance. Lippman (1956) applied a psychoanalytic approach to a wide variety of problems but with considerably more structure. He specified the approach to use in working with seventeen types of disturbance ranging from the effeminate boy to the child with organic brain damage. Redl and Wattenberg (1959) also brought direction to their approach as a result of their emphasis on learning as a part of therapy. Haring and Phillips (1962) conducted a study which showed that aggressive acting-out youngsters made significant educational gains in a special highly structured class over those children in a regular class. Structure in this case refers to clarification of the relationship between behavior and its consequences, to setting up dependable routines, and to the teacher adopting a consistent approach toward the child. Clarke (1958) reported two experiments, conducted in selected Seattle schools, employing a method called attitude consistency study. The first experiment was conducted in a junior high school. The teacher of the referred child received a recommendation from the school psychologist that one of five specifically defined consistent attitudes be adopted. At the end of the school year teacher ratings and the psychologist's reexamination were used to evaluate progress. The significant change was in the teachers' evaluations. These evaluations indicated that the teachers felt more comfortable with these children and that the children had fewer problems at school. A similar experiment conducted in an elementary school produced even more marked results. The explanation for this additional success might be that the child spent most of the day with only one teacher. It was concluded that more children were helped through the use of the attitude consistency study than with the conventional approach.

In the implementation of prescriptive teaching one problem was the communication of the consistent approach. Clarke and Fitzgerald (1958) had developed detailed written descriptions of their consistent attitudes, which were used to communicate the recommended approaches to the teachers. These were adapted to the prescriptive teaching program, with a sixth category added to the original five. Although modifications were made, the descriptions are based upon their original concept. The reader interested in the attitude consistency study should read the original sources, Clarke (1958) and Clarke and Fitzgerald (1958).

Although prescriptive teaching is a program based on individual diagnosis and prescription, there are groups of children whose individual needs can be met by the same approach. A specific and unique description of each approach has been laid down for the following types of children:

1. the socially defective child
2. the severely disturbed child
3. the child with neurotic conflicts
4. the child with paranoid projections
5. the acting-out child
6. the affectionless child

It is not the intention of the author to suggest that the following are the only consistent approaches that can be used effectively. The important element is consistency. Almost any consistent structure is more conducive to growth and confidence than no framework at all or a vague and fluctuating one. Unless a consistent approach is adopted, we reinforce the behavior that we are trying to eliminate. If we reflect the child's hostility, instability, etc., we tend to reinforce it. Any approach that is consistent and that reinforces positive social growth and behavior will be effective regardless of the personality or learning theory behind it.

It is important that the descriptions given should assist the teacher in adopting a consistent approach. While it may be argued that there are no absolutes in categorizing children, and no absolutes in the prescription, it should also be noted that there are no absolutes in implementation of the recommendations by the teacher. These descriptions place emphasis on clarity which will lead to consistency. A general description of the type of problem and the approach for each follows.

THE SOCIALLY DEFECTIVE CHILD.   These youngsters grow up without developing a set of acceptable values. They have not internalized the social norms which will make them completely acceptable in the school. These children exhibit conduct disorders in school. Some of them come from lower-class homes where behavior standards and values differ from those of the school and society or the middle-class ethic. They behave according to the codes of their family, neighborhood, or gang and have little concern for others outside their immediate group. They are likely to be aggressive, cruel, belligerent, and truant. Their intelligence is often underrated because they usually dislike schoolwork, especially routines, drill, and the abstract aspects. In large cities, some of these children live by their wits. They come and go as they wish in their homes. Often their parents take little interest in them. They steal and are impulsive and hostile. They find it difficult to make sustained effort and are restless in school. But these children may be well adjusted to their home and to their community; their problem lies primarily in the conflict of values between those of their homes and those of the school.

In working with these children, teachers have to strike a balance between sympathy, which such children regard as weakness or stupidity, and counter-hostility which would justify the child's retaliation. The teacher should not reflect the hostility that the child of the lower-class community is expressing toward the middle-class values of the school. The teacher by reflecting the child's hostility justifies its use by the child and reinforces aggressive behavior. The teacher's ability to establish and hold limits without hostility is essential. The teacher is more likely to be successful if he has ceased to moralize, has pruned the curriculum for these youngsters, and does not afford too much attention to the niceties of language. The teacher must be mature enough in his approach to absorb some of the hostility of such children. Generally these pupils are responsive to a warm teacher who is patient and provides opportunities for them to gain recognition. If the teacher has a group of such children in a class, individual treatment is very difficult. An individual approach would tend to make the child a traitor in the eyes of his group and family. Group work with the gang has been effective. Basically this is a social problem that in some cases is difficult to deal with as an individual problem.

THE SEVERELY DISTURBED CHILD. Some children may withdraw from social contact and detach themselves from the world. They may narrow their interests and become immobile. Common symptoms include refusal to eat, refusal to talk, and hallucinations. Some show infantile behavior, temper tantrums, extreme irritability, and aggressiveness. Many are extremely fearful, and in some cases, speech is affected. Screaming, squealing, and biting themselves are common behavior.

These mentally ill children are usually not retained in regular classes in the public school. It is extremely difficult to deal adequately with a seriously disturbed child in a regular classroom. In small special classes where the teacher can give sufficient support in using the following approach consistently, some severely disturbed and psychotic children have benefited. These children should be approached with an attitude of complete acceptance and receive affection and support at all times regardless of their reaction. The child may show no interest and may repel the accepting approach or even act out against it. Regardless of the response on the part of the child, he should be shown nothing but acceptance. This is a one-way process with the teacher always showing acceptance. This approach is used with those children needing maximum support to prevent further withdrawal. When this approach is combined with reinforcement of behavior in the direction of reality contact and communication, some quite positive results are achieved.

THE CHILD WITH NEUROTIC CONFLICTS. Internal conflicts make these children anxious and produce feelings of guilt. They generally suffer from an impaired self-image. They are hurt children, who have had unsatisfactory human relations. They feel rejected, insecure, and inadequate, often in spite of their favorable actual capacities and strengths. Constituting the largest group of exceptional children, they are usually referred to as neurotic or disturbed.

The teacher should offer this child affection and love on a mature level and take the initiative in being actively friendly. This approach does not imply that the teacher should fuss over the child or go out of his way, but he should help the child feel that the teacher is available to him for help and positive support. He gives support for little things and shows feeling toward the child and his best interests. He is positive in his approach, voice, and action. This approach sometimes involves giving the child an extra duty which can be overcredited. Punishment for this child frequently supports his derogatory self-regard. In this situation it is important that the child should understand that a reprimand is to help him learn to control his behavior and that "We like you but we cannot accept this behavior" is appropriate. The main objective is to improve the child's self-image by reducing anxiety while supporting an adequate self-concept.

THE CHILD WITH PARANOID PROJECTIONS. This child is very defensive, overly suspicious and untrusting, and usually blames others a great deal of the time. His perceptual field is distorted in that he sees in others the things he suspects. He feels that things are done against him and that in some cases people plot against him. He interprets gestures of friendship as attempts to get around him or put something over on him and makes alibis to protect himself. He is very cautious in forming relationships.

The approach to use consistently with this child is a passive one. Wait for the child to reach out. Make no moves toward the child, but be available if he reaches for support. Remain consistent but passive and friendly. Show acceptance but no affection until the child requests it. As the relationship develops, the teacher must not become aggressive about being friendly. Any gestures of friendliness, such as a hand on the shoulder, might be threatening to this child. It is therefore important to allow the child to initiate each step and show his desire for a closer relationship or understanding with his teacher. This child nearly always is likely to strain the limits of the relationship. He wonders if he can trust his new friend and may manipulate situations to see if the teacher will still be his friend. It is of utmost importance at this time to maintain the consistent approach prescribed.

THE ACTING-OUT CHILD. The aggressive or acting-out child is sometimes only testing the limits of authority. His behavior may be simply an expressive symptom of some minor or fleeting feeling of hostility, or it may be deeply embedded in his psychic structure. He is frequently a behavior problem in the school and may be delinquent in the community. Sometimes his acting-out behavior is a coping symptom, and he is seeking punishment for deep feelings of guilt.

The consistent approach to employ with the acting-out child is firmness. Definite limits are established for his behavior, and these limits are rigidly adhered to in spite of the reaction of the child. The purpose of this approach is to relieve guilt feelings and depression and also to provide maximum support for those who have insufficient strength to set limits for themselves. Employ a very direct approach toward this child. Kindness is included in this approach, and limits should be set in a firm, kindly manner. Give him lots of work to do. Work of a physical nature is frequently beneficial for this child.

THE AFFECTIONLESS CHILD. The problem of a child with a defective personality occurs infrequently, but the consistent approach recommended for this child has some utility in dealing with a variety of discipline problems. This child has little capacity to relate to others. He lies, steals, and deceives at will. He lacks the capacity for anxiety or guilt, and he learns little from his experience.

The approach to use with this child is to be very firm and unemotional. Be direct with a forceful show of confidence. The teacher lets the child know that there is no question about his demands or the demands of the situation. Make sure that the limits are clearly understood. This is a management device and will bring about control of this child's behavior. Do not be lenient or permissive as he will only take advantage. Use a show of force, or actual force if necessary, to enforce the limits. Because this child is prone to manipulate people, it is important that acceptable behavior be well established before the more friendly approaches are employed.

Teaching Methods (B)

From the case study and particularly from the differential diagnosis of the child's educational achievements and of his processing modes of learning, we devise a rationale for the first steps to be taken in remedial teaching. The diagnosis explains his present functioning so that a prognosis can be made about his behavior in various learning situations. This prognosis provides the basis for proposed modifications of teaching. Implementation of these modifications should always include feedback which checks the validity of the prognosis. Diagnosis, therefore, is a part of the teaching methods; it provides the prognosis which is the basis of proposed modifications leading to implementation which in turn validates the prognosis. The suggestions about teaching should be regarded as proposals which are validated by the ongoing diagnostic process.

READING INSTRUCTION. Reading methods are important in the school program because reading is one of the most complex things children learn to do. Reading, writing, and speech are aspects of language development which are achieved through maturation and experience. Reading problems occur when we lose sight of this fact and assume that a child is ready to read because he is in school. The discussion of perceptual modes of learning and personality development is pertinent to reading development. Looking more specifically at reading, we must consider it in relation to general language development. The child made speech noises before he learned to talk. Exploration of his environment, responses to social situations, imitation of speech, and maturation preceded effective use of the vocal mechanism in speech. His interest and experience with stories, along with his scribbling and increased awareness of visual symbols, precede reading.

Reading is interpretation of symbols with the meaning derived from outside the symbols. Meaning does not exist in words or groups of words until the child has had experiences that the words represent. He must experience or have the facts before language, whether listened to, spoken, read, or written, has meaning. To interpret symbols he must be able to reconstruct from his experience the meaning behind the symbol. This must precede interpretation of symbolic expression of abstract mental constructs. Language begins with symbolizing experience in the world of the mind. Generalizations constructed from experience with reality are symbolized before communication of abstractions is achieved.

Reading, a facet of the developmental process, is accomplished through the perceptual modes and is dependent upon maturation and experience. The formal phase of instruction usually begins in kindergarten or first grade and deals with symbols, pictures, and stories as well as general language development and background of direct and vicarious experience. If teaching of the mechanics of reading is attempted before the child has the perceptual development, reading disability results.

As a reader's eyes move along a line of print, he associates meaning with most of the words he sees. This is a complex process involving coordination of motor, perceptual, and associative processes. Reading is a self-reinforcing and therefore a self-motivating experience. As the child reads, the ideas, knowledge, feelings, etc., that he receives are the reinforcements of his reading. Reading is one of the few activities that is so self-rewarding that most people read best when alone. We can help motivate the child by listening to him read and by taking an interest in his progress, but the important motivation will come from his developing competency in reading.

Teaching methods can be directed to any aspect of reading improvement, such as (1) comprehension of the concepts in the reading materials, (2) understanding specific meanings of words, (3) ability to attack new words through word analysis, and (4) ability to read for specific information. Before attempting remedial reading one should become familiar with basic methods of reading instruction through standard textbooks such as Betts (1957) or Yoakam (1955).

There are several different reading programs designed for different purposes. Recreational reading is for enjoyment and entertainment. Developmental reading is graded sequentially for reading improvement and forms the structure of standard school programs. Corrective reading is carried out in the regular classroom and consists of help with specific difficulties. Adapted reading is designed for children with long-term or unmodifiable disabilities such as low intelligence or partial vision. Remedial instruction for children with severe reading deficits is usually conducted in small groups and concentrates on improving basic skills (Harris, 1961).

Research has brought to light certain problems related to reading difficulties such as poor eyesight, hearing defects, eye-span limitations, impoverished vocabulary, eye fixations, phonetic inadequacies, and stimulus deprivation. Treatment based on these factors has employed phonics, word analysis, word synthesis, flash cards, tachistoscopes, ophthalmographs, metronoscopes, and films and slides. A problem exists in trying to determine the cause of reading difficulties. Efforts are made to treat abnormalities, associated with reading problems, which are assumed to be the causes. Witness the programs of eye training to improve eye movements and eye span through exercises and various mechanical devices even though Traxler (1949) found that eye movements were related to comprehension and that increased emphasis on teaching for comprehension resulted in more maturity of eye movements.

Emotional disturbance is also given as the cause of reading problems. In some cases treatment of the reading problem resolves the emotional problem (Fernald, 1943). Frequently the question of whether a child is emotionally disturbed because he cannot read or cannot read because he is emotionally disturbed cannot be answered with assurance. Each technique has a place in treatment, but each has limitations. Only by employing techniques which are relevant to the handicap can we develop programs which meet the needs of children with a wide range of reading disabilities.

Every case requiring remedial reading is a case of failure which means defeat and a feeling of fear, frustration, and insecurity. Successful remedial-reading methods must reduce this feeling from the start. The child needs immediate and continued success. If remedial instruction does not rapidly restore his confidence, it is of little value. It should begin in an area of confidence with words, sounds, or perceptual tasks he can do easily. Each new step should be watched closely to assure that the pace is not too fast.

Children with perceptual-motor difficulties can begin with the physical activities recommended by Kephart (1960). The child can overcome these basic deficiencies by exercise on the walking board, balance board, and trampoline and can work up to training activities, such as scribbling, finger painting, and chalkboard directionality. These methods will be explained more fully in the discussion of adaptive physical education.

The child requiring further visual-motor training could progress to the kinesthetic tracing method of Fernald (1943). This method is particularly valuable for the child with visual-perceptual inefficiencies. The teacher writes the word with a felt pen on plain paper using blackboard-size cursive writing. The child says the word as he traces it with his finger. He repeats this process as many times as necessary in order to learn to write the word without looking at the copy. After he learns the word, he files it alphabetically in his own word file. In this method he employs visual, auditory, kinesthetic, and tactual modes simultaneously. Visual perception is still leading his kinesthetic development in this tracing method. In very rare cases where visual perception is so disrupted that it cannot lead adequately, more emphasis can be placed on tactual perception. The words are written with a wax crayon on rough drawing paper or on paper towels and traced by finger contact with the eyes closed. When the child has learned the form of the word through this tactual and kinesthetic method, he then traces the word with his eyes open. Another method is to have the teacher guide the child's hand while tracing the word in a shallow tray of sand or on a rough surface. Through these methods the tactual and kinesthetic modes are employed in training visual perception.

The Fernald method starts with the child's own story and teaches him the words he needs for the story. After it is written and he learns to read the written form, it is typewritten and he reads the printed form. Through writing freely and reading the written and printed copy the child develops word recognition, writing, spelling, and the meaning of words in context. This is an important method which can be used with many types of problems, such as reversals, mirror writing, and visual-motor problems. It can be used more casually with less handicapped children by simply writing the difficult word on the chalkboard and having the child trace it until he can reproduce it without looking at the copy.

The child with poor reading skills who does not need to go back to kinesthetic methods should begin remedial methods at his reading level. This level can be found by using various readers and reading tests. Efficient word perception is essential to all the processes involved in the total complex of reading. After reading level is discovered, the next step is to help the child find books and stories at his vocabulary level which contain subject matter of interest to him. Simple vocabulary so that he understands most of the words and interest in the meaning provide him with context clues for learning new words. By controlled vocabulary he becomes familiar with common words and builds up a sight vocabulary of words recognized by their shape. Dolch cards (1941) and other word games are also useful in developing a sight vocabulary.

When the child has developed the use of context clues and sight vocabulary, he is introduced to structural analysis. He begins with words which are made from two words from his sight vocabulary, such as "today," "upon," "storeroom."

The final word-attack skill for him to learn is phonetic analysis. This should not be introduced until the child can read using sight vocabulary and context clues and until he has started syllabication through structural analysis. He can then begin phonics by learning the vowel sounds in key words such as "big," "bag," "beg," and "bug." When he recognizes medial vowels in different words, he is ready for instruction in the sounds of single consonants, combinations, and blends. With his understanding of structural analysis and recognition that a vowel sound is the basis of a syllable, he is able to use phonetic analysis (Kottmeyer, 1947).

Remedial reading methods are complex, and this brief description is only intended to illustrate the principles of structure in teaching methods.

SPELLING. There are several common kinds of spelling difficulties. A child learning through the auditory mode may spell by sound. He does not see that his words look incorrect. He may spell "sugar" as it sounds to him, "shuger." The child with poor visual imagery omits and transposes letters or leaves out whole syllables. Remedial reading methods may help with spelling because the problems are related, but a child may be able to read reasonably well and still have spelling problems. A blurred or imperfect image might be adequate for recognizing a word but makes it impossible to reproduce the word correctly in writing.

Remedial spelling should begin with helping the child feel confident and relaxed. He should start with phonetic words which he pronounces while observing each syllable closely. After sufficient repetitions he writes the word saying each syllable as he writes it. If this process is unsuccessful, he should try kinesthetic methods using hand tracing.

ARITHMETIC. Many of the same perceptual problems encountered in reading are related to arithmetic handicaps. The number concept is rooted in the child's perception of objects in space. Extensive experience with counting games, abacus, play and real money, and measuring activities helps the child organize his environment and view his world in a quantitative fashion.

ADAPTED PHYSICAL EDUCATION. The therapeutic application of physical education constitutes an essential phase of newer developments in rehabilitation of the physically handicapped and emotionally disturbed. Rehabilitation services have made great strides during and since World War II, and much has been learned regarding physical activities for handicapped persons. In some public schools, handicapped and maladjusted children are excluded from physical education activities, and in other situations emotionally disturbed children are expected to participate. Pressure to make disturbed children participate in activities beyond their perceptual or motor development can cause psychosomatic illness. Some use illness as an excuse for avoiding physical education. Unless there is individualization of physical education, it will support these unwholesome developments in these children.

Three notable changes are occurring in physical education which are important to the prescriptive teaching approach. The first is that the physical education teacher is becoming a full-time teacher. Educators are examining the traditional role of the athletic coach and the need to have a winning team. In some schools this problem is being resolved by separation of team and competitive sports from physical education. The second is that the principle of physical education for all students is being accepted more fully. Part of this change is a shift in meaning from using ''physical'' as a noun to using it as an adjective. If physical education is thought of as education of the physical, then those who are not benefited physically are excluded. If physical education refers to education through physical activities, then programs for all children are possible. In the past many children were excused from physical activities on the basis that they did not fit in or that the activities would be harmful to them. Medical and rehabilitation research (Clarke and Clarke, 1963) indicates that physical activity is beneficial for postpolio cases, the cerebral palsied, victims of heart disease, amputees, substrength cases, epileptics, and postsurgical cases as well as for children suffering from obesity, poor motor coordination, postural defects, and emotional problems. In most cases these children need the values inherent in a good physical education program more than children who are without physical, mental, or emotional handicaps. The third important development is improvement in preparation of physical education teachers. Physiotherapy, rehabilitation, improved background in anatomy and physiology, and mental-health courses provided in modern teacher-training institutions prepare teachers for this more complex job.

Physical education teachers are becoming better equipped to plan programs that will be effective in realizing educational objectives. This planning involves adapting the program to meet individual needs. Usually the adapted program should be devised as an integral part of the educational program and not as a separate entity. The purpose of adapted physical education is to meet, through physical activities, the individual needs of handicapped children whose functional deficiencies are amenable to improvement through exercise. These children frequently possess inadequacies which interfere with their successful participation in the diversified and vigorous activities of the general physical education program.

Some prime considerations in initiating an adapted program are the administrative responsibility, coordination with other services, and the exercise system to be employed. To be effective the physical education department within the school should be given the responsibility of providing an appropriate program for every child. If administration in the school places a winning team ahead of physical education and if handicapped children are excused from physical education, an adapted program will have little opportunity for success. If we are going to provide adapted physical education for handicapped children, it should be in an integrated program.

The activity programs must be established within the confines of safety. The medical examination must necessarily be the starting point for the evaluation process related to adapted activities in prescriptive teaching. Defects, where vigorous exercise would be harmful, should be evaluated. The school health service should participate in, and be the liaison with, the private medical practitioner. The school psychologist or prescriptive teaching coordinator should be involved in planning the program for those children requiring physical activities for the remediation of perceptual-motor inefficiencies. Children who are emotionally disturbed can be provided with activities which reduce tension, improve coordination, and improve their opportunities for social interaction. Many of the activities recommended for the slow learner (Kephart, 1960) are beneficial also for some emotionally disturbed children. The coordination of the adapted physical education program with the psychological, private medical, and school medical services assures the implementation of diagnostic findings.

Of the number of systems which could be used to implement adapted programs, one called circuit training (Morgan and Adamson, 1958) appears to have considerable potential where the program is to take place in a regular class. According to the originators, circuit training enables large groups to train together by employing a circuit of consecutive activities around which each performer progresses. Each child performs individually for a prescribed time before moving on to the next activity station. A circuit can be established for the child with sensorimotor deficiencies which might include the walking board for developing balance, trampoline, rolling a ball to the wall and catching it when it returns, and tether ball. The next circuit he progresses to could include hopping, skipping, bouncing a rhythm ball, walking a line backwards and forwards, and walking on stepping stones forming various patterns. In this manner the handicapped child participates at his level and progresses circuit by circuit as he overcomes his perceptual difficulty. Children with severe sensorimotor handicaps should receive extra work, in a small group or individually, where the teacher can observe them closely and help them with their developmental problems.

The handicapped child's social development is encouraged by effective physical education programs (Mathews, Kruse, and Shaw, 1962).

The feeling of accomplishment among his own group promotes self-confidence and helps overcome the withdrawing, timid, or self-conscious behavior which is common among the handicapped. Adapted physical education, along with other appropriate educational modifications and provisions for guidance and counseling, has been demonstrated to be an effective means of providing opportunities for the success of these youngsters (Lerner and Martin, 1955, in a ten-year study of fifty-nine handicapped youths).

EMOTIONAL PROBLEMS. A child experiencing failure and disappointment at school may develop negative responses to the standard methods the teacher employs in an attempt to help him. He may avoid looking at the questions and answers which are marked wrong and thus miss the opportunity of learning from his mistakes. The cross after his answer becomes the symbol stimulus for his negative responses. A question mark made with a blue or green pencil instead of a cross made with a red one suggests to the child that he should look at his work and see where he went wrong. Some emotional blocks to learning may be avoided by changing the symbol stimulus for the child.

Children who are excessively hostile toward adults do not respond constructively to teacher encouragement or approval. Some of these children are not overtly aggressive but show their hostility by resisting learning and thereby avoiding adult approval. The writer worked with a group of such children and found that they learned rapidly with programmed instruction in a teaching machine. Since there was no adult figure in authority present, these children seemed to feel that working with a teaching machine was a self-rewarding experience. The results were most encouraging because there appeared to be some carry-over of satisfactions from this learning to the regular classroom situation. Programmed instruction has interesting possibilities for the teaching of disturbed children, although the present research is quite limited. Smith and Quackenbush (1961) report some positive results of experiments in teaching elementary mathematics with teaching machines in a special education setting for children with a wide variety of handicaps.

Many emotionally maladjusted children are subject to disturbance in their visual-motor areas. When they are seriously disturbed, coordination is poor, and the fine movements required in reading and writing may be difficult. Special instructional methods for dealing with visual-motor development are appropriate for improving physical coordination and can be an effective approach in an attack on the emotional problem. Physical activities can be used to correct perceptual distortions, thus reducing conflicts between the visual field and reality as perceived through other senses. This allows the child to walk and move about better and to handle objects and tools with greater ease. He falls and bumps into things less frequently and is less inclined to accidents. Walking, marching, and moving in rhythm to music is beneficial. Walking along a straight line and following large circles or squares drawn on the floor are helpful activities.

Lateral visual-motor development is a frequent problem of the disturbed child, and special exercises and games are available emphasizing left-right orientation. Gross motor tasks in work and play, such as large clay modeling, finger painting, and woodworking, are useful activities. These methods have the advantage of starting with activities which are not particularly threatening, and are not closely associated with the social interaction and academic learning difficulties which are contributing to the emotional disturbance.

In brief, visual-motor development can reduce the neurotic conflict resulting from the child's perceptual disturbance while, at the same time, it is diverting attention from stimuli which previously caused the disturbed behavior. This special method has considerable potential for the seriously disturbed. In teaching art to an inhibited child, the teacher uses methods which help develop freedom of expression (Randall, 1956). The child may be given more time in finger painting or more encouragement toward creative activities.

SPECIAL EDUCATION. Usually the teaching methods in special education are the special teacher's particular competency. The teacher of the deaf understands the methods of teaching speechreading or lipreading and language to his pupils (O'Neill and Oyer, 1961). Nonauditory communication for the deaf, special methods for the hard-of-hearing, and the problems of getting along with the hearing child are outlined by Brereton (1957). The teachers of blind and partially seeing children know the methods of teaching braille and of sight saving. Special education for mentally retarded, emotionally disturbed, brain-injured, and hyperactive children is discussed in Chapter 5.

Specific Objectives (C)

The general objective of intellectual development is the same for all children, but the specific objectives for the dull child and the bright child are different. The specific objectives of art for the blind child are modified in relation to his handicap. Color harmony, for example, is an aim which would be modified. The specific objectives of the music program for the child who is deaf, physical achievement for the child with a heart condition, and independence for the mentally defective child are modified consistent with the educational significance of the handicap.

The most important objective of education for severely retarded children is self-care. They have more sense of personal worth and are more independent when they can eat, dress, and wash themselves. The aim of communication does not include reading but emphasizes simple oral language.

Kornberg (1955) in discussing the goals for disturbed children suggests that instilling a culture and building good citizenship are long-run objectives. Specific objectives emphasize short-run or first steps in preparing a base for more effective conduct.

The child with an emotional disability has a good chance of overcoming the disability and its handicapping consequences. Sometimes a temporary modification of the specific objectives of education may facilitate his learning. If a child is too fearful to participate in a large group in competitive sports, forcing him to participate might be so traumatic that he does not learn. A temporary modification of the specific objective of integration into a group may permit him to participate with one other child in a situation which is less threatening. A child with a low frustration tolerance must be given frustration in small doses until he can learn to deal with a normal amount. Because learning is more likely to take place when success is within his grasp, the specific objectives are modified temporarily. The ultimate and general objective may be achieved later for the emotionally disturbed child.

Ancillary Services (D)

Because the services provided by administrators, consultants, psychologists, counselors, and social workers support instruction, they are called ancillary services. Services which are not instructional, or do not facilitate instruction, should not rightfully be school services (Froehlich, 1958).

ADMINISTRATION. The purpose of the school administration is to facilitate instruction. All the recommendations which become part of prescriptive teaching should have administrative consent. Reports should be approved by the administration before modifications are implemented in the classroom. The school principal is the final authority in matters of discipline, and therefore any recommendations regarding methods of control of the child should be made to the principal as well as to the teacher. Because consistency is essential to effective prescriptive teaching, the teacher and the principal must be in agreement regarding discipline. Frequently the school principal has to work with parents, and it is therefore essential that he be aware of the prescription for the child when discussing the problem. Implementation of recommendations regarding placement and personnel, materials, equipment, and school buildings is a responsibility of the administration.

The administration of the school provides a valuable resource for working with children whose self-image is inadequate. The principal of the school can do much in a supportive role for the child with derogatory self-regard. Because of his prestige position, the principal's recognition of and interest in this child will frequently produce very marked results. A word of encouragement or support from time to time can have notable influence in changing the child's self-concept.

CONSULTANTS. Prescriptive teaching makes use of special services available to the school system. Consultants, speech therapists, divisional supervisors, and curriculum consultants provide valuable resources.

Consultation with and referrals to these specialists in the school system are an integral part of the prescriptive teaching program. When there is effective coordination and communication within these services, it is possible to avoid many of the problems of the awkward diagnosis of multiple handicap. The child who is seriously emotionally disturbed may have as symptoms a speech defect and a health problem. Where coordination is poor, he may be classified as a speech problem, an emotional problem, or a health problem depending on who sees him first. The prescriptive teaching technique of diagnosis determines what is educationally significant about the handicap, and appropriate personnel are employed in the solution of the problem. This method may involve people from one or several professions, but it results in an integrated approach to both diagnosis and to treatment.

COUNSELING. Counseling services are a valuable resource within the school system. A counselor is effective in helping with the diagnosis through his interviews with the child and through the relationship that develops. He is also a valuable person in follow-up studies.

Counseling is effective in treating certain anxiety states in children. By talking out and sorting out problems, the child can frequently reduce his anxiety and function more effectively (Patterson, 1958). In a supportive role, the counselor can reinforce positive responses that the child makes. For example, he can give the child encouragement, can show interest, and can give additional praise and support for improved performance. With some unloved or rejected children the counselor can develop a therapeutic relationship contributing to emotional growth. Because counseling of this kind usually takes considerable time, only a few cases can be handled in this way.

The counselor must be aware of all the factors discussed in the case study so that he will avoid supporting weaknesses in the child. An all-inclusive sympathetic approach may make the client feel more comfortable but may be supporting deviance or weakness.

Frequently there are more direct ways of dealing with young children's behavior than by the symbolic method of counseling. The teacher, employing an appropriate approach in his daily contact with the child, can achieve significant results. The child may be better prepared in his symbolism and attitude as a result of counseling, but he must still face the problem of learning how to behave when he is in the classroom.

These limitations are mentioned because in many cases counseling has been regarded as the only solution when actually more effective means were available. Counseling is most effective with children who have a basis of anxiety regarding their behavior. For the child lacking in anxiety, counseling is not an effective way of solving problems unless a great deal of time is available. Counseling is a valuable resource but should not be regarded as the only means of solution to problems.

HEALTH SERVICES.   The school health services should be involved in the diagnosis of all referred children. Recommendations often involve the nurse in making further home visits, seeing the child on a continuing basis, and making referrals to other medical services. Some interpretations to the parents are best made by the school doctor or nurse. In some cases follow-up and further medical observation are part of the case method.

COORDINATION.   The school psychologist provides ancillary services as a consultant, diagnostician, counselor, and frequently coordinator of diagnostic and treatment services within the school. It is not implied that the school psychologist is the only person who should be assigned coordination responsibility. It is intended that the person with responsibility for coordination of a prescriptive teaching program should be primarily interested in education and the contribution that teaching makes to the treatment process.

The role of ancillary services in working with parents is of prime importance. When the parents are ready for help, a few interviews or an appropriate referral results in substantial gains. The possibility of involving the parents in more constructive approaches should always receive consideration.

The ancillary school services have an important part to play in the diagnosis of handicaps as well as in the provision of some school-centered treatment. This may involve the school social worker or visiting teacher, counselor, speech correctionist, school psychologist, principal, school nurse, and other medical personnel.

Placement and Personnel (E)

Placement of the child is usually limited by the educational facilities and teaching personnel available in the school or school system. Schools create problems when they try to move children along who are not ready. This is a particularly acute problem when teaching reading. For the child who is not ready, retention for an additional year in kindergarten, extended time in an ungraded primary division, or retention for an additional year in first grade is preferable to moving too rapidly. To be effective, retaining a child for a second year in a grade must be accepted positively by the parents and the child. The child must see it as an opportunity to learn rather than as punishment for failure (Steadman, 1959). If a child cannot find satisfaction in learning and in group acceptance, contingent on keeping up with group activity, he may find it in attention seeking, troublesome behavior, or withdrawal into fantasy. He cannot sit in school five days a week for forty weeks each year without satisfaction of some kind. He may start moving toward delinquency or illness and become a serious problem to himself and to society (Stringer, 1958). Successful grade placement must support the child by providing him with a situation in which interaction with his environment reinforces his feeling of competency.

Special classes enroll homogeneous groups of children with one type of exceptionality. These classes are usually located in regular public schools. When these classes operate in a self-contained fashion, the children are segregated or are separate from normal children for all or nearly all their classroom instruction. The integrated special class has the exceptional child enrolled in the special class but has him taking some of his academic instruction in regular classes. Regular class placement for the exceptional child is sometimes supported by the use of a resource room and teacher. The child is enrolled in the regular class or homeroom but goes to the resource room for special instruction and equipment.

Special education is a developing field with a substantial body of knowledge and methodology, but there exists considerable controversy regarding the placement of the exceptional child. There is a trend toward the belief that where possible through special help or equipment, an exceptional child should remain in his regular class at school. Where it is not desirable or possible, he should be removed from the regular class only to the degree to which the diagnosis indicates it is essential for his best treatment and education. It is thought that isolation from regular contacts with normal children can hinder the normal personality growth of the child and lead to feelings of rejection and inferiority. It is also important to realize that the physical placement of an exceptional child in a regular classroom neither guarantees his acceptance nor his integration with his classmates.

A review of research (Johnson, 1962) dealing with the efficacy of special class placement for mentally retarded children indicated that the majority of research studies did not support special class placement. Most studies indicated that retarded children showed greater academic achievement in the regular class but showed superior social adjustment in the special class. The social adjustment in the special class should be interpreted in terms of the protected environment.

Special class placement as a phase in the child's total education may be appropriate. Schwartzberg (1964) reports the case of a retarded reader of above-average intelligence who was placed in a special class for six months of his fifth school year. He gained confidence in his ability and twenty-nine months of measured reading development. On readmittance into the regular class he showed good adjustment to his peers and appeared to be accepted by them.

Normal children as well as the mentally retarded, deaf, blind, emotionally disturbed, and otherwise exceptional are being educated primarily so that they can take their appropriate places in society. The society in which these children will live as adults will not be divided into homogeneous groups. It is important that children receive their education in a milieu which is similarly diversified. As many handicaps have only situational significance, it is possible for children to remain in a regular class much of the time and have some special placement for their handicap. The principle from which placement should be made is that of integration where possible and segregation only where it is educationally relevant. The speech-handicapped child may benefit from special instruction in a group or in individual instruction while retaining regular class placement. The partially hearing child can take his language subjects in a special classroom and participate in industrial arts, physical education, art, and science with regular classes. If we discern a meaningful relationship between diagnosis and the provisions which might be made for the child by the school, we can resolve the question of integration and segregation of handicapped children.

It is evident that the handicapped child, such as the deaf, blind, or mentally retarded, needs special consideration. Emphasis should be on the desirability of retaining the child within the normal group wherever possible. This consideration involves the factor called School Plant because segregation and integration of handicapped children is dependent on the buildings and rooms provided. The child with low intelligence, placed in a special class for his academic subjects, may be integrated in art, physical education, industrial arts, home economics, and school social activities where his handicap is less significant. The deaf child needs special education so different from the hearing child that a special class is advisable. He must be taught language from its very rudiments because practically none of it has come to him incidentally. Once he has learned to read, he can be integrated with regular classes in many activities. It is probably better for him to remain in a special class for language subjects throughout much of his schooling.

The objective of total integration for the handicapped child must be considered in determining the degree of integration attempted. The therapeutic goal of a special class for emotionally disturbed pupils is to help them overcome their difficulties and move back into the regular program. Any unnecessary segregation from the regular program into special classes may be damaging to the child's self-concept and will contribute to his perception of himself as handicapped in ways which are unrealistic and inconsistent with his real abilities. Through the modification of his negative emotional responses, the troubled, tense, anxious, withdrawn, or unstable child will become more able to integrate socially. Even if he does remain somewhat unstable or peculiar, he will in most cases be integrated to a degree with normal society in adult life. Therefore, the degree of segregation within the school should be the minimum necessary to facilitate instruction. Where the mental or emotional disability is of a functional nature, the objective should always be to help the child learn to live a normal life. In cases of severe brain pathology and mental deficiency, the objective may be to prepare the child for life in an institution, a sheltered workshop, or other protected situation. Full integration with normal society is not feasible with our present limited knowledge and available facilities for children who have severe mental deficiencies. In these cases integration is not a prime objective, and segregation into special classes or special schools is desirable.

The blind, deaf, and orthopedically handicapped child has the potential for independence and self-support and can be integrated. The blind child may have some difficulty in studying music, but his handicap is not such that he cannot take music with the regular class. The partially seeing child, having adequate special equipment, can do much of his work in a regular class. The deaf child can participate in sports with the hearing child. When he is in a regular art class, he can see what the other children are doing and can carry out the assignments. The segregation of the exceptional child should be on the basis of the situationally significant aspects of his handicap.

Highly qualified special teachers are often in short supply, and less qualified personnel have to be employed for this work. The use of master teachers as consultants and the use of teacher aids or assistants increases the influence of the special teacher. The prescription regarding the teaching personnel is based on the teacher's qualifications, maturity, and personality.

In placement of an emotionally disturbed child it is advisable to consider the kind of social and emotional environment the teacher can provide. This environment is often highly dependent upon the personality integration and emotional well-being of the teacher. One teacher should not be given too many children with handicaps in the regular class, and the size of the class should be reduced when handicapped children are included.

Subject Matter (F)

The curriculum is modified in accordance with the special needs of the handicap. The hard-of-hearing child receives speech training to improve articulation, speech or lipreading to develop speech understanding, and auditory training to enhance listening skills and to ensure that he makes maximum use of his residual hearing with or without amplification. The curriculum for the blind child places emphasis on oral and tactile skills and braille. The child with an orthopedic disability resulting from accident, arthritis, cerebral palsy, congenital defect, or tuberculosis of the bone may have handicapping limitations in the manipulation of materials required for learning. The child with lowered vitality as a result of disabilities connected with heart conditions, rheumatic fever, birth injury, diabetes, and allergies may need a modified curriculum. In each case, whether the disability is of a physical or emotional nature, the modification of the curriculum should be based on the relevance of the handicap to the child's learning.

At the time in the child's school career when occupational planning becomes a consideration, the handicapping consequences of permanent disability should be considered in outlining curriculum. The program for a child with emotional instability should not lead to an occupation that is particularly stressful. A child with a disability of the respiratory function should not work toward a career in occupations which would place excessive demands on his lessened vitality or where he would work in dust or fumes which might result in irritation or damage to his respiratory system.

In planning for the subject matter to be employed in remediation of learning problems, the principles of structure in the learning process are the guides to follow. A sequence of activities is planned that provides for learning to overcome a deficient skill or perceptual inefficiency.

Instructional Materials (G)

For purposes of definition materials are differentiated from equipment on the basis of expendability. Materials are consumable supplies whereas equipment lasts longer and is not consumed in the learning process.

The instructional materials provide the media with which a child can learn. An emotionally disturbed child working with finger paints on large sheets of paper may be fulfilling a need to manipulate, to satisfy curiosity, and to achieve independent expression. Frequently, disturbed children need more activity with concrete materials to develop the processes of seeing, feeling, and doing. Early gross motor-development activities require large sheets of paper, brushes, and crayons.

Clay is another useful medium in developing expression and three-dimensional perception. Later, craft supplies such as wood, nails, weaving materials, and sewing supplies provide for creative expression and visual-motor development. Selection of appropriate materials helps channel creative imagination into constructive areas.

Instructional materials for sight saving with the partially seeing child include dull- or rough-finish exercise paper in an off-white color with lines 3/4 inch apart. Pencils with large, soft lead and felt pens are suitable for writing. Large sheets of paper and jumbo or kindergarten crayons are used for free drawings. Sight-saving chalks are specially designed to reduce eyestrain by giving greater visibility on the chalkboard. Dust-free chalk should be used where a child has a respiratory difficulty.

Workbooks provide practice with controlled vocabulary and for other subject areas. A variety of achievement tests is useful in working with remedial problems.

The hard-of-hearing or deaf child uses more graphic material since vision is his chief means of receiving instruction. The materials for special education of mentally retarded, emotionally disturbed, brain-injured, and hyperactive children are described in Chapter 5.

Special Equipment (H)

Special equipment is required for teaching many handicapped children. For the hard-of-hearing this includes a group hearing aid, record player, tape recorder, visual aids such as charts, a mirror for speech imitation, and a large amount of blackboard space. The equipment for the partially seeing child includes chalkboard of a special gray-green color, furniture with a light glareproof finish, and desks with movable seats and tops which are adjustable for height and angle. Specially designed magnifiers, talking books, tape recorders, typewriters, maps, globes, and charts are available for the partially seeing child. For the blind child, braille books, talking books, records, relief maps and geophysical globes, manipulative teaching devices, and abaci are employed.

Remedial reading uses equipment for testing and for teaching. Visual perception is evaluated by using a Snellen chart for detecting nearsightedness and visual acuity. The Keystone Visual Survey Tele-binocular checks nearsightedness, farsightedness, and astigmatism as well as vertical imbalance, lateral imbalance, far- and near-point fusion, and binocular visual efficiency. For remedial treatment there are available devices such as the tachistoscope and controlled reader. Dolch cards provide useful exercises while providing the novelty of playing a card game. For the kinesthetic tracing method the children require individual word files. The Iowa Reading Films (University of Iowa, 1959) give high school students practice in improving speed and comprehension.

Special aids and toys for handicapped children can be purchased or constructed. Perceptual-motor skill is developed through work with large beads, colored cubes, parquetry blocks, colored sticks, pegboards, interlocking plastic cubes, and abaci. Some specially prepared aids for children with severe motor difficulties are described by Dorward (1960). A device for visual-motor training which appears to have considerable potential is a light box or tracing table. The top is frosted plastic so that a design placed under the top is only visible when the light is on. The light is operated by a push button and is on only as long as the button is pressed. The child places his paper on top of the light box and presses the button. He may hold the light on until he finishes tracing the design, letter, figure, or word, or he may finish it from memory. The light can be operated by a timer for automatic control providing short exposure times which help the child hold the visual image as he continues his tracing. Seriously handicapped children can begin by making straight lines within rather wide bands and progress gradually to narrower bands. They can proceed to changes in line direction, curves, simple geometrical shapes, letters, and eventually to writing. This device should not be used with hyperactive children as the flashing of the light is too stimulating. Teaching machines, language laboratories, audio-visual aids, electric typewriters, and special individual aids may find their place in a program designed to meet individual needs.

School Plant (I)

Children with orthopedic handicaps and lowered vitality should be in school buildings which have been constructed for their restricted mobility. Many factors, such as transportation, accessibility of facilities, and ramps and stairs, should be considered when planning for these children. The room for the hard-of-hearing child should have acoustical treatment to reduce the noise level which would be amplified by hearing aids. Adequate shadow-free illumination for hard-of-hearing children facilitates lipreading. A wooden floor which carries vibrations makes it possible for them to enjoy dancing and rhythmical movements to music. Ample storage equipment for visual aids and projection equipment is an important plant consideration in special education. A room for blind children should be large enough for them to move about easily and explore tactually. The room where the blind child does much of his early academic learning should be acoustically treated to prevent extraneous noise from entering the classroom. Because the blind child depends on auditory cues which he will use later, the learning of these cues should not be contaminated by extraneous sounds.

Children who are hyperactive or overresponsive to stimuli can improve their learning in an environment containing a minimum of extraneous stimuli. Some brain-injured children have difficulty learning because they have difficulty sorting out stimuli. Everything that they see or hear appears in their responses. Limiting the stimuli, as much as possible, to the one associated with a specific learning, improves their opportunity of producing an uncontaminated response. When appropriate responses are established, these children can usually produce the responses in a more complex normal environment but need the simplified environment for learning new material.

The first environmental consideration for these children is to make the classroom as unstimulating as possible and still provide for learning. Illumination, for example, is essential in this classroom although light is stimulating. Lighting should provide ample illumination of whatever the child is to focus on, but it should be free of glare. The source of light should be concealed. Since color dynamics can contribute to the effectiveness of the physical environment on the child's learning, the room should be painted with a flat finish in a receding neutral color. The windows may have to be eliminated or covered with the same color. In this neutral environment the one item upon which attention is to be focused is in contrasting or highlighting colors. Acoustical treatment to insulate outside noise and soften sounds within the room helps control undesirable auditory stimuli.

A desirable seating arrangement for the child who is hyperactive does not require him to look past another child to see the teacher, demonstration material, or chalkboard. In the case of an extremely distractible child it may be desirable at times to place screens of the same neutral color as the walls at the child's sides to cut down on interference from peripheral vision, or he may work in a cubicle or booth.

The room should be large enough that these children need not be seated too close together. A quiet room should be available nearby to accommodate a child who may need a rest period away from the group.

These plant modifications are appropriate for children who are hyperactive, overresponsive to extraneous stimuli, and distractible, whether the cause is organic or emotional. The learning problem or handicapping consequence is similar for some brain-injured and some emotionally disturbed children.

Special education for most handicapped children should be regarded as a phase in their total education. Some require special placement for a relatively short period of time, while others require special placement for only part of the school day. Separate schools for special education make integration difficult. Special classrooms and facilities in regular schools provide for the integration and flexibility desired. Special schools are appropriate for severely retarded children who are not going to be integrated fully at school or in society.

Auxiliary Agencies (J)

Agencies, clincs, and services outside the school provide much-needed resources in the resolution of problems. The effective use of these resources depends upon communication, coordination, and integration of school and community services. Where mutual respect and trust exist between the agencies and the school, many problems which effect the child's progress at school can be resolved. It is not the function of the school to tell social agencies what to do; therefore the prescription will contain only a recommendation for referral to the appropriate agency. However, consistent two-way communication will enhance the effectiveness of both the school and the auxiliary agency. The techniques of referral depend on the agency involved and the necessary preliminary work that is required in making the referral. Where family problems exist, a referral to the family agency might be appropriate. The parents may need some help from the school counselor or psychologist in clarifying their need before they are ready for referral. Children in need of protection may be referred to the child welfare agency. A boy without a father may need support of a father substitute and a referral to Big Brothers may satisfy this need.

Some children receive psychotherapy from private psychiatrists, and some attend mental-health or child-guidance clinics. Maintenance of regular communication between the school and the treatment agency is of mutual benefit and provides improved treatment for the child. Prescriptive teaching can provide educational treatment which supports the therapy of the clinic. Similarly communication should be maintained for the child receiving other medical treatment, social work, or probation.

The parents' marriage problems may result in a disabling emotional condition in the child which results in poor school progress. This does not mean that marriage counseling should be the school's business. It is assumed that it is the school's responsibility to procure but not necessarily provide the help needed. The comprehensive diagnosis used in this program gives the school psychologist a vantage point from which he can recommend referrals to appropriate resources outside the school. In this context these resources become truly auxiliary services.

ORDER WITHIN THE MODEL

The order of the placement of variables in the model from most modifiable to least modifiable is the result of experience in one school system. A change in the order to fit a particular situation would make little difference in the operation of the model. In the present arrangement the modification involving the least number of people is Consistent Approach and the most modifiable cell is the closest to the front; therefore, the most modifiable cell is A-12. The least modifiable variable is Auxiliary Agencies because the acceptance of their help is the responsibility of the parent rather than that of the school. The most distant cell is the least modifiable; so there is a continuum from most modifiable, A-12, diagonally through the model to least modifiable, J-1. This places the most important variables closest to the observer and the least important farthest away.

Frequency of Recommendations

The frequency with which recommendations are made for modification of the school variables depends on a number of factors. Prescriptive teaching tends to encourage the development of new techniques as well as to communicate them. Therefore, the recommendations regarding methods will reflect the background and knowledge of the coordinator and the teaching staff. Other factors related to the frequency of recommendations are as follows.

THE COMMUNITY.   Concentrations of people with problems do occur. Areas characterized by social disorganization tend to have high delinquency rates. Communities of multi-family residences tend to have a high percentage of one-parent families. Poor housing, which is usually cheap housing, tends to have concentrations of people with poor economic resources.

THE REFERRALS.   Teachers differ in their opinions of what constitutes a problem. Their concept of a problem determines which children are referred. Many factors in the teacher's background influence perception of which child needs special attention. His professional preparation and in-service orientation also play a part in his concept of who should be referred.

THE SCHOOL SYSTEM.   When special schools are provided for specific handicaps, these handicaps will not be encountered as frequently in regular schools. The cases in this program were from schools which had some special classes for the deaf or hard-of-hearing, for the intellectually handicapped, and for the mentally superior. The severely physically and mentally handicapped were attending special schools for the retarded, cerebral palsied, blind, etc. This limited the number of referrals of children with these handicaps.

SPECIAL SERVICES AND CLASSES.   Placement is limited to the facilities provided and available. The recommendations for special placement or other special services depend to a large extent on the resources in the community and the special facilities within the schools.

ORGANIZATION.   The administrative responsibility in specific areas of the school system is a determining factor in the way in which the educational program is separated into elements for modification. For example, health services could be ancillary school services or auxiliary agencies. The guidance clinic might be a school service or a community agency.

SUMMARY

Prescriptive teaching is based on the modification of one or more of the ten variables in the educational program. It is not suggested that this is the only classification of the modifiable factors. The author found in writing teaching prescriptions that these categories were suitable classifications of the modifiable elements. In dealing with these factors in this chapter, descriptions of disabilities have been used. In application it must be kept in mind that the handicapping consequence to learning and the situational significance determine the required modification. Prescriptive teaching is concerned with what can be done in the classroom using what is educationally meaningful in dealing with a specific problem. We should not take the medical diagnosis of disability as a classification which tells us how to teach. The medical profession is particularly competent in the area of disability, and the teaching profession can be competent in the area of handicap.

The objective of the prescription for the handicapped child with a permanent disability is to facilitate his learning by helping him to make use of his available resources. The objective for a child with a functional disorder is to help him learn more appropriate responses and thus to overcome his disability.

This chapter did not attempt to cover in detail all modifications within these school variables. As the coordinator gains familiarity with the prescriptive teaching method, he will gain new insights into the school's potential which allow a wider scope for application of the method. Experience indicates that when a number of simultaneously integrated modifications are made, the improvement will be greater than when the modifications are made one at a time. The total in the integrated approach is greater than the sum of the parts.

REFERENCES

Bettelheim, Bruno. *Love Is Not Enough.* New York: The Free Press of Glencoe, 1949.

Betts, Emmett A. *Foundations of Reading Instruction.* New York: American Book Company, 1957.

Blair, Glenn Myers. *Diagnostic and Remedial Teaching.* New York: The Macmillan Company, 1956.

Brereton, Beatrice (Le Gay). *The Schooling of Children with Impaired Hearing.* Sydney: Commonwealth Office of Education, 1957.

Brogan, Peggy, and Fox, Lorene. *Helping Children Read.* New York: Holt, Rinehart and Winston, Inc., 1961.

Cassidy, Rosalind. *Counseling in the Physical Education Program.* New York: Appleton-Century-Crofts, Inc., 1959.

Clarke, David L. "A New Approach to Classroom Guidance," *The Education Digest,* 1958, 8:34–36.

Clarke, David L., and Fitzgerald, David M. *Attitude Consistency Handbook.* Seattle, Wash.: Seattle Public Schools Administrative and Service Center, 1958.

Clarke, H. Harrison, and Clarke, David H. *Developmental and Adapted Physical Education*. Englewood Cliffs, N.J.: Prentice-Hall, Inc., 1963.

Cruickshank, William M. *Education of Exceptional Children and Youth*. Englewood Cliffs, N.J.: Prentice-Hall, Inc., 1958.

Cutsforth, T. D. *The Blind in School and Society*. New York: American Foundation for the Blind, 1951.

Daniels, Arthur S. *Adapted Physical Education*. New York: Harper & Row, Publishers, Incorporated, 1954.

Dolch, E. W. *The Dolch Picture-Word Cards*. Champaign, Ill.: The Garrard Press, 1941.

Dorward, Barbara. *Aids and Toys for Handicapped Children*. Washington, D.C.: Council for Exceptional Children, NEA, 1960.

Dunn, Lloyd M. (ed.). *Exceptional Children in the Schools*. New York: Holt, Rinehart and Winston, Inc., 1963.

Fait, Hollis F. *Adapted Physical Education*. Philadelphia: W. B. Saunders Company, 1960.

Fernald, Grace M. *Remedial Techniques in Basic School Subjects*. New York: McGraw-Hill Book Company, 1943.

Froehlich, Clifford P. *Guidance Services in Schools*. New York: McGraw-Hill Book Company, 1958.

Haring, Norris G., and Phillips, E. Lakin. *Educating Emotionally Disturbed Children*. New York: McGraw-Hill Book Company, 1962.

Harris, Albert J. *How to Increase Reading Ability*. New York: Longmans, Green & Co., Inc., 1961.

Hathaway, W. *Education and Health of the Partially Seeing Child* (rev. ed.). New York: Columbia University Press, 1959.

Johnson, G. Orville. "Special Education for Mentally Handicapped: A Paradox," *Exceptional Children*, 1962, 29:62–69.

Kephart, Newell C. *The Slow Learner in the Classroom*. Columbus, Ohio: Charles E. Merrill Books, Inc., 1960.

Kirk, Samuel A. *Educating Exceptional Children*. Boston: Houghton Mifflin Company, 1962.

Kornberg, Leonard. *A Class for Disturbed Children*. New York: Bureau of Publications, Teachers College, Columbia University, 1955.

Kottmeyer, William. *Handbook for Remedial Reading*. New York: McGraw-Hill Book Company, 1947.

Laycock, Samuel R. *Special Education in Canada*. Scarborough, Ontario: W. J. Gage Limited, 1963.

Lerner, Ruth, and Martin, Marion. "What Happens to the College Student with a Physical Handicap?" *The Personnel and Guidance Journal*, 1955, 36:80.

Lippman, Hyman S. *Treatment of the Child in Emotional Conflict.* New York: McGraw-Hill Book Company, 1956.

Magary, James F., and Eichorn, John R. (eds.). *The Exceptional Child: A Book of Readings.* New York: Holt, Rinehart and Winston, Inc., 1960.

Mathews, Donald K., Kruse, Robert, and Shaw, Virginia. *The Science of Physical Education for Handicapped Children.* New York: Harper & Row, Publishers, Incorporated, 1962.

Morgan, R. E., and Adamson, G. T. *Circuit Training.* London: G. Bell & Sons, Ltd., 1958.

O'Neill, John J., and Oyer, Herbert J. *Visual Communication for the Hard of Hearing.* Englewood Cliffs, N.J.: Prentice-Hall, Inc., 1961.

Patterson, O. H. *Counseling the Emotionally Disturbed.* New York: Harper & Row, Publishers, Incorporated, 1958.

Randall, Arne W. *Art for Exceptional Children.* Lubbock, Tex.: Texas Technological College, 1956.

Redl, Fritz, and Wattenberg, William W. *Mental Hygiene in Teaching.* New York: Harcourt, Brace & World, Inc., 1959.

Riessman, Frank. *The Culturally Deprived Child.* New York: Harper & Row, Publishers, Incorporated, 1962.

Robinson, Alan H. (ed.). *The Underachiever in Reading.* Chicago: The University of Chicago Press, 1962.

Ross, Ramon. "Diagnosis and Correction of Arithmetic Underachievement," *The Arithmetic Teacher,* January, 1963, 10:22–27.

Schonell, Fred J. *The Psychology and Teaching of Reading.* New York: Philosophical Library, Inc., 1961.

Schwartzberg, Herbert. "The Case of Andrew Miller: A Retarded Reader of Above Average Intelligence," *The Elementary School Journal,* January, 1964, vol. 64, no. 4.

Smith, Donald E. P., and Carrigan, Patricia M. *The Nature of Reading Disability.* New York: Harcourt, Brace & World, Inc., 1959.

Smith, Edgar A., and Quackenbush, Jack. *Devereux Teaching Aids Employed in Presenting Elementary Mathematics in a Special Education Setting.* Devon, Pa.: Devereux Schools, 1961.

Steadman, E. R. "Fifteen Who Were Not Promoted," *The Elementary School Journal,* February, 1959, 59:217–276.

Strauss, A. A., and Lehtinen, Laura. *Psychopathology and Education of the Brain-injured Child.* New York: Grune & Stratton, Inc., 1947.

Stringer, Lorene A. "Promotion Policies and Mental Health," *The National Elementary Principal,* April, 1958, 37:32.

Traxler, Arthur E. "Research in Reading in the United States," *Journal of Educational Research,* March, 1949, 42:494.

University of Iowa. Iowa Reading Films, 1959.

Woolf, Maurice D., and Woolf, Jeanne A. *Remedial Reading*. New York: McGraw-Hill Book Company, 1957.

Wright, Beatrice A. *Physical Disability: A Psychological Approach*. New York: Harper & Row, Publishers, Incorporated, 1960.

Yoakam, Gerald A. *Basal Reading Instruction*. New York: McGraw-Hill Book Company, 1955.

5

THE EDUCATION OF
EXCEPTIONAL CHILDREN

Many exceptional children do not require special educational provisions. A child with an amputated limb may require special medical treatment and a prosthesis but may make satisfactory educational progress in a regular class at school. Children are educationally exceptional when they possess deviations requiring special educational facilities and teaching. Exceptional children are categorized by various authorities as follows: (1) mentally retarded, (2) gifted, (3) emotionally disturbed, (4) deaf and hard-of-hearing, (5) blind and partially seeing, (6) speech-handicapped, (7) orthopedically handicapped, (8) brain-injured and neurologically impaired, (9) socially maladjusted, and (10) chronically ill. Their need for special education is determined on the basis of the educational relevance of their exceptionality.

It is not the purpose of this chapter to serve as a substitute for intensive study of the relevant literature on the exceptional child and special education. The purpose is simply to illustrate the relationship between the problem and situation variables in the diagnostic structure and the modification of the ten school variables. The prescriptive teaching model is designed to help the school psychologist or other diagnostician determine an individual child's educational prescription. To achieve an adequate prescription for the educationally exceptional child requires that some members of the diagnostic team possess a working knowledge of special education. It is also necessary that the team be familiar with the local agencies involved in the family and child health and welfare fields as well as being informed regarding the school, its personnel, and ancillary services. The descriptions in this chapter are only of general provisions for exceptional children and should not be regarded as individual prescriptions. Furthermore, it is important to realize that many children have multiple disabilities and that it is frequently inappropriate to teach them on the basis of one diagnostic category. The reader is advised to become familiar with the up-to-date literature dealing with any exceptionality before making recommendations regarding special educational provisions.

The question is frequently raised as to the applicability of the methods of special education for more nearly normal children. What provisions should be made for the moderately disturbed child? How shall we deal with the exceptional child who does not require the total special program? Where appropriate special educational facilities are not available, should we try to provide them in the regular classroom? Answers to these questions are not readily available.

Usually the differences between the severely handicapped and the more normal child are matters of degree rather than differences of kind or type, but this is an inadequate basis of generalizing for all cases. Experience indicates that some techniques of special education can be applied successfully in the regular classroom. The principle of educational relevance provides a logical basis for trying out special education methods in adapted or remedial programs in regular classrooms.

Once the diagnostic structure is completed, the model can be used to determine the appropriate educational program. Because the diagnostic structure in the model was designed for the handicapped, it would need modification before it could be used to determine an educational profile for the gifted child. In the following examples each variable is keyed to the model.

Three exceptionalities—(1) the mentally retarded child, (2) the brain-injured and hyperactive child, and (3) the emotionally disturbed child—are included in the explanations.

THE MENTALLY RETARDED CHILD

A mental defective is a person who is socially incompetent, mentally subnormal, retarded intellectually from birth or at an early age, retarded at maturity, deficient as a result of constitutional origin (heredity or disease), and essentially incurable (Doll, 1941).

Two 6-year-old children arriving at school to enter the first grade may vary greatly in their capacity to benefit from formal academic education. One child has an IQ of 50 and the other 150. Their mental ages are 3 and 9 years respectively, a difference of 6 years. By the seventh grade when their chronological ages are 12, their mental ages will be 6 and 19, a difference of 12 years. Because a minimum mental age may be required for learning a given task, the child with a low IQ will have learning difficulties (Carrier, Malpass, and Orton, 1961). He cannot keep up with the normal child because his rate of mental growth is different (Goodenough, 1956). In the past many retarded children were excluded from school, but today's educators are increasing their acceptance of the challenge presented by having these children in the public schools.

Classification of Mental Retardation in Children

To date there is no universally accepted terminology or classification used when referring to persons with retarded intelligence, but certain terms are coming to have relatively broad acceptance by a substantial number of educators.

Two major problems exist regarding an accepted definition of mental retardation. One is that many disciplines, including medicine, social service, law, education, and psychology, have an interest in the retarded child and each profession tends to have its own classification and terminology. The other problem is a result of the high value placed upon intellect. Any term used to describe intellectual limitation is soon regarded very negatively. In attempts to see retardation more objectively or positively, the terminology has been changed from time to time.

A classification which has received considerable acceptance is that of the American Association on Mental Deficiency (Heber, 1961). Four levels of impairment of adaptive behavior are described:

Level I is described as mental handicap, mild but apparent and significant negative deviation from norms of adaptive behavior.

Level II is described as mental deficiency, moderate but definite negative deviation from norms of adaptive behavior.

Level III is described as mental deficiency, severe negative deviation from norms of adaptive behavior.

Level IV is described as mental deficiency, profound negative deviation from norms of adaptive behavior.

These classifications are closely related to the usual educational provisions for retarded children and will influence the placement of children in special classes. This will influence the curriculum and other variables in the programs. The AAMD manual includes measured intelligence, medical, and other classifications.

Educators in the past have relied rather heavily on the scores obtained on individual intelligence tests for the placement of mentally retarded children. While the test score is still the most reliable single predictor of school success, the IQ is not infallible and is subject to more variability than was generally believed (Dunn, 1963). The IQ scores employed in the classifications are useful for descriptive purposes, but in diagnosis of an individual child the IQ is only one of a number of factors to be considered.

It appears that educators usually have not used the AAMD demarcation lines in classifying children for special education. One reason for this is that most children classified as Levels III and IV fall below the groups where effective methods of teaching have been devised. A classification based upon the type of educational program is regarded as appropriate for use in the school system (Baker, 1959, p. 203). This classification refers to the retarded children as custodial, trainable, educable, and sometimes as slow learners.

CUSTODIAL MENTALLY RETARDED. This group has a profound level of impairment. The IQ is low grade or below 25. The term idiot was used in classifying these children (Williams, 1961). They are the totally dependent mentally retarded who would not survive without help (Kirk, 1962). They require nursing care, usually in an institution.

TRAINABLE MENTALLY RETARDED. This group has a moderate to severe level of impairment. The IQ is middle grade or 25 to 50. The term imbecile was used to describe these children. They are trainable and become semidependent. They can develop intellectually at about one-quarter to one-half the rate of the average child. They are so intellectually subnormal that they do not achieve literacy and are not educable in the usual sense. They do have sufficient ability, if given proper training, to develop self-care skills, to learn to converse at a simple level, and to perform uncomplicated tasks.

EDUCABLE MENTALLY RETARDED. This group has a moderate to mild level of impairment. The IQ is high grade or 50 to 75. The term moron is used to describe these children. They are marginally independent. They have the capacity to acquire the academic skills required for literacy. They are usually educated in special classes and later are employed at routine and service-type occupations and achieve independence in most normal situations.

SLOW LEARNERS. This group of children has low-normal or borderline intelligence, IQ 75 to 90. These children are frequently classified as low-normal, borderline, or backward. They are usually educated in regular classes or classes for slow learners in elementary schools but may require special occupational or study-work programs in secondary schools.

Diagnosis

Estimates of the prevalence of mental retardation based on theoretical distribution of intelligence are inaccurate predictors. Studies show a higher prevalence than the 0.13 percent with IQ below 55 which would occur in a normal distribution. The explanation for this is that the theoretical curve does not account for brain injury, cretinism, or mongolism and other physical and traumatic events which result in mental retardation. Brain injury occurs at all intellectual levels, but the highest prevalence is concentrated in the custodial and trainable categories. Surveys have shown the incidence of mental retardation to vary greatly from one locality to another. For these reasons, as well as the caution which is desirable before classifying anyone as mentally retarded, it should not be presumed that a certain percentage in any school system is retarded. This is particularly important in schools where IQ test scores have been the main basis of classification.

Although educators have found the scores on individual intelligence tests useful predictors of school success, other factors such as physical health, social conditions, and emotional disturbance also affect learning. A brief look at some of the known etiologies may be helpful in determining the educational outcomes.

There are many classifications of causes of mental retardation based upon such factors as the medical problems involved and the stages of embryonic development when injury occurred. Other classifications are based on heredity and environment and are called endogenous and exogenous, respectively. As these classifications have little educational relevance, the etiology will be discussed in relation to the diagnostic structure in the prescriptive teaching model.

Problem Variables

INJURY. Definite central-nervous-system pathology that is organically caused may result from injury during the prenatal or postnatal period, or from birth trauma, a genetic factor, or a combination of a genetic predisposition and certain environmental conditions. Infections in the mother during pregnancy may result in maldevelopment of the fetus. German measles (rubella) during the first three months of pregnancy can result in the child being mentally retarded as well as having other defects. A number of other diseases including syphilis, encephalitis, and toxemia produce organic defects. Birth injuries including anoxia or lack of oxygen can damage the central nervous system. If the oxygen supply to the brain is impaired for even a short time, permanent injury to brain cells will result. An inherent condition causing brain injury is the Rh factor; incompatibility of Rh-negative and Rh-positive blood in the parents can result in brain injury to the child shortly after birth. Encephalitis or brain fever caused by infection may result in brain injury after birth.

The differentiation of acquired organic conditions from genetic factors is difficult and sometimes impossible. Presently, mongolism is attributed to a genetic origin in which an extra or deviant chromosome is present. Genetic defects resulting in metabolism inefficiencies can cause injury because of an accumulation of toxic products such as phenylpyruvic acid. Two conditions now being researched are galactosemia which is the inability of the body to metabolize galactose and phenylketonuria which results in impairment of the enzyme required for metabolism of phenylalanine, an amino acid. Cretinism results from thyroid insufficiency. For many retarded children, the question of injury goes unanswered. As the diagnostic techniques in neurology are refined, a clearer picture of the effect of minimal brain damage will emerge.

DISABILITY. The majority of mentally retarded children are non-pathological or have no diagnosed organic defect related to the mental retardation. The nonpathological group has a functional disability of unknown origin which places them at the lower end of the normal distribution or they are members of the cultural-familial group. The cultural-familial group is composed of children from families of low attainment who have been reared in most adverse circumstances (Conant, 1961). They are from a culturally distinct minority who live in conditions where cultural deprivation and other forms of stimulus deprivation may be extreme. They frequently suffer from malnutrition, neglect, and a lack of intellectual stimulation throughout their preschool years. The nonpathological group has physical characteristics more nearly like children with normal ability and has fewer multiple organic defects than do the pathological groups described above.

Deficits in the intellectual functioning of retarded children are usually measured as immaturities or deviations from the norm for a particular age group. Because of a range of differences within each child, it is important to establish ratings for specific abilities as well as the general level or mental age. Many will have a consistent level of abilities across the functions tested and evaluated, while others will show different verbal and performance scores. Others who may have an expressive aphasia will show considerable ingenuity in a performance item. Where scatter of this nature is shown, a single derived score or mental age is of little value to educational planning. Where scatter occurs in test results, interpretation of disability should be given as a diagnostic profile rather than as a single score or mental age.

HANDICAP. The retarded neither learn as quickly nor achieve as much academically as children of normal intellect. The retarded child is not ready to learn to read when he starts school; if he is in the trainable group, he probably never will be ready, for his school progress will be limited to his rate of mental development. Much of the handicap is a by-product of the difference between society's expectancies and the child's abilities. Not only is he inclined to forget rapidly unless he has had much practice or overlearning, but he is very likely to be inept in transfer of training and to have a short attention span (Ellis, 1963). The mentally retarded have lower social status than the normal child (Baldwin, 1958). Another handicapping by-product may be a behavior problem and delinquency stemming from the discrepancy between his capacity and the requirements of his social environment (Blatt, 1960).

Situation Variables

NATURE OF PATHOLOGY.   Mentally retarded children are alike in two characteristics. They have a measurable degree of intellectual impairment on tests of intelligence, and they are having or have a prognosis of having learning difficulties. In all other human characteristics they vary greatly. Mental retardation covers such a range of intellectual impairment that the general or statistical descriptions do not apply to all the individuals in the group. Generally the mentally retarded compare unfavorably on most traits with children of normal or above-normal intelligence. They have poorer physical development and motor coordination than the average (Francis and Rarick, 1960). Some mental retardation is the result of infection or other organic impairment. Regardless of the etiology mental retardation is a chronic condition requiring long-range planning.

THERAPEUTIC PROCEDURES.   Medical research has made considerable progress in the prevention and treatment of some mental retardation. Prevention has resulted from treatment which is effective in eliminating causes of central-nervous-system impairment. Antibiotic drugs which control infection and prevent high fever and delirium in young children help prevent brain injury. Improved prenatal, parinatal, and postnatal care contributes to prevention. Specific successful treatment is essentially prevention of injury, because brain damage that has occurred is permanent. An obstetrician can avoid mental retardation in a baby born with Rh-factor incompatibility if he knows the parents' Rh factors. Prevention is accomplished by tranfusing the baby's blood at birth. Cretinism is avoided by thyroid treatment. In cases of phenylketonuria and galactosemia special diets can reduce significantly damage to the brain tissue which would normally result from these metabolic defects. Medical science is studying many problems relating to retardation but so far has no specific treatment for the majority of retarded children who have suffered stimulus deprivation.

TIME FACTORS.   The earlier brain damage occurs, the greater the handicapping consequences. It appears that the central nervous system requires more extensive assemblies to establish intellectual functions than it requires to operate them (Hebb, 1949). The cultural-familial or stimulus-deprived child's retardation will be reduced, the earlier his environment is modified to be intellectually stimulating. Some of these children attending nursery schools have shown remarkable progress. The longer the child's intellectual potential is undeveloped, the more permanent his retardation becomes (Kirk, 1958).

SOCIAL CONDITIONS. Neurologically impaired children come from every social and economic level. The large group of cultural-familial retarded comes from families where the values and mores are in conflict with the middle-class values of schools. The child lives in conditions of cultural and intellectual deprivation. The parents are usually retarded intellectually, and there is no reading material in the home. The children are neglected and the family is often characterized as a multi-problem one. There is a high prevalence of broken homes, alcoholism, illegitimate births, economic instability, crime, and physical health problems within these families. When the school becomes part of the social situation for the child, it is important not to increase the handicap of the child by emphasizing the middle-class value system of the school.

Parents at all social levels have difficulty accepting the fact of having a retarded child even when the diagnosis of the child is reliably established medically, psychologically, and educationally (Ross, 1964). This problem is particularly acute in middle-class families. This lack of acceptance has handicapping relevance when the parents' cooperation is required in seeking placement of the child in a special class or school. It continues to be a problem for some even after the child is placed in a special class. As long as parents have unrealistic goals for their retarded child, it is questionable whether they have actually accepted that the child is retarded (Heiser, 1955; Worchel and Worchel, 1961).

School Variables

Of the four educational classifications of mentally retarded children only the trainable, educable, and slow learner are the usual responsibility of public schools. The school variables for these three classifications will be discussed briefly.

The Trainable Mentally Retarded Child

Provisions for trainable children have been made in residential institutions, public school classes, special day schools, and day-care centers. The following description applies particularly to a public day school for retarded school-age children. They are admitted after diagnosis, by an admission committee. Admission is generally granted to a child with IQ 25 to 50 who is able to get along with other children in a class and who is toilet trained. He also has to be able to behave well enough not to create major disruptions in the classroom program.

Ↄ CONSISTENT APPROACH (A). Teachers and assistants working with trainable children need to employ a very consistent approach. Training requires that the same thing be done in the same way many times. Attention in training is paid to the performance of the task at hand or the specific skill being mastered, whereas in educating, attention is paid to generalizing and understanding abstract meanings. The trainable child will make his best progress if the teacher consistently focuses attention on the activity at hand and reinforces the child's active participation.

TEACHING METHODS (B). Instructional methods are based on the concept of structure and progression in the stimuli presented, with emphasis on doing. The child is given very simple tasks at which he can succeed. If he is to learn color discrimination and naming, the teacher may have to lead him or even help him manually to start picking up colored cubes and putting them in the same colored box. When he picks up the cube, names it correctly, and places it in the correct box, he is rewarded or reinforced by a word of praise. In a class where correctly completed assignments were rewarded with a star, the productivity of individuals in the class increased significantly. The stars were put in the child's star book and a material reward was exchanged for the book of stars.

This kind of sequence from immediate to a more delayed reinforcement seems meaningful to many mentally deficient children. They do not respond to an explanation of it, but they do respond as the sequence unfolds. Activities are gradually lengthened in duration in view of the child's increased attention span (Ellis, 1962). Since lectures are not an appropriate teaching method, a lesson must be broken down into simple steps and each step taught separately and mastered before the next step. Then the sequence is repeated many times on succeeding days. It should be overlearned for retention and returned to from time to time for reinforcement. Teaching procedures are based on an awareness and understanding of the uneven, poorly integrated levels of development of the mentally deficient child.

SPECIFIC OBJECTIVES (C). The major objective for the trainable child is self-care. Training should help him learn to dress and undress himself, to take care of his bathroom needs and cleanliness, and to follow adequate daily routines. He should become as independent as his limitations allow through training in self-care. Socialization is a goal which is related to his independence and safety in home, school, and community. Learning to speak, to follow directions, to wait his turn, and to share with others are part of social adjustment. Although the trainable child is not expected to become self-supporting, he should learn to be useful. He can become helpful in the home and later derive satisfaction in a sheltered workshop, in a supervised work situation, or in an institution. Safety is an important objective which school can help him achieve through careful sequential training in real or practical situations.¹

ANCILLARY SERVICES (D). These children have more physical defects than normal children; therefore, health services are particularly important. More frequent routine examinations and help with visual and auditory deficits are required. Through training, the child's visual and auditory acuity may change. Speech therapy is beneficial for some, and speech consultation for the teacher can assist him in teaching speech to the child. Psychological evaluation and follow-up contribute to understanding of individual progress, and the school psychologist can advise the teacher regarding problems of instruction and working with parents.

PLACEMENT AND PERSONNEL (E). Opportunities for integration of these children at school are quite limited, but they appear to do better if kept in their own home and community (Cain and Levine, 1961). A special day school or class provides the usual placement.

Most teachers are prepared to educate children; to facilitate their appreciation of literature, art, and music; to help them generalize and conceptualize; to teach them to read, write, and understand symbolically. They know less about training, which is essentially a conditioning process. A common error of teachers beginning this work is to underestimate the value of simple activities and games used in training and to want to do something "important" such as teaching reading. Techniques of training generally receive rather less emphasis in teacher preparation for this special field than does the etiology of retardation. Because the etiology has little educational relevance when determining the teaching techniques or in establishing present functioning, limitations, and abilities of the child, most teachers have to learn techniques of training on the job. Experience, workshops, and in-service training are the most effective means of developing adequate teachers for the severely retarded where colleges do not have laboratory or demonstration programs. Specific abilities in recreational games, arts and crafts, industrial arts, music, and homemaking are valuable skills. Ability in teaching reading and arithmetic is not necessary. This brings into question the usual requirement of having a regular teaching qualification plus special training. A special certification might be more appropriate particularly in light of the shortage of teachers and the tendency to place regular teachers in charge of these classes because of the shortage of special teachers. Working with parents is an important function of the special teacher, and he should have preparation in methods of counseling or interviewing parents. Teachers who are patient and who appreciate small gains are suited for this work.

Teacher aids or assistants are useful in giving the teacher time for preparation of instructional material and other important activities, such as case conferences and in-service work with other teachers, and in increasing the pupil-teacher ratio.

SUBJECT MATTER (F). Learning for these children is so difficult and requires so much time that it is essential that time is not wasted on unnecessary content. Parental pressure to have the child learn to read should be resisted. Reading may have high cultural significance for the family but little educational relevance for the child (Hudson, 1960). When he is learning traffic safety, he should be taught to recognize and respond to traffic signals. He can be conditioned to respond to "stop," "go," "walk," "do not walk," "danger," "keep out," and so forth. He can also learn "entrance," "exit," "men," "women," and other words of value to his social competency.

Counting and recognition of numbers can be taught to many trainable children. This skill is valuable in many social situations and in their future placement in sheltered workshops. A worker who can count to ten can package or bundle products reliably. Counting accurately to five or ten or multiples thereof is most useful, whereas counting to large numbers is of relatively less worth. Simple quantitative concepts, the vocabulary "big," "little," "long," "short," "more," "less," and, for the more able, time concepts are worthwhile. Arts and crafts such as weaving on a simple loom, cutting and pasting, drawing and coloring, and simple woodwork develop motor control as well as perceptual abilities. The older students can progress to gardening, housework, sewing, cooking, washing, and classroom chores. Games which include activities required for development of various manipulative skills as well as social development play an important part in the program. Songs, stories, and dramatization develop language and can be used to teach physical hygiene, grooming, dressing, socialization, etc.

Maria Montessori (1912) developed a program of activities for retarded children. This included many activities with objects such as blocks, cutouts, and embossed letters which were employed as self-teaching or auto-education devices. The principles of the Montessori method are valid today in selecting activities for developing self-help, social abilities, motor skills, and occupational usefulness. Self-help activities include eating, dressing, toilet training, washing, and grooming (Baumgartner, 1960). Social abilities are fostered through practice in obeying rules, following directions, completing assignments, and employing courtesy and manners. Motor skills are developed through exercises involving walking, marching, running, climbing, balancing, jumping, and arm movements in catching, throwing, and rolling a ball. Occupational usefulness is developed through household chores such as washing dishes, washing, ironing, sewing, answering the telephone, gardening, sweeping, and dusting (Rozenzweig and Long, 1960).

INSTRUCTIONAL MATERIALS (G). Expendable supplies are selected with reference to the poor coordination and difficulties with differentiation that these children have. Weaving materials that are large, strong, and in clear contrasting colors provide appropriate learning opportunities. Large crayons and paper are more useful than small ones. In woodwork, learning to drive many large nails should precede driving smaller ones. With these principles in mind suitable materials can be selected for instructional purposes.

SPECIAL EQUIPMENT (H). Selection of equipment is based on its value in training as well as on its strength, durability, and simplicity of operation. Because manufacturers' specifications are sometimes misleading when used in selecting equipment for poorly coordinated children, it is wise to visit and correspond with people experienced in special education. Much of the equipment will be similar to that found in a regular household. Stoves, dishes, cooking utensils, garden tools, etc., should be strong and simple. Things which require fine adjustments consume the teacher's time unduly. Educational supply houses have some kindergarten and primary equipment which is suitable. Teachers should be encouraged to design equipment for the particular needs of their children.

Some teachers have tried using teaching machines and programmed instruction for the trainable retarded child (Stolurow, 1960*a*; 1960*b*; 1961). At the Rainier School (Birnbrauer, 1962) teaching machines operating on the multiple-choice system were used with children who could not write. A "programmed-learning classroom" was developed in which all formal learning was programmed. Visual-motor and later cursive writing was taught by use of a light box. This machine provides a surface on which the child writes following the image revealed by a flashing light. The model or image of the correct response is revealed intermittently so that when the light is off the child sees only his own writing. Although the procedures are in a developmental stage, it is suggested that an entirely programmed classroom for some trainable and educable retardates is feasible. Ellis (1960) has explored some possibilities of implementing operant conditions through programming for the trainable retarded child.

Programmed instruction for training purposes has not been fully explored. Although the programs described above were not designed exclusively for the trainable retarded child, they do indicate some applications of training through programmed instruction. They also illustrate the fact that it is not necessary for the child to be able to read and write to be able to use programmed instruction.

Many training devices can be programmed so that they provide automatic feedback or reinforcement. A traffic signal connected to a barrier which allows the child to proceed when the light is green can provide training in waiting for the green light. Sorting and matching training devices can be connected to a buzzer which sounds when the correct response is produced, reinforcing the child's correct response. These devices are self-instructional in that usually the child knows when the task is completed correctly.

SCHOOL PLANT (1). A central location is desirable for a day training school. Children are transported, usually by bus service provided by the school system or by the crippled children's or other associations. Plant facilities should resemble those of the home and workshop. Except for modifications to facilitate instruction, the building can provide normal home situations for learning to cook, serve meals, wash dishes and clothing, mow lawns, weed and water gardens, and care for shrubs. Care for the house, washing the car, polishing shoes, storing clothing properly in closets, and working in the shop can only be successful if the plant provides similar facilities to those the child will use outside of school.

AUXILIARY AGENCIES (J). In addition to the regular agencies there are a number of specialized agencies that work with handicapped children. The title auxiliary agencies when applied to the work of the Council for Exceptional Children, American Association on Mental Deficiency, and the National Association for Retarded Children, is misleading in that these groups were mainly responsible for the establishment of special schools. In most districts schools were established first, outside the public school system, by interested citizens and groups. They provide an excellent resource for many kinds of assistance and are particularly helpful in working with parents of retarded children. Group work with parents is beneficial as is the support given individually to a parent having difficulty accepting the fact of having a retarded child.

The Office of Vocational Rehabilitation of the U.S. Department of Health, Education, and Welfare makes available grants for sheltered workshops. School systems, civic groups, Goodwill Industries, the Salvation Army, and associations for the retarded provide work programs which include subcontracts and piecework for industry, restoring used or damaged articles, and producing items for sale. In sheltered workshops the graduates from schools for trainable children can be productively employed in a wide variety of jobs. An excellent handbook (Fraenkel, 1961) is available for establishing sheltered employment which is an integral part of a comprehensive program for the trainable child.

The Educable Mentally Retarded Child

The preschool educable mentally retarded child may be only slightly delayed in his development of speech and other accomplishments, and therefore he may not be diagnosed as retarded. Unless intelligence or readiness tests are routinely administered to all pupils before they enter school, the child's problem may go undetected until he experiences failure in school. Pupils who obtain IQ scores 50 to 75 at six years of age have mental ages from 3 to 4½ years. The child near the upper limit of this group is not likely to be delayed in his general development sufficiently to cause parents to suspect that he is retarded. Most educable mentally retarded children enter school at six years of age and are only suspected of being retarded when they fail to learn to read. This is to be expected as their rate of mental development is approximately one-half to three-quarters that of an average child. Generally, these children have similar appearance to normal children although they have more physical defects as a group. Many have good physical health, vision, and hearing.

They have sufficient intellectual potential to enable them to acquire limited skills in academics and to enable them to become self-supporting adults in casual service-type jobs and unskilled employment.

CONSISTENT APPROACH (A). It is usual for educable retarded children to have experienced considerable defeat and rejection in regular classes before they were considered for special placement. They often develop negative attitudes toward themselves, teachers, school, and society. It is important that the teacher have a consistent approach which is encouraging and motivating for these children. He should be positive in his approach and avoid showing disappointment in their slowness. Starting with very simple tasks with almost assured success followed immediately with praise and external rewards is an effective approach.

TEACHING METHODS (B). A variety of teaching methods are employed in educating the educable retarded child. The methods are all designed to help the child grow by providing situations to which he can react and thus develop habits, establish attitudes, and master content. The methods based upon the philosophy that the child's happiness is most important tend to center around activities that are the child's preference. The methods based upon the training of specific senses, such as vision, hearing, touch, and kinesthesia, center around concrete physical activities. The methods based upon academic or tool subjects center around adapting regular programs and methods for simpler presentation. The methods based upon practical and vocational training center around arts and crafts such as woodwork and homemaking. The methods based upon the unit of experience center the activities and academic work around a central topic or theme. Because knowledge about the relative values of these methodologies is limited at present, the employment of a variety of methods should be encouraged.

Generally, methods based upon the principle of providing much experience with concrete materials as a basis of understanding a more abstract idea are effective. This principle requires that special attention be paid to frequency of repetition, pacing, and step size in the presentation of the subject matter. This approach requires that the child use his new skill in a variety of situations. One idea is presented at a time following the sequential steps based on the structure of learning. Learning is supported through the use of a variety of the processing modes of learning. Transfer of acquired skills from one situation to another is taught. These children tend not to make generalizations spontaneously. Instruction needs to be systematically presented without too much reliance on incidental learning.

Teaching methods for educable students may be classified as adapted and therapeutic. A child who is below the normal range in most or all school subjects and does not have specific disabilities requires a program adapted to his slower pace. Instruction is adapted to his level of ability. Adapted teaching in this case means teaching appropriate to his mental age and development.

A child with specific inefficiencies in a processing mode of learning over and beyond his general developmental retardation may profit from clinical or therapeutic teaching procedures designed to remedy specific deficits. For example, a child who has difficulty with laterality and has difficulty in learning to read or write may benefit by perceptual training beginning with motor activity (Kephart, 1960; Delacato, 1959). He may participate first in physical activities involving balancing on a walking board and walking a line to develop a centralized left-right concept. This would be followed by a kinesthetic method for reading and spelling which develops eye-hand coordination in implementing the laterality concept (Fernald, 1943).

Practical and vocational education is more than "making things" or "learning a trade." As well as learning the particular skills required for a job, vocational training should include teaching the child how to relate to his coworkers and his supervisors. He should learn punctuality and the other responsibilities expected of a worker. The methods of teaching these behaviors should be an integral part of teaching the technical and manual aspects (Hutt and Gibby, 1958). Learning of proper attitudes and ways of behaving are functions of the whole personality of the child, and vocational training should be one way in which the child is helped to achieve social maturity.

Although emphasis is placed on structure and organization in the teaching methods, self-determination of the student should not be excluded. The children themselves should be encouraged to assume responsibility for their own behavior. They should be given adequate guidance so that they can work out their own rules of conduct. Kirk and Johnson (1951) suggest that the teaching methods for retarded children should be organized in harmony with good mental-hygiene principles and that the child's attention should be focused through positive suggestions and an atmosphere of acceptable social behavior. They recommend that the child be allowed to plan activities within his range of interests and abilities and that techniques such as sociodrama be used for developing insights into real-life situations.

Recent developments in programmed instruction, audio-visual techniques, language laboratories, and other teaching aids provide new and in many cases improved techniques for teaching these children.

Until recent times the media of formal education were teachers and books. Today we have teachers and books as well as motion pictures, recordings, language laboratories, television, teaching machines, and programmed instruction. All these can provide methods of instruction for the educable retarded child. The language laboratory, for example, which has been used generally for the teaching of foreign languages, can be used to assist the retarded child to learn to speak and read his own language correctly. Programmed instruction for the educable retarded has received considerable attention from researchers (Stolurow, 1960a; 1960b; 1961).

Programmed instruction is still in the developmental stage, and the present findings are only an indication of the potential for special education. Research indicates that programmed instruction is clearly feasible for the educable mentally retarded. For example, Price (1962) compared results achieved with groups of retarded children employing programmed instruction which required constructed answers and multiple-choice responses with a control group receiving conventional instruction. An arithmetic program was presented through use of a teaching machine. Both programmed instructions and conventional teaching produced significant improvement in addition, but only the multiple-choice program produced significant improvement in subtraction. Naumann and Woods (1962) reported an automated basic-spelling program for the educable mentally retarded child. The teaching machine had "play appeal," and the children responded favorably to the programmed instruction.

Stolurow (1963) reviewed the research and concluded that programmed instruction may be more efficient than alternatives presently available and that much more study needs to be done. Programmed instruction provides a method whereby the application of the psychology of learning can be made to the teaching of educable mentally retarded children.

SPECIFIC OBJECTIVES (c). A general goal for the educable retarded is to develop abilities necessary for independent living. This educa-

maybe

tional goal is the same as for average children. A difference occurs when the general educational aim is stated as specific objectives. The objective of academic competence may mean that he achieves a grade-four reading level, that he can read and understand instructions and labels, that he can write a letter, that he can count, do simple calculations, and make change. The objective of personal adequacy means that he should learn to get along with other people at school, at home, and on the job. It also means that he should develop emotional security, health habits, and wholesome leisure-time activities. The objective of occupational competence means that he should learn to participate in work for the purpose of earning his living. He should develop occupational competence through vocational guidance and training at school. Planning of a program involves careful consideration of specific objectives. Of the many statements of objectives the following are representative. Kirk and Johnson (1951) present a meaningful brief statement of objectives. Orr (1962) relates objectives specifically to curriculum ingredients. Goldstein and Seigle (1958) employ a multidimensional structure in defining objectives. They compiled a curriculum guide which (1) defines functions which continue throughout life, (2) delineates academic accomplishment for the educable mentally retarded, and (3) states specific activities ordered sequentially and related to the child's developmental level. With these as guides, courses of studies can be organized which meet the needs of educable retarded children.

ANCILLARY SERVICES (D). All supporting school services appropriate for average children are important to the educable child. Health services and speech therapy, for example, are required by a greater number of retarded than average children.

It is particularly valuable to have special classes for the educable children in school where principals are understanding and accepting. Integration is difficult or impossible where the school administration does not fully accept the retarded child. An understanding principal can do much to assist these children in their social development by seeing that they are included in many activities and in making and interpreting school rules so that they are meaningful to the retarded child.

Counseling and vocational guidance are a vital part of a good educational program for these students. Intellectual impairment results in less spontaneous or incidental understanding of self. In a one-to-one counseling relationship the student can explore his individual needs and learn more about the nature of his disabilities and assets. If the counseling interview deals in concrete terms with the client's experiences, he can develop realistic understandings of his capabilities. Counseling for the educable mentally retarded child is different because of the student's immature verbalization and lack of realistic generalization. This does not mean that counseling is ineffective. Discussion which centers around and focuses attention on what the student did, what he felt competent in doing, what he liked to do, and what he would like to try to do appears to encourage self-actualization. The retarded student needs more assistance in entering an occupation. A study of vocational training (Hutt and Gibby, 1958) indicated that the mentally handicapped should learn a particular vocational skill for a particular job where a demand exists in the community. Engel (1950) compared 2,755 retarded with 10,000 normal employees and found that the retarded successfully held jobs in mechanical, material, and personal service. They were handicapped when they were in aesthetic, commercial, scientific, and social fields. More recent studies of smaller populations support the same conclusions (Peterson and Smith, 1960; Dinger, 1961).

PLACEMENT AND PERSONNEL (E). The usual educational placement provided for the educable retarded child who receives special services is in a special day class in the regular school. During the past few years a number of studies designed to assess the efficacy of these special classes have appeared.

The findings of the majority of the studies comparing the achievement of the educable retarded in special class and in regular class favored the regular class placement. Thurstone (1959) found that mentally handicapped children in special classrooms achieved less academically than those in regular classrooms. He suggested that the retarded child in a regular classroom profits from stimulation provided by normal children. Johnson (1962) reviewed the research and concluded that the educable retarded child achieved more academically in the regular class. Some studies showed that while superior academic achievement was noted for the regular class group, the special class group showed superior social adjustment (Stanton and Cassidy, 1959; Mullen, 1962).

Ainsworth (1959) worked with children placed in three different school environments—special class, regular class with itinerant special teacher, and regular class with no special services. The largest academic gains were made by children attending special classes and regular classes with no additional special services. There were no significant differences among the three groups with regard to ratings of personal characteristics or in decrease of seriously deviant behavior. Only the regular group with no special services showed significant improvement on occurrence of observed behaviors. The studies of social and emotional adjustment of retarded children in special and regular classrooms have to be interpreted with reference to the protected situation in the special classroom. There is insufficient evidence regarding which school placement is related to better occupational and life adjustment after leaving school.

Johnson (1962) concludes it is a paradox that mentally handicapped children having specially trained teachers, being enrolled in classes with fewer children, and having more money spent on their education should be accomplishing the objectives of their education at the same or at a lower level than similar mentally handicapped children in regular classrooms.

Integrated placements have not been subjected to research as have special and regular placements. The appropriateness of the educational program as related to the educational handicap of the child may provide a better basis for placement than an IQ score between 50 and 75. Laycock (1963) recommends the two-track plan for the educable retarded, that is, those with IQ scores under 65 in special classes and those with IQ scores over 65 in regular classes. The New York City special program was studied (Wrightstone, Forlano, Lepkowski, and Sontag, 1959) and the one- and two-track plans were compared. The adaptive group had a better prognosis for independent living. They usually had IQ scores in the above-65 range. The nonadaptive group had a poorer prognosis for completely independent living and usually had IQ scores below 65. Prescriptive teaching offers no final answer to the very complex issue of placement for these children but attempts to place children where the educational experiences will be appropriate to their individual needs. In providing this kind of educational experience we should consider some of the following placements.

Preschool and kindergarten programs for these children can assist many in overcoming some or all of their handicap. Kirk (1958) reports research which demonstrates that certain children need to be placed in special preschool programs at as early an age as possible. Enriching preschool programs are desirable for educable mentally retarded children who live in conditions of extreme cultural deprivation (Conant, 1961). Most of the program of nursery school and kindergarten is applicable with special emphasis on oral communication and self-care.

The provision of perceptual and motor training such as the readiness activities outlined by Kephart (1960) can result in overcoming some of the consequences of deprivations of retarded children. This training emphasizes work with gross motor movements, eye-hand coordination, posture, laterality, and directionality. An extra year in nursery school or kindergarten is frequently considered beneficial.

The primary grades provide the first opportunity for special service for many retarded children. Usually these pupils are not recognized as retarded until a grade-one teacher is working with them. An ungraded primary division provides better opportunities for the retarded child to learn at his own rate and avoids some frustrations that the graded primary imposes. Primary special classes contain children with chronological ages 6 to 10 years with mental ages from 3 to $6\frac{1}{2}$ years. These classes emphasize social adjustment, self-care, readiness activities, and oral communication skills. The child is usually moved to the regular program or to the intermediate special class when his mental age is 6 to $6\frac{1}{2}$ years.

The intermediate special class is for children of 10 to 13 years of age with mental ages from about 6 to 9 years. These children should be ready for more formal instruction in basic school subjects. They are usually moved to a secondary program on the basis of age.

The secondary special class pupils range in age from 13 to 18 years and have mental ages from 8 to 12 years. Preparation for an occupation is emphasized in the secondary program. These classes located in regular public schools provide opportunities for integration and socialization which are lacking in separate schools.

The classroom teacher for these children should have special preparation in teaching the educable retarded and in remedial instruction. The educable retarded require an educational program adjusted to their abilities which can be implemented by a special teacher for the basic academic subjects of reading, writing, and arithmetic. The intermediate and secondary students can take physical education, art, music, industrial arts, and home economics with regular teachers of these subjects, and where appropriate they should be integrated in these subject classes with normal children.

SUBJECT MATTER (F). Children in a primary special class usually have preschool mental development. Much of the curriculum of regular nursery and kindergarten is applicable. Environmental enrichment with many things to see, touch, and experience kinesthetically will stimulate intellectual development in the stimulus-deprived child. Sensorimotor training will begin with work in areas of gross motor movements, eye-hand coordination, laterality, and directionality.

Training in the processing modes should focus on visual and auditory memory; scanning, copying figures, and form perception and discrimination can be experienced through games which are highly interesting to young children (Carlson and Ginglend, 1961).

When retarded children play, they not only have fun but usually develop mentally, physically, and socially, frequently beyond general expectation. Play helps the retarded child's mental development if it centers around his becoming more observant of things in his environment, his ability to notice things and remember, and his ability to hear things and remember. The first ability to develop is that of visual discrimination and memory, including ability to work puzzles, to pick out things alike, to pick out something that is different, to match, to sort, to find what is missing from a familiar pattern, to reproduce patterns, to observe, and to recall. Auditory development and discrimination include ability to follow spoken directions, to identify rhythms and tunes, to identify animal sounds, and to finish a song, story, or poem. Play helps the retarded child when we discover what the child can do and let him do it often.

Intermediate curriculum is more structured than primary. When students are ready, emphasis is placed on the tool subjects. Concrete examples and illustrations are used to make reading and arithmetic meaningful.

Promotion to secondary school is based more on the student's reaching adolescence than on his academic attainment. Here he is taught additional basic school subjects and a broadened curriculum including practical reading and arithmetic, science, social studies, home economics, and industrial arts. Practical tasks with which he will be confronted in later life, such as handling money, reading road maps and timetables, and filling out application forms for employment, constitute much of the academic program. The other major aspect is preparation for work. He might try working with the janitor, helping in the cafeteria or office, and taking shop courses as his in-school work program. The U.S. Department of Labor has helped school districts establish study-work programs. These part-time placements in community work experiences are gaining acceptance by both schools and employers. Specific job training in school and on-the-job training complement each other in providing occupational adjustment. At school-leaving age some students may not be ready for independent vocational placement and require an intermediate step provided by a transitional placement in a sheltered workshop.

INSTRUCTIONAL MATERIALS (G). The student's mental age is the most significant factor in selecting materials for him. It is necessary to improvise, adapt, and adjust materials to his rate of learning. Such a wide variety of materials is available for each grade level that it is possible to select items which serve the same educational purpose as those items used in the regular grades but are more suited to the greater experience and physical development of the older retarded child. It is preferable that the retarded child not be using the same instructional materials as the younger normal child in the lower regular grade in the same school.

SPECIAL EQUIPMENT (H). Because the retarded child needs more repetitions of words than the average child, books must be selected to provide this experience. Programming is a way of structuring the whole presentation of an amount of subject matter. Teaching machines and programmed instruction provide proper sequential presentation of materials to be learned, clear directions, and immediate reinforcement of the student's correct efforts. Special simplified machines and programs (Smith and Quackenbush, 1961) are being developed and tested for special education. A light box is a useful device for teaching the form of letters and shapes as well as visual-motor skills. Objects such as large nuts and bolts which can be handled, put together, and taken apart give experience with form and spatial relationships. Many real objects to work with and adequate storage are important equipment considerations.

SCHOOL PLANT (I). The size of the classroom and most of the basic furnishings and facilities are not different from those required for a regular class. Because the class size is smaller, a normal classroom seems adequate for the extra equipment needed for the educable retarded student.

AUXILIARY AGENCIES (J). Most of the same agencies interested in the trainable are available to the educable student. One additional resource is the State Vocational Rehabilitation Agency which works with the retarded youth when he reaches sixteen or more years of age and is eligible for on-the-job training.

The Slow Learner

The slow learners compose the largest group of mentally retarded children in schools (Johnson, 1963). Because they are usually in the borderline range of intelligence including some low-normal children, the question regarding whether they should be classified as mentally retarded can be debated. The AAMD classification (Heber, 1961) includes some of this group, on the basis of adaptive behavior, in Level I. The basis for the slow learner's classification is educational retardation rather than IQ; most slow learners will be in the borderline range of 75 to 90, but some children with IQ scores in this range will not be slow learners.

An adjusted program conducted in the regular classroom is usually the most appropriate placement for the borderline child in elementary school. Extra time in an ungraded primary division gives him time to develop the mental maturity needed for regular school progress without the same sense of failure he would have in a graded primary division. Other adaptations are those which can be made in a regular classroom consistent with his special needs. Cleugh (1961a) has edited a book describing teaching techniques for the slow learner in the primary grades, and Ingram (1960) and Johnson (1963) have written textbooks covering the total school program for the slow learner.

Implementation of the concept of universal secondary education has presented educators with a new challenge. These children traditionally would fall farther and farther behind in school each year and drop out of school early. Because their maximum mental growth is achieved at a mental age of about 11 to 13½ years (Johnson, 1963), they usually cannot continue to progress in the regular secondary school program. At this point special educational programs seem appropriate. These programs may be essential to the proper development and utilization of our human resources (Kruger, 1963). The following is a brief description of the school variables to be considered in a special program for the slow learner in secondary school.

CONSISTENT APPROACH (A). In adopting a consistent approach to employ in working with the slow learner in secondary school, the teacher should be aware of the value system which has been operating throughout the child's school life. Academic achievement and intellectual ability have high status, and this child is in the lowest quartile academically and intellectually. Special placement provides the teacher with an opportunity to adopt an approach which reflects a different set of values—a set of values more appropriate for this child. If the teacher places higher value on the child's practical and nonacademic achievements, the child may be better able to make use of his abilities. The teacher's approach should reflect interest in the adolescent child's activities and place high value on the manual and service occupations.

TEACHING METHODS (B). The teaching methods are adapted to meet the occupational and social interests and abilities of the slow learner. The program is built to help the child achieve vocational and social competence, for it is in these that the slow learner can most likely find his areas of competency. Application of the unit method by which varied experiences are integrated into practical and meaningful action is used to promote development of occupational and social competence (Ingram, 1960).

The basic principle of this method is that experiences the student has outside school give meaning to the classroom instruction, and classroom instruction has value outside the school. In this program approximately half the time is devoted to school instruction, and half the time is devoted to out-of-school work experiences. In the junior high school programs this involves trips and visits in the community to learn firsthand about things taught and discussed in the school shops, laboratories, and classrooms. In the senior high school program the student is learning on the job through a work-study or work-experience program.

The teacher must be responsible for the work-study program because the classroom instruction is integrated with the work experience. There must be sufficient time for the teacher to contact employers and visit the student on the job, because the program centered within the school is built around the student's vocational needs (Johnson, 1963).

SPECIFIC OBJECTIVES (c). The specific objectives for the slow learner in the secondary school will be described as academic competence, social adequacy, work experience, and employment.

Academic competence for the slow learner is (1) the ability to follow oral or written instructions; (2) the ability to handle everyday number concepts in practical situations; (3) the ability to transfer information and skills from school to real life situations; and (4) maintenance of good work habits.

Social adequacy for the slow learner involves (1) the knowledge and understanding required for adequate social integration at school, at work, and in the community; (2) respect for law and order; (3) acceptance of responsibility; (4) consumer effectiveness; (5) maintenance of health and safety practices; and (6) productive use of leisure-time and participation in extra-curricular activities.

Work experience is provided to (1) acquaint the student with an awareness of his own limitations and assets; (2) familiarize the student with up-to-date occupational skills and knowledge; (3) assist the student to develop specific skills required on the job; and (4) establish a direct contact with employers and employment agencies.

Employment is a specific objective because these students are on a terminal program designed to assist them assume a place in the world of work.

ANCILLARY SERVICES (D). Counseling and vocational guidance facilitate the social development of these students (Super, 1957). Occupational information and vocational guidance are the responsibility of the teacher and the ancillary counseling and guidance services of the school.

The psychological assessment of the slow learner and aptitude testing in particular are of value in this program. The school psychologist, counselor, and administrator may provide ancillary consultive services for parents of slow-learning students.

PLACEMENT AND PERSONNEL (E). Placement in this program assumes three preconditions: (1) slow learners have largely achieved as much in academic skills as it is realistically possible for them to learn (Johnson, 1963); (2) the student is not seriously emotionally disturbed; (3) the program will be offered for three years in the senior high school so that the student can complete his secondary schooling in this program.

The student who has reached the age of sixteen years should be placed in a program of work experience or job tryouts which may lead to full employment. At least 50 percent of the student's time should be devoted to occupational experience.

The teacher for the secondary class for slow learners should be a generalist competent to provide instruction in all the basic academic skills and content areas (Johnson, 1963).

SUBJECT MATTER (F). The subject matter in this program is selected to form a bridge between the child and a more independent phase of his development. Although his academic growth is leveling off, there are facets of his education that require specific attention. He will be out in the world in two or three years, and therefore his education should be along practical lines.

Academic work should be based on a central topic or theme of interest to, and within the ability of, the student. It should not be a "watered down" version of the regular curriculum.

Occupational education includes discussion and practice of (1) finding, applying for, and holding a job; (2) following directions; (3) vocational goals and skills; (4) getting along with fellow workers; (5) traveling in the city; (6) general job training; (7) acquisition of vocational information; and (8) maintenance of social adequacy on the job (Kirk and Johnson, 1951).

Vocational training, home economics, and industrial arts should be largely geared to the individual needs of the student. Regular secondary vocational courses are suitable for those with sufficient ability. Home maintenance is emphasized because these people will have homes of their own or be members of homes as children and as adults (Kirk and Johnson, 1951). Study of home building and maintenance exposes both boys and girls to several occupational areas such as building trades, homemaking and personal service, and household mechanics.

INSTRUCTIONAL MATERIALS (G). Teachers who have had experience in teaching slow-learning classes have suggested that textbooks, workbooks, and reference materials should be chosen to suit the students' reading level, but that regular texts and workbooks are not suitable because they are frequently labeled for the regular grade level, which in the case of the slow learner is often well below his placement. Newspapers, special-interest magazines, and technical instruction books are suitable classroom reading materials. Business forms, application forms, time sheets, requisitions, etc., provide practical writing materials. Craft materials of many kinds are media for pre-occupational skill training.

SPECIAL EQUIPMENT (H). The emphasis on practical training requires that commonly used business, industrial, and domestic equipment be used. For example, the classroom should be equipped with a cash register, adding machine, and telephone. Audio-visual aids such as tape recorders and projectors can serve as media for auditory and visual training.

SCHOOL PLANT (I). The class should be housed in a regular high school or, where available, in a vocational high school. The class should have its own homeroom which is equipped for a variety of activities.

AUXILIARY AGENCIES (J). Vocational preparation of the slow learner requires the cooperative efforts of many specialists and community agencies. The attitudes of persons in the community and in particular the attitudes of potential employers are of prime importance (Hutt and Gibby, 1958). The Board of Industrial Relations can clear the way for the work-experience programs. The labor councils and the teachers can work together in establishing the working relationships with labor unions. The State Employment Service can assist students in securing part-time and full-time employment. Many groups such as service clubs, chambers of commerce, and parent-teacher associations can be auxiliary agencies to this program.

THE BRAIN–INJURED AND HYPERACTIVE CHILD

Ever since the publication of the first volume of *Psychopathology and Education of the Brain-injured Child* by the late Alfred A. Strauss in conjunction with Laura Lehtinen (1947), children who have neurological handicaps have received increased attention from specialists in medicine, psychology and education. A second volume (Strauss and Kephart, 1955) furthered this interest. Previously, experimental psychologists, neurologists, biochemists, and physiologists were trying to increase the sum of knowledge about the function of the central nervous system but their gains were too limited to be of significant value to educators and others concerned with environmental modification for the brain-damaged child. Even today, with the advances made in electroencephalography and radiology, information about the structure and function of the central nervous system does not adequately explain the learning abilities and behavior of the individual. Strauss helped to resolve the problem when he revealed common psychological characteristics among a number of children diagnosed as having cerebral palsy, epilepsy, aphasia, and exogenous mental retardation without any motor disability. Later, Cruickshank, Bentzen, Ratzeburg, and Tannhauser (1961) developed a program based upon the similar psychological characteristics among hyperactive, brain-injured, and emotionally disturbed children without brain damage. This program resulted in similar treatment for both certain brain-injured children and certain emotionally disturbed children with no diagnosed specific or generalized neurological damage.

Intracranial impairment is related to cerebral palsy, epilepsy, and exogenous mental retardation as well as some less well-known disabilities resulting from injury during pregnancy or birth or caused later by disease, accident, or incompatibility between the Rh factor of the blood of the mother and child. Epilepsy may take the form of *grand mal* seizures, with major convulsions usually followed by deep sleep, or *petit mal,* which may result in loss of consciousness for a few seconds or in periods during which the child is confused and irrational and of which later he has no memory, as well as many other minor motor and mental aberrations.

Cerebral palsy takes many forms. The three commonest are spasticity, or tightness of the muscles; athetosis, or writhing purposeless movement; and ataxia, or impaired balance.

Exogenous mental retardation may vary in degree and be the major symptom or may occur in combination with any of the other disabilities. The child may have communication handicaps. Aphasia may be receptive in that the child does not receive meaning from spoken or written words, or it may be expressive in that he does not communicate in reading, writing, or speaking. More specific aphasic difficulties are alexia, or inability to read; dyscalculia, or inability to do arithmetic or learn numbers; agraphia, or inability to learn to write; and apraxia, the inability to carry out voluntary or purposeful acts.

Since cerebral damage is generally not limited to a single area in the brain, these conditions are frequently accompanied by vision defects, hearing loss, and speech disorders. The list of conditions described above is far from complete but will give the reader some idea of the variety and complexity of the behavioral problems included in the category of brain injury. The term brain injured describes such a wide variety of disorders that it is of questionable value as a diagnostic entity for the educator wishing to modify his program for the child.

A group of children who have considerable commonality in their observable characteristics are referred to variously as brain injured and hyperactive, or as having the Strauss syndrome (Stevens and Birch, 1957). These children in a normal environment are persistently hyperactive and increase their activity disproportionately to stimulation. They have poor motor coordination and organization of behavior. Mild provocation results in erratic responses. They exhibit disinhibition of motor activity and distractibility. Psychologically, they are described as having the following difficulties. They have visual-motor perception deficits in distinguishing one entity from another, distinguishing figure from background, reproducing figures from memory, and identifying total configuration. Because of poor perceptual integration, they have difficulty perceiving apparent moton. They become attracted to detail and unable to respond effectively to the total stimulus. They perseverate or are unable to shift from one stimulus to another. Although their poor performance is attributed to a deficit in the central process itself, it appears that auditory and kinesthetic perception generally tends to suffer less impairment than visual-motor perception. The conceptual development of the brain-injured and hyperactive child in an unstructured situation is markedly different from that of a normal child. Testing tends to show intellectual scatter and their performance IQ is frequently lower than their verbal IQ. We have described a syndrome of cerebral dysfunction which may result from injury, maldevelopment, delayed maturation, or intense emotional stress. The instructional methods used, in this application of the prescriptive teaching approach, were developed by the following authors: Cruickshank et al. (1961), Gallagher (1960), Haeussermann (1958), and Strauss and Kephart (1955). Experiments have been conducted which showed that the structured approach was superior to other methods tested. Anyone working with a child having this syndrome should read the detailed descriptions of these programs (Cruickshank et al., 1961; Gallagher, 1960).

Problem Variables

INJURY. Individual neurological examinations, using electroencephalograph tracings and X-rays, detect evidence concerning the presence or absence of organic brain damage. This examination attempts to locate the position and extent of the lesions and relate it to the area's functions as well as the functions that are due to mature at a later stage of development. At present these questions frequently cannot be answered with certainty but with more precise instrumentation, technique, and increased knowledge of the deeper regions of the brain, the neurologist will be able to diagnose more specifically. When the neurological diagnosis can include information about capacities for retraining tissue neighboring injured areas, the diagnosis will contribute more to educational planning.

DISABILITY. Functional deficits associated with this syndrome of central-nervous-system impairment could be stated most simply as inadequate central processes in handling stimuli. Specifically, the child is unable to hold attention or perseverates and cannot release attention. His behavior is unpredictable. Lack of laterality is common along with other visual-motor disabilities and restricted concept formation.

HANDICAP. The handicapping consequences resulting from lack of cortical control may involve a varying number of learning areas. Physical motion is awkward, with the result that the fine motor coordination required in reading and writing is poor. His lack of behavioral inhibition interferes with his learning. Disharmony in intellectual functioning interferes with both verbal and nonverbal responses. This may result in developmental aphasias or in inadequate vocabulary. The specific handicaps for a child can only be determined when the problem variables are considered in conjunction with the situation variables.

Situation Variables

NATURE OF PATHOLOGY. There are two etiologies for this oversensitivity to stimuli. One is a type of brain injury and the other is a type of emotional disturbance. In the functional disorder or emotional disturbance it is possible for a child to overcome the total handicap when he learns how to handle stimuli more productively. The brain-damaged child may have injuries in areas of the brain that result in disabilities which will be permanent, and the best that can be done is to overcome the consequences of the disability.

THERAPEUTIC PROCEDURES. Medical treatment of the brain-injured or hyperactive child is quite limited. In some cases sedation helps to slow the child down and makes learning easier. These children should be under careful medical supervision because medication sometimes has an exciting effect rather than a calming one.

TIME FACTORS. Although brain damage is permanent and frequently not progressive, the age of the child at the time of the injury is important (Hebb, 1949). Many assemblies and phase sequences are formed during infancy. The established assemblies are so diffuse that they are not usually wiped out by local injuries. Exceptions are found where damage to specific brain areas results in aphasia or other specific disabilities. Established abilities are usually retained because remaining assemblies or sequences reproduce the complete memory. If injury or emotional trauma impedes assembly before a skill is established, then the organization cannot be formed adequately and the phase sequences are distorted.

The earlier the child receives educational therapy, the less handicapping consequence will result from this disability. The longer the child has to cope with imbalance in his attentional state in an unstructured environment, the more drastically his learning processes are affected.

Early treatment is equally important for the emotionally disturbed child. Without treatment he is confronted with the same functional problem and has little opportunity to learn to organize his perceptions in a normal stimulus-rich environment.

SOCIAL CONDITIONS. Family, community, cultural, and school values and attitudes should be studied in attempting to understand the social conditions of the hyperactive child. Usually, hyperactive children have a particular social problem which increases the handicapping consequences of their disability. Their distractibility and excessive sensitivity to stimuli are usually responded to in the home and school by increased stimulation. Frequently, parents say that they cannot understand why the child is so restless and then explain that they are after him all the time to leave things alone, to be quiet, and so forth. The teacher reports that he has tried everything and to no avail. The child has been encouraged, lectured, punished, moved from one place to another within the classroom, sent out of the room, sent to the office, and been interviewed by several consultants, counselors, etc. Under ordinary circumstances, children who cannot deal productively with stimuli are given more stimuli with which to deal. Unless there is adequate interpretation of the child's perceptual disorder and unless the stimuli are reduced, the child will have increased difficulties. The school can provide a structured social situation and a special place in which he can grow and learn.

School Variables

When the assembled information indicates that the child has the characteristic hyperactivity associated with injury to the central nervous system or with developmental deviations of a functional nature, then it is recommended that a program be planned to help overcome the basic and specific dysfunctions underlying his underachievement. He needs a particular kind of environment in which to gain or partially recover normality. In order to learn effectively he needs a selected and regulated set of experiences that help him assume or resume responsibility. In contrast to the normal child who makes perceptual order out of rather complex and only moderately ordered stimuli, the hyperactive child needs to have the stimuli ordered so as to correct his disordered perception. In this way the perceptual distortions of the hyperactive child are modified, and assemblies within the central nervous system are established which make it possible for him to deal effectively with stimuli in the normal situation.

CONSISTENT APPROACH (A). In adopting a consistent approach to use in working with a hyperactive child, the important idea for the teacher to keep in mind is the central concept of structure in providing ordered educational experiences. Emphasis is on the present status of the child and on what can be done to overcome or ameliorate the condition so that the child moves toward maintenance of general normality in living.

Initially, the program is completely teacher-directed. The child is given little or no opportunity for choice throughout the school day. The teacher must be capable of meeting the child's needs within the structured school environment. From the beginning of implementation of this approach the program is completely simplified and devoid of choice and conflict. Experiences of failure are minimized if the teacher establishes routines for the child concerning how to enter the school and classroom, where to put his belongings, and where to sit, as well as other experiences until the close of the school day.

He avoids expressions of intense feeling and focuses attention on the task at hand. Most attempts to motivate and stimulate these children result in boisterousness, uncontrolled laughter, running around the room, looking out the window, or increased sensitivity to noise, etc. Cases of organic brain damage react particularly unfavorably to this kind of environmental stimulation.

TEACHING METHODS (B). The basis of instructional methods for brain-injured and hyperactive children is setting up dependable classroom routines and giving at first very specific and limited tasks which can later be extended and embellished as emotional self-control and educational applications increase.

Work should begin where the child is able to succeed. At the beginning this is tentatively determined by examining samples of the child's work. It is studied for reversals, spatial relationships, kinds of errors, erasures, perseveration, and incompleteness. In reviewing the results of reading-readiness and other group tests, one should be more concerned with how a score was achieved rather than with the score itself.

It is usually recommended that the child start on a perceptual level task such as sorting blocks for color. Two small boxes and a group of colored blocks are placed before him. A red block is placed in one box, and the child is told to put all blocks like this in the box; another color is then put in the second box. This process is repeated and expanded until he can sort primary and secondary colors and later shades of the same color. Similar methods are employed in teaching the child to recognize shapes and symbols. When he recognizes form and color through sorting, he can be introduced to copying designs by

drawings of squares, circles, and crosses or by constructing designs on
the pegboard. Block designs are built first on top of the design on the
card and then separate from the picture. In sorting and matching
pictures, numbers, and letters, he can use color cues he has learned
earlier. When recognition of symbols is established, visual-motor
training through drawing the symbols by following dotted lines and
cutting out with scissors develops eye-hand coordination. Finally in
this sequence he develops recall or afterimage by reproducing the
color or shape after the original design is removed from his sight.

All extraneous stimuli are reduced by increasing the stimulus value
of material to be learned and removing or subduing all other stimulation. Order in the material presented, with gradual progression from
simple to complex, controls extraneous stimulation in the presentation
itself. Physical activity during study is reduced by seating him at
considerable distance from other children. If distraction is still excessive, have him face a wall or a corner of the room, or work in a booth,
depending on the severity of his difficulty. Make directions concise
and meaningful, one step at a time, and be sure he understands what
is expected. Demonstrations are usually better than explanations.
Consistency in methods of teaching and clearly defined limits will
help the child find himself.

Observation of the child will show when he is ready for the next
step or when we have moved too fast and he needs to go back. Progress
comes slowly at first, but when he has confidence in himself he will
learn just as much and just as fast as he can. Watch that drill is not
encouraging perseveration. If he seems to be doing the task over and
over ritualistically, change to another task to divert him. Records,
which will help teacher and child see the progress being made, support
self-confidence. Samples of each child's work are the best records and
contribute to ongoing research that should be part of the teacher's
method.

SPECIFIC OBJECTIVES (c). The specific objective of the structure
in this program is to break up rigidity and perseveration in the brain-
injured and hyperactive child and to clarify relationships between
behavior and consequences. The goal is to help the child grow by
providing preparatory experiences and by moving the regular age or
grade challenge farther away. In other words, it is not the objective
for these children to keep up with normal children until their perceptual disabilities have been resolved.

ANCILLARY SERVICES (d). A number of school services may be involved in the diagnosis of the hyperactive child. The family history

should be available, whether it is gathered by a social worker or other pupil personnel workers familiar with techniques for dealing with the home. The teacher should have an interview with parents regarding the program, but it is more effective if he is not involved at the level of a case study.

Involvement of the school health department, whether the medical diagnosis was by a private physician or through a public health service, is essential so that communication and consultation are effective. The speech therapist and school psychologist may be involved in diagnosis. While all these services are of value in diagnosis, it is essential to the prescriptive teaching program for these children that the teacher is the one person carrying out the prescribed school program and that other personnel are consultants for him. The coordinator of the program should be the main consultant in the initial stages of the program until the concept of structure is understood by the teacher and consultants.

The child should not be taken out for counseling or speech therapy until well along in his perceptual development. When he can cope adequately with stimuli in the structured situation, he may be able to make better observations of social situations. Until the process of differentiation or the emergence of figure-ground relationships is under way, his perception of events is so immature that counseling is ineffective. Furthermore, the lack of environmental structure and the permissive social situation which will be appropriate in counseling him later are detrimental in the school setting at this stage. When his discrimination and differentiation develop and hyperactivity is reduced, he should start visits to the counselor. These interviews should be conducted in quiet surroundings and the client allowed to tell of his experiences. A counselor working with these children employing a passively friendly approach can provide an opportunity for exploration of a social relationship which will not be excessively stimulating. It is particularly important that the counselor not be actively friendly at this stage. The child with his new ability to perceive relationships in the spatial world must be allowed to explore social relationships in a semistructured counseling situation. This counseling relationship can establish a bridge to an expanding social world.

Interviews with parents should be provided on a regular basis by the visiting teacher, social worker, counselor, or psychologist. Group work with parents of children with similar problems is effective.

PLACEMENT AND PERSONNEL (E). If the information indicates that a child has the characteristics of brain or central-nervous-system injury or developmental deviations, it is prescribed that he have a quiet uncluttered place in which to work and grow. What school activities can he do that normal children do? Which of his activities are immature? Should he go on as a normal child where he can? Should he have therapy where he deviates? Whatever placement is decided upon, learning tasks should be within the learning capacity and within the limits of frustration and attention span of the child. The following four placements should be considered:

1. Regular-class placement can be adapted to meet the needs of the disturbed child if his behavior is not too deviant and the teacher has the interest, patience, and time to devote to the individual handicapped child. A corner for the child to work in and special materials should be provided. The regular classroom with these provisions cannot meet the needs of a hyperactive child who is very distractible and overly responsive to auditory stimulation.

2. An integrated placement for the child who performs adequately in some areas is advisable. The child having difficulty with visual-motor perception may be able to maintain his regular place in music, adapted physical education, and certain functions such as lunch period and social activities while learning to overcome his disability in a special class for perceptually handicapped children.

3. Many brain-injured and hyperactive children derive greatest benefit from being in a special day class where the principle of structure can be applied consistently until such time as they develop adequate perceptual organization to be able to employ the project method in their studies. Integration should then be a gradual process starting with their areas of competency.

4. A few very hyperactive children with accompanying physical or mental handicaps and inadequate homes may need treatment in a residential school. Any segregation should be viewed as a phase in the child's development with integration of the child in the normal home and school environment as the objective. Segregation is justified only when the normal situation cannot provide appropriate learning tasks within the learning capacity and within the limits of frustration and attention span of the child.

The program demands that the teacher have special qualities. A teacher specializing in working with hyperactive children should be methodical and well organized. He must be able to give clear, brief instructions and be consistent in follow-through. He needs to understand the structure of the prescriptive teaching approach and be able, step by step, day by day, to build his teaching on this structure. He must be accepting and understanding of the restless, hyperactive, and socially disturbed child while at the same time he must not participate with the child in his upsets. Special training would be an asset, but at present, courses dealing with teaching hyperactive children are taught on only a few campuses. Syracuse University has perhaps pioneered in this field more than any other school (Cruickshank et al., 1961). Effective, interested teachers who read about these methods can learn to apply them on the job and achieve desirable results.

Children in this program need close and constant supervision. A teacher assistant can share this responsibility giving the teacher some time for other duties such as interviews with parents or professional personnel. The assistant should have a personality similar to the teacher and carry out the same control as the teacher. Professional pretraining is usually not provided for the teacher assistant; however, careful on-the-job training must be given. Additional help in preparing materials for instruction can also be provided.

SUBJECT MATTER (F). Because a special class for hyperactive children has a wider therapeutic purpose in addition to helping children progress with their schoolwork, the curriculum is planned to overcome the specific dysfunctions underlying underachievement. The prescribed program will include those activities that will meet individual needs in developing finer muscular control, eye-hand coordination, form perception, figure-ground relationships, establishing left-right progression, and integrating behavioral responses. For example, a perceptually disturbed child may have to return to early levels of development and there establish perceptual integrations. (Delacato, 1959). For a child with severe visual-perceptual difficulties, tactual perception precedes visual perception, so he feels hard and soft, rough and smooth surfaces with his eyes closed, then with his eyes open. He then sorts objects into hard and soft, rough and smooth, and so forth. He uses games which identify objects by feel, and finally he identifies pictures of hard and soft objects. These activities develop coordinations necessary for the school subjects of reading and writing which will be introduced later. Auditory training is facilitated through listening games and through contrasting loud and soft sound, high and low pitch, fast and slow beat. Behavioral integration is encouraged by activities which require the child to follow directions starting with simple tasks and building until the child can carry out a normal sequence.

INSTRUCTIONAL MATERIALS (G). Materials for the hyperactive child should be clear and simple, presenting one concept at a time. In a stimulus-free environment the one item the child is to see should be clear and bold. Color cues and color contrast are employed. Paper should not be glossy, and it should be in plentiful supply so that only one response per sheet is required in the early stages. Use large pencils and crayons. The materials are somewhat self-tutoring and assist the child in working by himself. Simple stencils help the child learn the form of squares, triangles, circles, etc. Later, stencils of animals can be used for drawings which are then colored. Some commercial materials produced for primary work are suitable. Workbooks and primers can be cut up and pasted on cards so that only one assignment is presented. Some programmed materials and vocabulary cards are useful when the child has overcome his major perceptual disturbances.

SPECIAL EQUIPMENT (H). The same principle of structure is the basis for selection of equipment for the room. Very hyperactive or disinhibited children may be better able to concentrate when isolated behind a screen. The provision of a screen provides for flexibility to meet individual needs. A child can be seated near a side wall with a screen placed so that he can see the front of the room and the chalkboard for group instruction and still be isolated from the distractions of other children and the room. Tables which can be used for individual pupils can be placed facing the wall for hyperactive pupils who cannot stand the isolation of a booth. Tables can be arranged in positions so that the teacher has control of the attention of the class while at the same time the children are separated. Black is the preferable color for chalkboards and large sight-saving chalk provides maximum contrast. The room should be kept free of displays. All teaching equipment and materials, except that being attended to, should be stored out of sight in a cabinet or special room. Each child should have a storage space of his own which is out of sight. Jumbo pegboards using square and round pegs, and later standard boards have many uses. The child can work out designs and gain coordination before he is able to draw. Double-deck pegboards with the top made of plexiglass develop depth perception. Form boards and color-matching boards develop color, size, and shape discrimination. The teacher who is aware of the need for new devices that will reach a particular child will find some equipment available commercially but will also have to devise some himself.

The child's clothing should not be distracting; the material should be soft and the design simple. Clothing worn by the teacher should be neutral and without contrasting buttons and ornaments. Female teachers should not wear jewelry or excessive makeup (Strauss and Lehtinen, 1947).

SCHOOL PLANT (I). A classroom located away from the work and play areas of the school is most suitable. Windows which have the lower part painted over reduce glare and stimuli from outside. The color of the walls, woodwork, furniture, and floor should match. There is a lack of evidence to prove which color is best, but it is generally agreed that a neutral color is most satisfactory. The finish should be flat and the lighting diffused to avoid glare. Acoustical treatment to reduce noise is essential. Wall-to-wall carpeting reduces the noise level from within the classroom more than any other modification. Reduced space controls stimuli. The individual cubicle in the special room provides a situation where the child can attend completely to his learning experiences. Cubicles are usually built along the back of the classroom so that the child faces the back wall away from the open side. The partitions are high enough and deep enough to obviate peripheral distractions. The only materials in the cubicle are those he is working with on his desk. In other words, the cubicle is a nonstimulating environment into which the structurally controlled stimuli are introduced. In this situation many hyperactive children experience their first feeling of success in learning. Every detail of construction, plumbing, lighting, heating, and air conditioning should be considered in providing a quiet, stimulus-free environment within the classroom. All extraneous or unessential stimuli should be reduced or eliminated in their visual, auditory, and tactual impressiveness.

AUXILIARY AGENCIES (J). Frequently the child with intracranial lesions is diagnosed at a neurological clinic, and the emotionally disturbed child has had psychiatric evaluation. Follow-up studies and evaluations by specialists in these agencies are of value to the school, to the home, and to the clinic personnel. A reassessment once or twice a year with a conference of the clinic and school personnel provides in-service training.

If the home environment is disturbed, a referral may be made to an appropriate source of help such as a family agency, as would be the case for any problem child from a difficult home situation. Usually there is no social agency outside of the school which can help with the hyperactive child until his perceptual difficulties are reduced. He may then try his new perceptual skills in regular activities in the community, such as Boy Scouts, community center, or special interest groups.

THE EMOTIONALLY DISTURBED CHILD

The emotionally disturbed child is one who is unhappy and insecure within himself, who has poor relationships with other people and with his environment, who has excessive hostility or fears or fantasy life, or who has too many nonorganic physical complaints or too little control over his body functions without organic cause.

As an adult, he will exhibit a higher degree of vulnerability to behavior problems, general health problems, poor interpersonal relationships, inability to function sexually, inability to profit from experience or lead a happy life. In its more pervasive form this vulnerability may lead to psychosis, neurosis, suicide, repetitive automobile accidents, alcoholism, narcotic addiction, or criminal behavior.

When a child's early experiences are not salutary for him, unwholesome tendencies may be started. His intellectual development may be retarded, or he may fixate on immature ways of expressing and demanding affection. He may become excessively submissive or excessively aggressive. He may express his disturbance in physical illness or in pathological fears or desires. These symptoms will not serve him well when he is required to display endurance and adaptability later in life.

The assumption that unsatisfactory homes produce emotionally disturbed children has not been supported by some recent research. It may be valid to state that a particular home is unsatisfactory in a specific way for a specific child, but this fact does not provide a sound basis for explaining all emotional disturbances.

In a thirty-year follow-up study of children referred to a child-guidance clinic, O'Neal and Robbins (1958) employed a control group of children from public schools who were matched for age, IQ, sex, race, and residence with the children attending the child-guidance clinic. The public school children were intended to be only a control group, but the investigators became interested in their characteristics. The criteria of selection had yielded a healthy successful group which had no excessive absences, no grades repeated, no disciplinary action recorded, and had IQs of over 80. The success of the control group at school and as citizens was interesting in view of the fact that children were drawn from disadvantaged classes and that a history of broken homes was found in one-third of the cases. These homes did not appear to produce emotional disturbance in the children.

In a report of a large-scale study of emotionally handicapped children in California public schools, Bower (1961) states that emotionally handicapped children, like other children, have varied socioeconomic backgrounds, have average intelligence, and generally live with their parents. He also found they were like other children in that they came from families of various sizes and occupied various positions in their families. His findings showed that they differed from other children in that they were (1) emotionally handicapped and (2) educationally retarded. He concluded that each of these conditions continually plays havoc with the other, with the result that both continue to become increasingly worse until essential steps are taken to remedy the situation.

In discussions relating to child-rearing practices it seems that parents are advised to do impossible and contradictory things. They are told to do things for their child so he knows he is loved and to give plenty of affection so that he will not feel rejected. But they are also told not to overprotect so that he will not be frustrated at school and to let him settle his own problems. They are told not to repress and inhibit him lest he become disturbed, but to set limits lest he develop a poor superego. Anyone familiar with the literature for parents can fill a long list of conflicting and contradictory advice. This is not an attempt to deny the importance of the home and early experiences. It is an attempt to point out the inadequacies of our generalizations about how parents should behave. It is more profitable under these circumstances to study the child's present functioning, to work with the child in an environment conducive to improving his responses and self-concept, and to work with the parents in helping them understand the child's difficulty than it is to generalize about how the child should have been raised.

Definition of Mental Health

Another difficulty in the treatment of emotionally disturbed children exists because of a lack of a useful definition of mental health and because we have not reached the point where mental health is a quantifiable concept. The problem is stated succinctly by Smith (1959) when he says that mental health is a value judgment and that science has not yet learned how to deal surefootedly with values. A definition (Deutsch and Fishman, 1963, p. 2123) which is quite inclusive states: "Mental health is a state of being which is relative rather than absolute in which a person has effected a reasonably satisfactory integration of his instinctive drives. His integration is acceptable to himself and his social milieu as reflected in the satisfactory nature of his interpersonal relationships, his level of satisfactory living, his actual achievement, his flexibility, and the level of emotional maturity he has attained." Although this definition in practice involves a culturally determined value judgment of the good life, it is an improvement over the less dynamic maladjustment concept. The deviation or maladjustment approach rated mental health on the basis of the ordinariness of behavior as contrasted to the unusualness of behavior. Some unfortunate aspects of rating emotional disturbance as a deviation from some norm are that (1) this approach does not differentiate between creativity and illness; (2) the norm is culturally determined and may have little relationship to the individual's health; (3) the approach tends to focus on behavior rather than on the stimulus situation; and (4) the approach defines improvement in terms of greater conformity to social norms. The recent shift of the mental-health movement away from exclusive concern with mental illness toward greater concern with positive mental health has not been accompanied by proportionate gains in research and scientific understanding. Mental health as a value is more of a slogan or rallying cry than a scientific concept (Scott, 1958). Mental illness or emotional handicap is more easily defined in terms of limitations, such as lack of speech, refusal to eat, and underachievement at school. Because we can define mental illness and not mental health, we know what to treat the disturbed child out of, but we do not know what to treat him into.

This book does not attempt to give a satisfactory definition of mental health although the author feels that mental health and mental illness are not only our number one health problems but are important to the peace of the world and survival of the human race. When the objectives or desired outcomes of treatment are not clearly defined, we look at disability in terms of specific limitations in the repertoire of responses of the individual child. By overcoming the limitation or disability, the individual can become a more fully functioning person and therefore a more creative person. This process may not provide a completely satisfactory answer for the school as some creative children are considered to be problems in some schools.

For our purposes we will regard children as emotionally handicapped when their responses are unrewarding to themselves and inappropriate to the degree of being unacceptable to others. In a regular class they underachieve and disrupt the class. The incidence of emotional disturbance and mental illness is higher than other problems. Bower (1961) found 10 percent of schoolchildren disturbed to the extent that they were in need of psychiatric help. Only a few, 0.5 percent, were found to be so severely handicapped emotionally that they needed special placement or intensive treatment.

Identification

Identification by classroom teachers and referral to school psychological services usually precede referral to mental-hygiene clinics. Teachers generally are accurate in recognizing children who are emotionally disturbed. Standardized personality tests and sociometric studies are useful screening devices which can be employed by teachers. Children appearing in need of help are referred to the school psychologist for further evaluation using more complex psychological instruments, such as projective techniques and tests of visual-motor ability. Depending on the severity of the problem, a school-centered case study and/or referral to a mental-hygiene clinic may follow. The diagnosis of emotional disturbances and mental illnesses is a function of the mental-health clinic. Here the social worker provides the psychosocial history, the psychologist administers intelligence, projective, and other tests, and the psychiatrist is the medical specialist who has the main responsibility of integrating his information from interviews with the psychologist's and social worker's evaluations. The psychiatrist has legal responsibility in the mental-health field and should be represented whenever planning is undertaken for emotionally disturbed children.

Emotional disturbance is a blanket term covering a number of diagnostic categories. It is beyond the scope of this chapter to deal fully with any one category, let alone the whole range of emotional disturbances. All the techniques of instruction employed in prescriptive teaching are aimed at preventing and reducing emotional disturbances. Here we shall deal with some severe conditions requiring special educational facilities. We have already dealt with the hyperactive emotionally disturbed in the section on the brain-injured and hyperactive child. We shall now look at teaching the emotionally disturbed child.

Emotional disturbance can be viewed, in one frame of reference, as the result of a certain type of undesirable learning. The child has an inherent urge to grow and to achieve emotional maturity, and when events interfere with normal development, emotional disturbance occurs. Growth can be facilitated by modification of the events causing the disturbance. This assumption is based on the view that the law of homeostasis is applicable to psychological processes.

Problem Variables

INJURY. Emotional disturbance is defined as a disability without clearly defined physical cause or without structural damage to the brain. Obviously a child could be emotionally disturbed because of a physical injury, disability, or disfiguring scar, but the emotional disturbance results indirectly from his altered self-concept.

DISABILITY. When disturbed processes are in control, a child is unable to make productive responses. He may not be able to eat or to tolerate food if force-fed. He may respond to different situations in a ritualistic manner because he has a distorted view of certain situations which have one aspect in common. He may be acting-out in a physically and verbally assaultive manner or be withdrawn and uncommunicative as his typical way of responding to a wide variety of situations. Abnormal fears, desires, and compulsions are common disabilities.

HANDICAP. The consequences are numerous and range from severe physical symptoms to behavior which is handicapping in only one situation. Eczema, asthma, digestive disturbances, and migraine are typical physical symptoms of emotional disorders. Impaired cognition, memory dysfunctions, perseveration, restrictions of social interaction, and excessive fears create learning handicaps and inadequate self-concepts. Exaggerated fear of animals could cause specific reading difficulty associated with stories about animals. Because many primary grade stories are about animals, this fear could result in a quite general reading problem. Traumatic experiences with parents or other adults could result in difficult teacher-pupil relationships. Some emotionally disturbed children are thought to be mentally retarded because of the totality of the handicapping consequences to their learning (Devereux, 1956).

Situation Variables

NATURE OF PATHOLOGY. Emotional disturbance is a condition in which a child is chronically fearful or has inordinate desires. He habitually distorts some aspect of his perceptual field.

THERAPEUTIC PROCEDURES. Play therapy and psychotherapy for the child along with counseling for the parents are the usual clinical treatments for the emotionally disturbed child. When this help is provided for the child and his parents along with a modified or therapeutic educational program, the child's opportunity to overcome his disturbance is greatly improved (Laycock, 1963). Medication in the form of tranquilizing or relaxing drugs is helpful for some children. A study of the effect of using chlorpromazine with emotionally disturbed boys with reading problems indicated that this reduced their hyperactivity and was an effective adjunct in their remedial-reading program (Freed, 1958). In general the improvement associated with tranquilizing drugs is a reduction of hostile behavior and hyperactivity. This control of behavioral symptoms may enable the child to participate in psychotherapy, remedial instruction, and socialization.

TIME FACTORS. The earlier that educational provisions and environmental and relationship modifications are made for emotionally handicapped children, the more successful is the treatment. A point needing continuous consideration is that emotional disabilities are not necessarily permanent and as a matter of fact are more readily modifiable than many other conditions. Reid and Hagan (1952) found that half the severely disturbed children placed in residential treatment centers were released within one year. Schoolchildren tend to have more emotional disturbances during puberty (Wattenberg, 1955).

SOCIAL CONDITIONS. Many conditions within the home are related to emotional disturbances in children. Deprivation of maternal affection, excessive inconsistency and mobility, marital discord, extreme sibling rivalry, etc., are considered to be causes. An emotionally disturbed child in any social group is a disrupting influence, and both the situation and the child's disturbance probably interact to support each other.

School Variables

The modifications discussed here are those considered appropriate for a special class for emotionally disturbed children in a public school.

These children are able to live with their parents or in a foster home and attend day school. Because emotional disturbance is not a static condition, and because environmental modifications result in changes of the child's behavior and personality, flexibility is required in planning. Special placement is regarded as a phase in the total plan of educational therapy. Some of the modifications can be carried out in the regular classroom, but the severely disturbed child needs a program sufficiently different that special placement is advisable. A long-range study (Bower, 1961) of 45,000 California schoolchildren found 1,200 emotionally handicapped. Half were placed in special programs, and half were left in regular classrooms. The results indicated the superiority of special programs and the inadequacy of providing only mental-health consultations for disturbed children in regular classes. The reader planning any program for emotionally disturbed children is advised to read this comprehensive report.

CONSISTENT APPROACH (A). The central concept of the consistent approach is the principle of structure outlined earlier. An emotionally disturbed child needs a particular atmosphere and ordered educational experiences in which to assume or resume responsibility, to learn effectively, and to move toward self-actualization. Haring and Phillips (1962) studied experimental programs for working with disturbed acting-out children. The experimental classes were given a highly structured school day. The approach emphasized what could be done about an undesirable situation to overcome or ameliorate it. The control groups consisted of regular classes with consultative assistance and special classes employing permissive approaches and an adapted or modified curriculum. They reported that the experimental classes using the structured approach made significant gains over the control groups in academic achievement and behavior.

Some authorities object to this approach especially when applied to all types of emotional disturbance (Laycock, 1963). Prescriptive teaching, as employed by the author, is based upon a concept of structure which provides for a variety of approaches to meet the needs of individual children and is opposed to one approach applied indiscriminately. The approach employed by the teacher should reflect the therapeutic plan, but the teacher need not adopt the role of the psychotherapist. The teacher should allay the child's anxiety whereas the psychotherapist may wish to arouse anxiety. A withdrawn child in an understanding environment provided by the teacher's acceptance may be able to break through the defenses of his private world and come to grips with reality. An acting-out child may be helped to curb his aggressive behavior through the firmness and dependability of the teacher's approach. Both children are striving to bring order out of emotional chaos, and both need warmth and understanding from the teacher; but the approach employed by the teacher is different for each of these children. Experience with the six approaches discussed in Chapter 4 suggests that when they are employed appropriately and consistently, they can provide a dependable environment wherein the child can resolve emotional problems and make progress toward more effective learning. Heil, Powell, and Feifer (1960) reported a research project showing that teachers who employed structure, self-control, and orderliness achieved significant results.

TEACHING METHODS (B). Starting to teach a special class for disturbed children should be different from starting with a regular class because most of the children have had traumatic experiences at school and with groups. The teacher begins at the proper place for each child according to the educational diagnostic profile. He does not start by asking the child personal questions but begins by assigning him a task that is easy and pleasant. Work is planned in advance, and a dependable school routine is established from the first day. A young child starts on a perceptual-level task such as sorting blocks for color, size, or form and later goes on to writing, arithmetic, and reading. The teacher should not expect sustained effort from a disturbed child. Assignments should be short at the beginning of the program and should alternate between physical activity and quiet desk work. It is advisable to use routines in giving out paper and getting down to work. Routines improve the classroom situation so that it is easier for the child to maintain self-control. Rules and routines are to facilitate action, not to prevent it, and therefore must not frustrate the child but free him for the real task of learning. As the group develops, some routines can be established by democratic means. The teacher supports the child's self-control by (1) proximity control, that is, by being close to the child and making his physical presence felt; (2) signals, such as a warm smile, nod, or shake of the head; (3) interest in what the child is doing and reinforcement of positive responses; and (4) humor, or helping the child see that it is all right for him to laugh at his mistakes.

A disturbed child's anxiety makes him more likely to fail. In many cases the harder he tries, the worse he does. It is essential that the child be successful from the beginning in the special class. This does not mean avoiding areas of previous failure. It means starting at a level at which he can be successful. Children with perceptual-motor difficulties will receive instruction and engage in activities which develop form perception. Physical activities which develop perceptual skills are particularly beneficial for emotionally disturbed children who tend to have perceptual problems and poor coordination. The techniques employed by Kephart (1960) and described earlier are beneficial in overcoming these deficits. Walking a line, balancing, rhythm games to music, and training in ocular control and form perception build perceptual foundations for academic learning and reduce emotional tension. Muscular activity following emotional stress reduces the physiological reaction to extreme emotion (Fait, 1960).

The structure of the learning experiences should clarify the relationship between behavior and consequences. This clarification is accomplished through setting up dependable classroom routines, giving at first very specific and limited tasks which can be extended and embellished later as the child gains in emotional self-control and application to studies. When a child tries to avoid or postpone a disliked subject or assignment, it is usually advisable that he be given a very brief assignment which he must finish before he is allowed to go on to a more enjoyable activity. Where blocking is the result of a phobia, the problem stimulus is presented along with one which produces pleasure until conditioning overcomes the block. Assigned work is given priority at the beginning of the day with recreation, artwork, finger painting, etc., following completion of more formal assignments.

When an emotionally disturbed child arrives at school in a disagreeable mood or has an upset during the school day, it is frequently desirable to give him time to settle down. If he provokes others excessively, he should be removed from the group for a short period of time. The teacher's concern places emphasis on a solution or resolution of the problem in preference to queries as to why the child behaved as he did. The teacher does not participate with the child in his upset but only participates in reinforcing a solution to the present problem.

It is the situation for which a child cannot muster an adequate response that overwhelms and creates severe anxiety states. Emotional upsets block clear thinking, preclude deliberation, and destroy ability to formulate an appropriate course of action. Excessive motivation or anxiety narrows perception and therefore limits the response. If the child feels that too much is at stake or that learning this lesson is too important, he increases his chance of failing. Learning for disturbed children takes place best under conditions of moderate motivation. This is accomplished by focusing on the immediate and reinforcing correct responses rather than attempting to convince him that his future success and happiness depend upon his learning to read.

Teaching machines and programmed instruction have been used with disturbed children. The Devereux Schools (Smith, 1961) have used programmed materials in special education, and their results are encouraging. Programming is a way of structuring the presentation of materials to be learned and providing clear directions and immediate reinforcement of the student's correct efforts. Gallanter (1959) reports some of the early work with exceptional children. The author's experience in using programmed materials with disturbed children indicates that these materials have considerable potential. Teaching machines may have an appeal to a child who has not been successful with books, and selected responses have an advantage for the child with writing difficulties. This effect of uniqueness is only short-lived but seems to help overcome some blocks. Obviously we are not suggesting that the child substitute button pushing for writing, but while he is developing his visual-motor coordination and writing skill, the machine can provide some other learning and help support his feeling of adequacy. The principle of programming has been applied to the whole classroom for emotionally disturbed children. With full environmental control, automatic programming techniques, and adequate reinforcing agents, disturbed behavior may be quite rapidly brought under stimulus control. Sensitively arranged changes in programming of discriminative and reinforcing stimuli may readily speed up acquisition of discrimination. The development of programmed materials and particularly programmed rooms, while still in its infancy, holds promise of a brighter future for disturbed children and is a challenge to the ingenuity of school psychologists.

Diagnosed psychotic children are frequently not retained in regular public schools. Some attend special day schools and others are institutionalized. Their status remains an enigma for school authorities. The author has attempted to employ conditioning techniques with several he has encountered in the school system. The outcome in terms of overcoming the psychosis is uncertain, but the technique seemed to be an improvement over other methods of dealing with them in the school setting. Appropriate classes were not available so they were placed in

classes for slow learners. Recent studies employing operant conditioning suggest new opportunities for educational therapy for these severely disturbed children.

There is general agreement regarding the effectiveness of operant
conditioning (Patterson, 1963). It is effective in shaping the behavior
of even severely disturbed children and has been successful in restoring speech to catatonic schizophrenic patients who had not spoken for
many years (Isaacs, Thomas, and Goldiamond, 1960).

Operant conditioning is the shaping of behavior through the reinforcement of spontaneous behavior approximating the desired response and gradually eliciting and rewarding responses closer and
closer to the desired response. The key to this behavioral approach is
that environment must be manipulated to allow strong reinforcing
consequences to become attached to the behavior that is desired. In the
classroom rewards or token reinforcers are dispensed immediately
upon occurrence of the desired response. To increase occurrence of a
particular behavior, it is only necessary to ensure that reinforcement
occurs relatively soon after the behavior. The principle of operant
conditioning has been used successfully in treatment of emotional
problems as well as abnormal behavior (Eysenck, 1960).

SPECIFIC OBJECTIVES (C). For children in this special class educational therapy is not directed toward solving underlying unconscious causes of neurotic symptoms. The major aim is to make it
possible for the child to tolerate emotional stress and live more comfortably even under difficult conditions. He is in this class so that he
may receive special instruction which will support development of his
perceptual modes of learning and overcome distortions in his perceptual field. The objective is for the overcoming of emotional blocks and
for perceptual-motor development which will allow him to return to a
regular class and maintain normal progress. The special class employs
educational techniques as therapy to assist the child in overcoming
deficits but does not attempt to maintain normal academic progress.

ANCILLARY SERVICES (D). The teacher implementing this program
for a special class will frequently need much reassurance from the
school psychologist. He may need support for his means of handling
an upset in the classroom. Helping him analyze how he dealt with a
problem is an important function of the psychologist. Counseling at
school or psychotherapy at the mental-health clinic should be a regular part of the program for disturbed children. All the school services
should be available to this as to any other class, but special attention
must be given to working with parents of disturbed children.

PLACEMENT AND PERSONNEL (E). Special education can provide emotionally disturbed children with improved opportunities for developing strengths and abilities to deal with problems. Bower (1961) describes a large-group long-range study of educational provisions for the emotionally disturbed child. Of the 1,200 emotionally disturbed children in the study, 600 were in special classes, and 600 were in regular programs. This study indicated significant improvement for those in the special classes over those in the regular classes.

A selective placement in a class for disturbed children with a teacher who has special training and skill in dealing with emotionally handicapped children appears to be justifiable. The class is usually limited to six to twelve children. The optimal class size depends on a number of factors such as (1) the severity and variety of disturbances, (2) teacher aids, (3) ancillary services, (4) programmed materials, and (5) degree of integration. If the class consists of children with similar educational needs, more group instruction can be used. Teacher aids can contribute to raising the pupil-teacher ratio. Ancillary services can relieve the teacher of some liaison work with parents and community agencies. Suitable programmed materials and other commercially prepared aids allow the teacher to use more time for instruction. Where children are integrated for part of the day with regular classes or are taking an adapted physical education program with the physical education instructor, the special class can be larger.

There are obvious advantages in having a child in his own home while he is attending school for educational therapy. The restoration of harmony and understanding between parents and child is a major purpose of treatment. Treatment of him and of his parents can go hand in hand and reduce the danger of conflict being set up between different standards of the home and school environments.

The success of a special class for emotionally disturbed children will depend on the selection and training of the teacher. The teacher for this class must be motivated to work with emotionally disturbed children and be emotionally mature and secure. Teachers whose own neurotic needs result in overdomination or overprotection of children should be excluded from working with these children. Some teachers who say that they love children may have a neurotic need for children to love them and place excessive strain on the emotional reserves of the child. Emotional stability is, therefore, a prime requisite for the teacher. He must be able to enter into or understand the child's emotional disturbance without becoming too emotionally involved in the child's upsets. The teacher should have special training in the methods of promoting the emotional growth and development of these children. A teacher with a background in remedial teaching who is provided with adequate ancillary services can provide education which has therapeutic results (Gage, 1963).

The special teacher for the emotionally disturbed child is a therapeutic educator who can work effectively with unusually challenging children who have difficulties in perception, communication, and sensory development. These children may achieve one day and regress the next. To deal constructively with these children the teacher should have full membership in the mental-health team and understand the psychological procedures, family influences, and social and personality dynamics for each child. He must be able to provide educational experiences which lead toward the therapeutic goals.

Since most disturbed children are in regular classes, the role of the regular teacher is of prime importance. La Vietes (1962) described the contribution of the regular teacher in educating the disturbed child. Douglas (1961) described the special teacher's role in the education of the emotionally disturbed and advocated that the teacher should operate as a teacher and that his goal should be to have the child return to the regular class.

SUBJECT MATTER (F). Disturbed children have distorted views of information which in some cases cause academic retardation. Selection of subject matter is aimed primarily toward relieving the perceptual distortion rather than toward remedying the academic retardation. Subject matter which develops the perceptual modes, teaches discrimination, and facilitates perceptual-motor growth is covered in other parts of this book and in the references. Frequently the physical activity recommended for perceptual development also reduces tension and seems to divert the child's attention from the family or social situation which threatens him.

When a group is over the most severe symptoms of disturbance, role playing is an effective approach to settling problems of interpersonal relationships. Psychodrama provides opportunity for expression of difficulties which are too complex for expression in words only. It provides a situation in which the child can, by active participation, live through a problem he has encountered. It involves action which goes beyond mere verbal expression or listening. It is concerned with an individual problem, but the activity takes place in a social situation where spontaneity is the essential element. In using this technique we must not turn the classroom into a clinic and overinterpret play as therapy or psychodrama. We are only trying to help the child find solutions to social problems. His adjustment through an appropriate form of action will depend partially on his ready-made responses. An inexperienced driver seeing a car coming toward him may let go of the steering wheel, throw up his hands, and let the car crash. A more experienced driver may perform brilliantly and escape by split-second timing and have his emotional seizure later when he can cope with it. Experience with driver-training devices which only simulate the real experience are effective and safe means of learning. Role playing, psychodrama, and play therapy can simulate or symbolize reality and provide experience which develops useful responses for real life situations.

INSTRUCTIONAL MATERIALS (G). The prescribed activities dictate the materials, and these have been discussed in relation to the activities in Chapter 4 and in other parts of this chapter.

SPECIAL EQUIPMENT (H). Teaching machines and other equipment for the disturbed child should be of simple rugged construction because of his poor coordination. He may lose fine control at times and use undue force in trying to manipulate equipment. Pegboards, punchboards, and machines where dialing the correct answer is required develop coordination. Much of the equipment suggested for the hyperactive child is suitable. Flexibility in providing for individual stimulus control is desirable to meet individual needs and progress. Desks or tables of sturdy construction which can be moved to face the wall or be placed in other suitable positions in the room provide flexibility. Movable screens can sometimes help the child who is very distractible gain stimulus control. It is important to avoid excessive isolation of the child and therefore flexible equipment is desirable. The objective is to control the amount of stimulation or distracting influences in the classroom to the degree that the child can handle them constructively.

SCHOOL PLANT (I). The classroom should be in a quiet location away from the main activity areas of the school. Distractions should be minimized by the same plant considerations as for the hyperactive child, but the classroom does not have to be as devoid of stimuli. Some booths large enough for the teacher to sit beside the child are useful for individual instruction as well as for individual work. More responsibility is placed upon the individual for control of extraneous stimuli. A side room where a seriously upset child can be isolated and where a child can rest is a definite asset. Observation for visitors from an adjoining room through one-way glass is preferable to having visitors in the room. The ideal design for a programmed classroom probably has not appeared at this time; therefore flexibility and experimentation should be part of the plan for a special classroom.

AUXILIARY AGENCIES (J). The mental-health or child-guidance clinic will most likely be the major agency active with this child. Therapeutic educators function as members of the mental-health team, and teaching procedures must reflect the therapeutic plan. Both the psychiatrist and the educator have much to learn from each other. Only by cooperation, communication, and coordination of efforts can we, the educators, make full use of the therapeutic potential of the school.

SUMMARY

The prescriptive teaching program for exceptional children has been illustrated by showing the modification of school variables for mentally retarded, brain-injured and hyperactive, and emotionally disturbed children. The next chapter will show the application of the approach to specific cases of handicapped children.

REFERENCES

Ainsworth, S. H. *An Exploratory Study of Educational, Social and Economical Factors in the Education of Mentally Retarded Children in Georgia Public Schools.* Athens, Ga.: University of Georgia, 1959.

Allinsmith, Wesley, and Goethals, George W. *The Role of Schools in Mental Health.* New York: Basic Books, Inc., Publishers, 1962.

Baker, Harry J. *Introduction to Exceptional Children* (3d ed.). New York: The Macmillan Company, 1959.

Baldwin, Willie K. "The Educable Mentally Retarded Child in the Regular Grades," *Exceptional Children*, 1958, 25:106–108.

Baumgartner, Bernice B. *Helping the Trainable Mentally Retarded Child.* New York: Bureau of Publications, Teachers College, Columbia University, 1960.

Bettelheim, Bruno. *Love Is Not Enough.* New York: The Free Press of Glencoe, 1949.

Birnbrauer, J. S. "The Rainier School Programmed Learning Class-
    room," Seattle, Wash.: University of Washington, 1962, 14 pp.
    (Ditto.)

Blair, Glen Myers. *Diagnostic and Remedial Teaching.* New York: The
    Macmillan Company, 1956.

Blatt, B. "Some Persistently Recurring Assumptions concerning the Men-
    tally Subnormal," *Training School Bulletin,* 1960, 57:48–59.

Bower, Eli M. *The Education of Emotionally Handicapped Children.*
    Sacramento: California State Department of Education, 1961.

Brereton, Beatrice (Le Gay). *The Schooling of Children with Impaired
    Hearing.* Sydney: Commonwealth Office of Education, 1957.

Cain, Leo F., and Levine, Samuel. *A Study of the Effects of Community
    and Institutional School Classes for Trainable Mentally Retarded
    Children.* U.S. Office of Education, Cooperative Research Project
    no. SAE 8257, San Francisco: San Francisco State College, 1961.

Capobianco, Rudolf J., and Cole, Dorothy A. "Social Behavior of Men-
    tally Retarded Children," *American Journal of Mental Deficiency,*
    January, 1960, 64:638–651.

Carlson, Bernice Wells, and Ginglend, David R. *Play Activities for the
    Retarded Child.* Nashville, Tenn.: Abingdon Press, 1961.

Carrier, Neil A., Malpass, Leslie F., and Orton, Kenneth D. *Responses of
    Bright, Normal, and Retarded Children to Learning Tasks.* U.S.
    Department of Health, Education, and Welfare, Office of Educa-
    tion, Cooperative Research Program, Project no. 578, Carbondale,
    Ill.: Southern Illinois University, 1961.

Clarke, Ann M., and Clarke, A. D. B. *Mental Deficiency.* London: Methuen
    & Co., Ltd., 1958.

Clarke, H. Harrison, and Clarke, David H. *Developmental and Adapted
    Physical Education.* Englewood Cliffs, N.J.: Prentice-Hall, Inc.,
    1963.

Cleugh, M. F. (ed.). *Teaching the Slow Learner in the Primary School.*
    London: Methuen & Co., Ltd., 1961(*a*).

Cleugh, M. F. *Teaching the Slow Learner in the Special School.* New
    York: Philosophical Library, Inc., 1961(*b*).

Conant, J. B. *Slums and Suburbs.* New York: McGraw-Hill Book Com-
    pany, 1961.

Cruickshank, William M. *Psychology of Exceptional Children and Youth*
    (2d ed.). Englewood Cliffs, N.J.: Prentice-Hall, Inc., 1963.

Cruickshank, William M., and Johnson, G. Orville. *Education of Excep-
    tional Children and Youth.* Englewood Cliffs, N.J.: Prentice-Hall,
    Inc., 1958.

Cruickshank, William M., Bentzen, Florence A., Ratzeburg, Fredrick H.,
    and Tannhauser, Marian F. *A Teaching Method for Brain-injured*

and Hyperactive Children. Syracuse, N.Y.: Syracuse University Press, 1961.

Delacato, Carl H. *Treatment and Prevention of Reading Problems: The Neuro-psychological Approach.* Springfield, Ill.: Charles C Thomas, Publisher, 1959.

Deutsch, Albert, and Fishman, Helen. *Encyclopedia of Mental Health.* New York: Franklin Watts, Inc., 1963.

Devereux, George. *Therapeutic Education.* New York: Harper & Row, Publishers, Incorporated, 1956.

Dinger, Jack C. "Post-school Adjustment of Former Educable Retarded Pupils," *Exceptional Children,* March, 1961, 27:353–360.

Dolch, Edward William. *Helping Handicapped Children in School.* Seattle, Wash.: Garrard Publishing Company, 1948.

Doll, Edgar. "The Essentials of an Inclusive Concept of Mental Deficiency," *American Journal of Mental Deficiency,* October, 1941, 46:214–219.

Dorward, Barbara. *Aids and Toys for Handicapped Children.* Washington, D.C.: Council for Exceptional Children, NEA, 1960.

Douglas, Katherine B. "The Teacher's Role in a Children's Psychiatric Hospital Unit," *Exceptional Children,* January, 1961, 27:246–251.

Dunn, Lloyd M. (ed.). *Exceptional Children in the Schools.* New York: Holt, Rinehart and Winston, Inc., 1963.

Ellis, Norman R. "Amount of Reward and Operant Behavior in Mental Defectives," *American Journal of Mental Deficiency,* January, 1962, 66:595–599.

Ellis, Norman R. "Clinical and Training Implications of Operant Conditioning Methods with Mental Defectives," paper presented at American Psychological Association, Chicago, 1960.

Ellis, Norman R. (ed.). *Handbook of Mental Deficiency: Psychological Theory and Research.* New York: McGraw-Hill Book Company, 1963.

Engel, A. M. "Employment of the Mentally Retarded," *Vocational Rehabilitation of the Mentally Retarded,* Rehabilitation Series 123, Washington, D.C.: 1950, 80–107.

Erdman, Robert. *Educable Retarded Children in Elementary Schools.* Washington, D.C.: National Education Association, 1961.

Eysenck, H. J. *Behavior Therapy and Neurosis.* New York: Pergamon Press, 1960.

Fait, Hollis F. *Adapted Physical Education.* Philadelphia: W. B. Saunders Company, 1960.

Fernald, Grace M. *Remedial Techniques in Basic School Subjects.* New York: McGraw-Hill Book Company, 1943.

Finley, Carmen J. "Arithmetic Achievement in Mentally Retarded Children: the Effect of Presenting the Problem in Different Contexts," *American Journal of Mental Deficiency,* September, 1962, 67:28–286.

Fraenkel, W. A. *The Mentally Retarded and Their Vocational Rehabilitation: A Resource Handbook.* New York: National Association for Retarded Children, 1961.

Francis, R. J., and Rarick, G. L. *Motor Characteristics of the Mentally Retarded* Cooperative Research Bulletin, no. 1, USOE35005, Washington, D.C.: 1960.

Freed, H. "The Use of Tranquilizers in a Child Psychiatry Clinic," paper read at American Orthopsychiatric Association, New York, March, 1958.

Gage, N. L. (ed.). *Handbook of Research on Teaching.* Chicago: Rand McNally & Company, 1963.

Gallagher, James J. *The Tutoring of Brain-injured Mentally Retarded Children.* Springfield, Ill.: Charles C Thomas, Publisher, 1960.

Gallanter, Eugene. *Automatic Teaching.* New York: John Wiley & Sons, Inc., 1959.

Goldstein, Herbert, and Seigle, Dorothy. *A Curriculum Guide for Teachers of the Educable Mentally Handicapped.* Circular Series B-3, no. 12, Springfield, Ill.: Office of the Superintendent of Public Instruction, 1958.

Goodenough, Florence L. *Exceptional Children.* New York: Appleton-Century-Crofts, Inc., 1956.

Goodenough, Florence L., and Tylor, Leona E. *Developmental Psychology.* New York: Appleton-Century-Crofts, Inc., 1959.

Haeussermann, Else. *Developmental Potential of Preschool Children.* New York: Grune & Stratton, Inc., 1958.

Haring, Norris G., and Phillips, E. Lakin. *Educating Emotionally Disturbed Children.* New York: McGraw-Hill Book Company, 1962.

Hebb, D. O. *Organization of Behavior.* New York: John Wiley & Sons, Inc., 1949.

Heber, Rick. *A Manual on Terminology and Classification in Mental Retardation.* Pineville, La.: American Association on Mental Retardation, Second Edition, 1961.

Hegge, T. G., Kirk, S. A., and Kirk, W. D. *Remedial Reading Drills.* Ann Arbor, Mich.: George Wahr Publishing Company, 1940.

Heil, Lewis W., Powell, Marion, and Feifer, Irwin. *Characteristics of Teacher Behavior Related to the Achievement of Children in Several Elementary Grades.* Brooklyn: Office of Testing and Research, Brooklyn College, 1960.

Heiser, Karl F. *Our Backward Children.* New York: W. W. Norton & Company, Inc., 1955.

Hudson, Margaret. *An Exploration of Classroom Procedures for Teaching Trainable Mentally Retarded Children.* CEC Research Monograph, Series A, no. 2, Washington, D.C.: Council for Exceptional Children, 1960.

Hutt, Max L., and Gibby, Robert G. *The Mentally Retarded Child.* Boston: Allyn and Bacon, Inc., 1958.

Ingram, Christine Porter. *Education of the Slow Learning Child.* New York: The Ronald Press Company, 1960.

Isaacs, W., Thomas, J., and Goldiamond, J. "Application of Operant Conditioning to Reinstate Verbal Behavior in Psychotics," *Journal of Speech and Hearing Disorders,* 1960, 25:8–12.

Johnson, G. Orville. *Education for the Slow Learners.* Englewood Cliffs, N.J.: Prentice-Hall, Inc., 1963.

Johnson, G. Orville. "Special Education for Mentally Handicapped: A Paradox," *Exceptional Children,* 1962, pp. 29, 62–69.

Jordan, Thomas Edward. *The Mentally Retarded.* Columbus, Ohio: Charles E. Merrill Books, Inc., 1961.

Kephart, Newell C. *The Slow Learner in the Classroom.* Columbus, Ohio: Charles E. Merrill Books, Inc., 1960.

Kirk, Samuel A. *Early Education of the Mentally Retarded: An Experimental Study.* Urbana, Ill.: The University of Illinois Press, 1958.

Kirk, Samuel A. *Educating Exceptional Children.* Boston: Houghton Mifflin Company, 1962.

Kirk, Samuel A., and Johnson, G. Orville. *Educating the Retarded Child.* Boston: Houghton Mifflin Company, 1951.

Kirk, Samuel A., Karnes, Merle B., and Kirk, Winifred D. *You and Your Retarded Child.* New York: The Macmillan Company, 1955.

Kornberg, Leonard. *A Class for Disturbed Children.* New York: Bureau of Publications, Teachers College, Columbia University, 1955.

Kruger, Daniel H. "Trends in Service Employment," *Exceptional Children,* 1963, vol. 30, no. 4.

La Vietes, Ruth L. "The Teacher's Role in the Education of the Emotionally Disturbed Child," *American Journal of Orthopsychiatry,* October, 1962, 32:854–862.

Laycock, Samuel R. *Special Education in Canada.* Scarborough, Ontario: W. J. Gage Limited, 1963.

Lindgren, Henry Clay. *Mental Health in Education.* New York: Holt, Rinehart and Winston, Inc., 1954.

Lippman, Hyman S. *Treatment of the Child in Emotional Conflict.* New York: McGraw-Hill Book Company, 1956.

Magary, James F., and Eichorn, John R. (eds.). *The Exceptional Child: A Book of Readings.* New York: Holt, Rinehart and Winston, Inc., 1960.

Masland, Richard L., Sarason, Seymour B., and Gladwin, Thomas. *Mental Subnormality*. New York: Basic Books, Inc., Publishers, 1958.

Montessori, Maria. *The Montessori Method*. Philadelphia: Frederick A. Stokes Company, 1912.

Mullen, Frances A. *Effect of Special Classes on Personality and Adjustment of Educable Mentally Retarded*. 40th Annual CEC Convention, Columbus, Ohio, April, 1962, pp. 137–141.

Naumann, F. E., and Woods, W. G. "The Development of an Automated Basic Spelling Program for Educable Handicapped Children," *AID*, August, 1962, 2:160.

O'Neal, Patricia, and Robbins, Lu. "The Relation of Childhood Behavior Problems to Adult Psychiatric Status: A 30-year Follow-up Study of 150 Subjects," *American Journal of Psychiatry*, May, 1958, 114:961–969.

Orr, K. N. *Cardinal Objectives in Teaching the Educable Mentally Retarded*. Terre Haute, Ind.: Indiana State Teachers College, 1962.

Patterson, C. H. "Control, Conditioning and Counseling," *The Personnel and Guidance Journal*, April, 1963, 41:680–686.

Perry, Natalie. *Teaching the Mentally Retarded Child*. New York: Columbia University Press, 1960.

Peterson, Leroy, and Smith, Lloyd L. "A Comparison of the Post-school Adjustment of Educable Mentally Retarded Adults with That of Adults of Normal Intelligence," *Exceptional Children*, April, 1960, 26:404–408.

Prescott, Daniel A. *The Child in the Educative Process*. New York: McGraw-Hill Book Company, 1957.

Price, James E. *A Comparison of Automated Teaching Programs with Conventional Teaching Methods as Applied to Teaching Mentally Retarded Students*. Tuscaloosa, Ala.: Partlow State School for Mental Deficients, 1962, 10 pp. (Offset.)

Randall, Arne W. *Art for Exceptional Children*. Lubbock, Tex.: Texas Technological College, 1956.

Redl, Fritz, and Wattenberg, William W. *Mental Hygiene in Teaching*. New York: Harcourt, Brace & World, Inc., 1959.

Reid, J. H., and Hagan, Helen R. *Residential Treatment of Emotionally Disturbed Children*. New York: Child Welfare League of America, 1952.

Ross, Alan O. *The Exceptional Child in the Family: Helping Parents of Exceptional Children*. New York: Grune & Stratton, Inc., 1964.

Rothstein, Jerome H. *Mental Retardation: Readings and Resources*. New York: Holt, Rinehart and Winston, Inc., 1961.

Rozenzweig, L. E., and Long, Julia. *Understanding and Teaching the Dependent Retarded Child*. Darien, Conn.: Educational Publishing Corp., 1960.

Sarason, Seymour B., Davidson, Kenneth S., Lighthall, Frederick F., Waite, Richard R., and Ruebush, Britton K. *Anxiety in Elementary School Children.* New York: John Wiley & Sons, Inc., 1960.

Schlosberg, H., Skinner, B. F., Miller, N. E., and Hebb, D. O. "Control of Behavior through Motivation and Rewards," *American Psychologist,* 1958, 13:93–113.

Schonell, Fred J. *Backwardness in Basic Subjects.* Toronto: Clarke, Irwin & Company, Ltd., 1956.

Scott, W. A. "Research Definitions of Mental Health and Mental Illness," *Psychological Bulletin,* 1958, 55:29–45.

Smith, Edgar A. *Reinforcement Psychology in Special Education.* Devon, Pa.: The Devereux Foundation, 1961.

Smith, Edgar A., and Quackenbush, Jack. *Devereux Teaching Aids Employed in Presenting Elementary Mathematics in a Special Education Setting.* A Devereux Reprint. Devon, Pa.: The Devereux Foundation, 1961.

Smith, M. Brewster. "Research Strategies toward a Conception of Positive Mental Health," *The American Psychologist,* November, 1959, 14:11–24.

Stanton, Jeanette E., and Cassidy, Viola M. *An Investigation of Factors Involved in the Educational Placement of Mentally Retarded Children: A Study of Differences between Children in Special and Regular Classes in Ohio.* U.S. Department of Health, Education, and Welfare, Office of Education, Cooperative Research Program, Project no. 043, Columbus, Ohio: Ohio State University Press, 1959.

Stevens, Godfrey D., and Birch, Jack W. "A Proposal for Clarification of the Terminology Used to Describe Brain-injured Children," *Exceptional Children,* May, 1957, 23:346–349.

Stolurow, Lawrence M. "Automation in Special Education," *Exceptional Children,* October, 1960, 27:78–83. (*a*)

Stolurow, Lawrence M. "Teaching Machines and Special Education," *Educational and Psychological Measurement,* Autumn, 1960, 20:429–448. (*b*)

Stolurow, Lawrence M. *Teaching by Machine.* U.S. Department of Health, Education, and Welfare, Office of Education, Cooperative Research Monograph no. 6, Washington, D.C.: 1961.

Stolurow, Lawrence M. "Programed Instruction for the Mentally Retarded," *Review of Educational Research,* February, 1963, 33: 126–135.

Strauss, A. A., and Kephart, N. C. *Psychopathology and Education of the Brain-injured Child.* New York: Grune & Stratton, Inc., 1955.

Strauss, A. A., and Lehtinen, Laura. *Psychopathology and Education of the Brain-injured Child.* New York: Grune & Stratton, Inc., 1947.

Super, Donald E. *The Psychology of Careers.* New York: Harper & Row, Publishers, Incorporated, 1957.

Tallman, Irving, and Levine, Samuel. "The Emotionally Disturbed Child in the Classroom Situation," *Exceptional Children,* 1960, 27:114–126.

Thurstone, Thelma G. *An Evaluation of Educating Mentally Handicapped Children in Special Classes and Regular Classes.* U.S. Department of Health, Education, and Welfare, Office of Education, Cooperative Research Program, Project no. 513, Grambling, La.: Grambling College of Louisiana, 1959.

Wallin, J. E. Wallace. *Education of Mentally Handicapped Children.* New York: Harper & Row, Publishers, Incorporated, 1955.

Walsh, Mary C. "Safety Education for Children with Mental Handicaps," *Exceptional Children,* October, 1962.

Wattenberg, William W. *The Adolescent Years.* New York: Harcourt, Brace & World, Inc., 1955.

Williams, Harold M. *Education of the Severely Retarded Child.* Washington, D.C.: U.S. Department of Health, Education, and Welfare, 1961.

Worchel, Tillie L., and Worchel, Philip. "The Parental Concept of the Mentally Retarded Child," *American Journal of Mental Deficiency,* May, 1961, 65:782–788.

Wrightstone, J. W., Forlano, G., Lepkowski, J. R., and Sontag, M. A. *A Comparison of Educational Outcomes under Single-track and Two-track Plans for Educable Mentally Retarded Children.* New York: Board of Education, 1959.

6

THREE EXAMPLES OF TEACHING PRESCRIPTIONS

All diagnostic resources which are appropriate for the case should be explored and their information consolidated so that the coordinator is reasonably satisfied as to the adequacy of the evaluation before proceeding. Obviously an inaccurate or incomplete diagnosis might result in unsuitable school modifications. The accumulated information regarding the problem and situation variables is located in the cells of the diagnostic structure at the top of the model. Only when the diagnostic structure is complete should it be used in modifying the school variables.

In order to determine the consistent approach to use in teaching the child, the completed diagnostic structure of the model is moved to level A. The modification of this school variable is made in relation to the handicap. When the appropriate approach has been determined, the diagnostic structure is moved down to level B. The process is repeated until all the school variables have been considered.

Three children were selected to illustrate the procedure employed in developing the teaching prescription. They were selected because they represent a wide variety of problems for the individual child. As seen from a learning point of view, case 1, Lily, was essentially an emotional disability resulting from a physical impairment. Case 2, Bobby, was an emotional or personality problem with no organic or physical impairment. Case 3, George, was primarily a physical problem with some emotional involvement in the total handicap of his multiple disability.

These children were selected because they also represent a range of problems for the school. Lily had a problem of academic underachievement in a normal classroom. Bobby had a serious behavior problem in and outside class. George had a multiple disability and required special placement.

Furthermore, these three children were studied by a wide range of diagnostic teams. The team approach was used for each, but the emphasis and composition of the team varied. The assessment for Lily was accomplished by a school-centered team composed of school and public health personnel. For Bobby the evaluation was mainly the responsibility of the school psychologist. George was studied by a team which was clinic centered with the school having only a small part in the total evaluation.

CASE 1, LILY

An eleven-year-old girl, Lily was referred because she was underachieving and the teacher was at a loss to explain her drop in accomplishment. The school history showed her to be an average student in ability and achievement until recently. She had never been a behavior problem, but recently had become very quiet and submissive. She was the youngest of three children in a family where no serious problems were known to the school. The medical record indicated that Lily had normal health until recently when she had an attack of rheumatoid arthritis. Her right hand had been affected, and she had been left with a deformity in the joints of her second and third fingers. The following procedures were used to fill in the rest of the needed information.

The psychological evaluation was based on interviews, an individual intelligence test, and projective tests. This evaluation indicated that she had normal intelligence but that her self-image was inadequate. She saw herself as severely handicapped, the world as a gloomy place, and the future as dark and unrewarding. She spoke of herself as a cripple.

The school doctor was able to procure information from the family physician about Lily's condition and the treatment she had received so far. She had been hospitalized for one week and was receiving physiotherapy as an outpatient. She was also taking cortisone.

The public health nurse visited the parents. They were very sympathetic toward Lily and showed concern for her, because they felt that her fate would be the same as that of her grandmother who was badly crippled with arthritis. Lily had also mentioned this in her interview with the school psychologist.

The process of converting these educational, psychological, social, and medical data into pedagogical terms involves working with a complex of interrelated variables.

PROBLEM AND SITUATION VARIABLES

The procedure which follows is keyed to the model as an aid to visualization of the relationship between the variables. The numbers refer to the cells in the diagnostic structure, and the letters refer to the school variables.

Nature of Pathology

INJURY (1). Rheumatoid arthritis is a general condition affecting the whole body, particularly the connective tissue; its exact cause is not known. There is a tendency for it to run in families, and it is more prevalent in women than men. Infection, cold, damp weather, and emotional stress seem to bring on acute attacks. Lily had several acute phases of the disease with fever and pain in many joints. These phases passed in a short time, but the two fingers remained swollen and painful. Although the nature of the condition was general, the specific injury was to the joints of the two middle fingers of her right hand.

DISABILITY (2). The nature of the disability was loss of motion in the fingers. The secondary disability might be some loss of cognition as a result of pain distraction.

HANDICAP (3). The nature of the condition at the handicap level was the hindrance caused by the lack of mobility in the fingers.

Therapeutic Procedures

INJURY (4). The cortisone and physiotherapy were not regarded as cures for the disease. They reduced the crippling effect, made the patient more comfortable, and made increased mobility possible. It was not stated that the therapeutic procedures would result in change of the injury. The suggestion was that future injury would be less if proper therapeutic procedures were used.

DISABILITY (5). Therapeutic procedures might reduce the disability by increasing motion in the affected fingers and by reducing the pain accompanying the disease.

HANDICAP (6). The handicapping consequence of the therapeutic procedures was the impaired self-concept of the child. Taking cortisone every day and visiting the hospital every week for therapy had an effect on the child's self-concept. It became clear during the interviews that hospitalization and outpatient treatment played an important part in Lily's concept of herself as a severely handicapped person.

Time Factors

INJURY (7). The duration of the illness could not be predicted although it was considered to be long term.

DISABILITY (8). The injury was considered to be permanent. The disability could change in time depending on the progress of the disease. The pain would decrease if the acute phase did not return. The onset of the illness took place at puberty when Lily was beginning to consider herself as becoming a young lady and her self-concept was particularly vulnerable to negative feelings.

HANDICAP (9). The handicapping consequences of the injury and some of the physical disability would be long term, but the consequences to her self-image might be modified in a comparatively short time.

Social Conditions

INJURY (10). The family attitude toward Lily may have had some effect on her arthritis because emotional and psychological problems are frequently associated with the onset of this illness.

DISABILITY (11). The parents were very solicitous and sympathetic toward Lily, but their attitude gave the impression that they felt she was doomed to a life of pain and incapacitation. Treating her as an incapacitated person placed limitations on her mobility which increased her disability. Doing too much for her reduced her opportunities to do things for herself.

HANDICAP (12). Her grandmother, who was an important figure in Lily's perceptual field, was severely handicapped with arthritis. The grandmother's condition and the parents' attitude were social considerations which contributed to the impaired self-concept which was Lily's major handicap to learning.

Diagnostic Summary

To summarize the levels of injury, disability, and handicap which have been dealt with above, the injury at that time was not extensive and involved primarily structural changes to the joints of two fingers. The more general aspects of the condition were given consideration but were not classified as specific injury.

The disability was loss of motion in the affected fingers, pain, and the effect of the cortisone which was some loss of mental alertness.

The handicapping consequence of these factors was reflected in the impaired self-image of the child. It is not implied that this is the only handicap but that her impaired intellectual functioning and drop in academic accomplishment were primarily related to her perception of herself as a cripple and of her future as unrewarding and painful. Another handicapping consequence resulting from the loss of motion in the affected fingers was situationally significant in only a few activities. The necessity to avoid things which would strain or injure these joints was another handicapping consequence.

Because the cause of arthritis was not known, because some of the factors in Lily's case were not definitely established, and because the organic, social, and psychological elements were in a state of flux, it was essential that this diagnosis be revised as changes took place and further information was available.

SCHOOL VARIABLES

In order to arrive at the most appropriate teaching prescription, consideration was given to each cell of the diagnostic structure. All the known relevant factors in the total diagnostic constellation were used in prescribing modifications of the variables in the educational program.

CONSISTENT APPROACH (A). The purpose of prescribing a consistent approach was to modify Lily's self-concept and to make it more consistent with the reality of her disability. Lily felt inadequate in spite of her actual adequacy and strength. The approach, which was to reaffirm her confidence in herself, included giving additional support, showing feeling, and employing methods to motivate and encourage her. The recommendation was for the teacher to take the initiative in being actively friendly, to give support and show feeling toward her and her interests, to use a positive voice, and to credit her achievement whether large or small. These approaches were intended to reinforce her self-confidence and replace her self-doubt.

TEACHING METHODS (B). Lily was to be given an extra monitor duty which could be somewhat overcredited. She was to take certain class records to the principal's office each morning. In this special activity she was not in competition with anyone else, and the activity could receive additional support from the teacher, the principal, and the office staff. This provided another opportunity for Lily to modify her perception of self from that of a cripple to a person who could make a unique contribution. Similarly, for the parts of the physical education program where Lily was excluded, it was recommended that she be given extra work such as keeping score and taking inventory of equipment.

SPECIFIC OBJECTIVES (C). At this time it seemed advisable to modify the specific objectives in physical education regarding full participation in team sports. The medical opinion was that the risk of injury made this participation undesirable.

ANCILLARY SERVICES (D). It was recommended that Lily receive counseling on a continuing basis for additional support and encouragement for achievement.

The school doctor consulted with the family doctor. With the information from the school, the family physician agreed to interpret the medical aspects of arthritis to Lily and her parents in a manner which could be positive and still be consistent with the reality of the condition. It was highly probable that Lily would not become as severely incapacitated as her grandmother, and it was hoped that the parents would adopt a more optimistic outlook.

The school nurse was going to explore the desirability of a referral to the mental-hygiene clinic. This recommendation was made on the basis of the medical opinion regarding the emotional factors, which could be a contributing cause in rheumatoid arthritis.

The school administration was included in the discussions of the recommendation and was involved in carrying out part of the additional support and encouragement which Lily was to receive.

PLACEMENT AND PERSONNEL (E). Lily was to be retained in the regular class, and the approach was carried out by her regular teacher. The homeroom teacher showed interest in helping Lily and was anxious to try the recommended approach.

SUBJECT MATTER (F). Lily was to participate in all the courses in the elementary school. The modification of physical education to meet her individual needs was the only change; catching a ball, for example, was an undesirable activity for her at this time. She was to participate in the rest of the program and be given some useful activity in place of the parts she did not take.

INSTRUCTIONAL MATERIALS (G). Lily could work with standard classroom materials so there was no recommended modification.

SPECIAL EQUIPMENT (H). The orthopedic disability was not sufficient at the time to warrant equipment modification.

SCHOOL PLANT (I). No plant modification was recommended.

AUXILIARY AGENCIES (J). The referral to the mental-hygiene clinic depended on the attitude of the parents toward psychiatric consultation.

CASE 2, BOBBY

Bobby was selected as an illustration because in his case there was apparently no injury or organic involvement. His disability was of a functional nature involving emotional disturbance.

Bobby was $10\frac{1}{2}$ years old when referred and was in an accelerated class for bright and gifted children doing grades four and five work. He had made good grades at school but had not made the progress which would be expected on the basis of his individual intelligence-test rating, a Stanford-Binet IQ of 136. He had been placed in the accelerated class to ascertain if he would be intellectually stimulated. His academic achievement deteriorated in the accelerated class in most areas with the exception of mathematics. He had been at the top of his class in mathematics, and he retained this superiority.

The reasons given for referral were his excessive fighting with other boys and not answering questions when asked about his behavior. When in difficulty he would not speak. He had a manner which was described as "having a chip on his shoulder." He had the reputation of being the number one problem in an elementary school with a population of about 1,000 children.

Bobby had a perfect health record. He was well developed physically and was handsome and well groomed.

With this information available at the school, the investigation and diagnostic procedures were started. In reporting this case only the essentials will be included for the sake of brevity.

The psychological evaluation showed Bobby to be very distrustful of people. He was reluctant to enter into relationships and was very defensive of his own private world. He felt persecuted and picked-on by other children and adults. He was constantly on the alert for any injustice which might be done to him, and he expected that he would be treated unjustly. He gave an impoverished Rorschach record with only thirteen responses, and he rejected three of the cards entirely. His responses were the easy ones, and he approached the test with great caution. Bobby was a very suspicious boy with paranoid projections. (A more complete psychological report is included in Chapter 7.)

Contact with the parents had been quite limited. The mother had visited the school on two occasions, both times feeling that some injustice had been done; she had come to complain. She would not enter into discussion of Bobby's behavior with either the teacher or the principal. She felt that there was nothing wrong with Bobby and that the school was prejudiced against him.

The public health nurse had made several home visits in an attempt to explore the possibility of a referral to the mental-hygiene clinic. The interviews took place at the door as the nurse was not invited into the house. The mother was not willing to discuss Bobby's behavior. She said if there was anything to complain about, such as his physical health or care, the nurse should make this complaint, but otherwise it was none of her business how Bobby behaved. She declined any invitations to visit the school counselor or school psychologist. The father's employment had been somewhat unsteady, and they had moved around a great deal. At one time the family lived with the father's brother. This domestic arrangement ended in a fight and the family moved. There was little other information available about the family. Because they appeared to be untrusting of the school or the health service, it was difficult to obtain accurate information regarding the nature of the social and cultural situation within the home. The evidence that was available was consistent with the attitude that Bobby showed at school.

The nature of the pathology appeared to be a disability in the affective area. Bobby was unable to trust people and this limited his repertoire of responses; he reacted to overtures of friendship with as much suspicion as he reacted to hostility. He felt that if people were unkind to him, it was to be expected because they were against him; if they were nice to him, they were just trying to put something over.

The handicapping consequence of this disability was primarily in the field of social interaction and communication. The distortion in his perception resulted in a greater handicap in the accelerated class where more group discussion, group projects, and social interaction were expected. The one activity where the children did not work together was mathematics, and in this Bobby could function quite well. It was also probable that he perceived mathematics as less revealing of himself. In the accelerated class the children sat around tables to do social-studies assignments and discussed the work in groups. In creative activities such as writing and art, Bobby could not function because he did not want to reveal himself.

The nature of the pathology was described as a functional disorder affecting primarily his emotional response with the handicapping consequence in social interaction. The diagnostic and treatment resources available to Bobby were limited to those that could be provided by the school, in school time. The nature of the social and cultural considerations caused Bobby's behavior to be seen by the school and by other children as hostile and disrespectful toward authority. The parents appeared to be untrusting and suspicious of the school and public health agency. Additional information indicated that the parents had difficulty in getting along with their own relatives and with other people.

The nature of the time factor in relation to the duration of the disturbance was that this behavior was a family trait and had been in existence all Bobby's life. A change in his way of perceiving would take time. Relating time to treatment, the sooner some modification of Bobby's negative emotional responses could be started, the better the prognosis became.

PROBLEM AND SITUATION VARIABLES

Only six cells in the diagnostic structure were occupied as a result of no involvement at the injury level and therapy being limited to the school variables.

Nature of Pathology

INJURY (1). None.

DISABILITY (2). Bobby's limitation in his responses was his inability to differentiate between those people and situations which were threatening to him and those which were only perceived as threatening. He was overly suspicious of most people.

HANDICAP (3). He was impeded in his social interaction with peers and with adults. Verbal communication was restricted to a superficial level which would not reveal very much of himself.

Therapeutic Procedures

INJURY (4). None.
DISABILITY (5). None.
HANDICAP (6). None.

Time Factors

INJURY (7). None.

DISABILITY (8). On the basis of the school history it appeared that the disability had existed from before the time he started school. Without help the prognosis regarding the duration of the disability was poor. Bobby needed to learn to discriminate between those situations he should regard with suspicion and those he should trust. If modifications were made to provide him with opportunities to learn such discrimination, he might overcome some of his disability.

HANDICAP (9). The handicapping consequence of the disability had increased with time. The lack of socialization was noticed in the first grade, but a number of children in the class appeared to have difficulties in getting along with other children. His case did not attract particular attention then, but by grade five Bobby was the most difficult child in the school. It appeared that the handicap increased as time passed.

Social Conditions

INJURY (10). None.

DISABILITY (11). Evidence regarding the home situation was consistent but was so limited that what was put in this cell should be regarded as assumption rather than fact. It appeared that there was considerable family solidarity and that Bobby's disability was a family trait. There was no evidence of difficulty within the immediate family group. There was some evidence that the family had difficulty in relating to the community.

HANDICAP (12). The handicapping consequence socially was that Bobby was not accepted by his peers, and his relationships with adults were unsatisfactory. Frequently people reflected Bobby's mistrust, and some showed open hostility toward him. This supported and probably reinforced his suspicion. His inhibited responsiveness of expression and social interaction affected his learning and resulted in underachievement in most subjects.

SCHOOL VARIABLES

CONSISTENT APPROACH (A). The consistent approach recommended was passive friendliness; it would give Bobby the best opportunity to learn how to trust people. This was an accepting approach at all times with the teacher responding only to the extent that Bobby requested help or friendship. The teacher was to avoid close contact such as a hand on the shoulder or any other physical contact. He was to try to convey the attitude of being available if Bobby reached out for help. He would not reflect the hostility that Bobby showed. If Bobby's behavior was inappropriate, the teacher was to tell him what he should do and insist that he get back to work. The objective was to reduce suspicion and to provide an environment where Bobby could reach out and test his ability to trust people in easy stages.

ANCILLARY SERVICES (D). The ancillary services which could support Bobby in overcoming his handicap were provided by the school administration and the school psychologist. It was recommended that when Bobby was sent to the office for his misconduct, the principal should not challenge him to explain himself but rather should explain very carefully the circumstances which brought Bobby to the office. Bobby was to be given opportunities to express himself but was not to be pressured into explaining. In the past when he had been under pressure, he usually would not speak or made some excuse which was not thought to be true. It was suggested that the principal be kindly but unemotional in dealing with these disciplinary matters. He was to take extra time and care to explain simply and clearly in what way Bobby's behavior was unsatisfactory.

The school psychologist was to see Bobby on a regular basis. The intention was to see if someone, completely accepting in his approach, could be accepted by Bobby. He would use the passive approach also, but the one-to-one situation would give Bobby a better opportunity to reach out and form some kind of relationship.

PLACEMENT AND PERSONNEL (E). Placement in a regular class at the grade-six level for next term was recommended. Experience with the accelerated class indicated that this was too much for Bobby at this time.

AUXILIARY AGENCIES (J). Auxiliary services were not used, but the recommendation was made that further contacts should be made with the home in case the parents felt they would like a referral to a mental-hygiene clinic.

CASE 3, GEORGE

This case was selected as an illustration of diagnosis which was the responsibility of a clinic outside the school.

George was a member of a special class for hard-of-hearing children located in a regular public school; he had made satisfactory progress considering his hearing problem. He was quiet and conforming in his behavior. In science lessons he had at times shown indications of a superior intellect. Although he appeared to be trying very hard to do exactly what was required, he seemed to lack spontaneity in his responses. He complained about his shaking which he said made writing difficult and tiring. His teacher had referred to his problem as poor coordination and nervousness.

In preparation for the fitting of a new hearing aid, George was seen by a medical specialist for a diagnosis of his hearing loss. This doctor referred him to the cerebral-palsy clinic for assessment, which was done by a team in the outpatient department of a large hospital. The coordinator of this diagnostic team was the medical director of the clinic. Reports were received from the medical doctor, child psychiatrist, neurologist, speech therapist, occupational therapist, physiotherapist, social worker, clinical psychologist, and school psychologist.

The assessment was the clinic's responsibility. The school psychologist was on the team to represent the school. Since this comprehensive assessment cannot be adequately reported in the space available here, a brief summary will be given followed by the teaching prescription.

Developmental History

In this family there were three older brothers alive and well, making good progress at school. The mother made a favorable impression and superficially at least had an accepting attitude toward George's disability. She said that the other members of the family were embarrassed and irritated by his clumsiness and scolded him for this.

George was thirteen years nine months old. The birth was premature with a birth weight of 4 pounds 6 ounces and a pregnancy duration of twenty-nine weeks. Membranes had ruptured at five months with loss of amniotic fluid. He was colicky during the first year. Deviation of the left eye was noted. He was slow to sit and walk, and little speech developed until the age of five. When he entered school at the age of six, a hearing deficit was discovered. After a hearing consultation, George was fitted with a hearing aid and was placed in a class for hard-of-hearing. His speech was still difficult to understand at this time. Although George had very little illness, he was presented to a series of doctors for medical examination from time to time because of his clumsiness and his shaking. His mother became quite hostile toward doctors because they had not given an immediate diagnosis; she had not taken him for an examination for over four years.

Assessment

The diagnosis was cerebral palsy of the post-kernicterus–choreaathetosis type. This condition resulted in a serious motor disability in the form of muscle imbalance causing a constant shifting to maintain position and requiring conscious effort to repeat movements. The incoordination and tremor increased under emotional tension.

His hearing loss was severe in the upper frequencies in both ears. He was unable to distinguish speech sounds with the right ear. A little understanding of speech was possible with the hearing range of his left ear. Speech was typical of hard-of-hearing children and was complicated by continuous activity of the tongue resulting from the athetosis. Although he wore a hearing aid, he lip-read well and used the hearing aid only to assist speechreading. Although vision in his left eye was adequate, there was some internal strabismus involving predominantly the right eye.

George was a personable, cooperative boy. His schoolwork was carefully done. In a two-minute writing test, he averaged fifty-six letters per minute (grade five averages sixty letters per minute). He could read at grade-six level. He had superior intelligence with a marked deficit in verbal learning. He had difficulty in the perception and performance of hand-eye coordination and synthesis.

He manifested considerable insecurity and lacked confidence in his abilities. Misunderstanding of his physical incoordination by his family had made him anxious. Among strangers he became apprehensive lest he misinterpret what was said. He was lacking in feelings of personal worth and competence.

George's communication difficulties tended to predominate, but his motor disturbance was considerable. His intelligence was superior, but his self-regard was poor.

PROBLEM AND SITUATION VARIABLES

Nature of Pathology

INJURY (1). George's brain damage was diagnosed as cerebral palsy resulting from injury occurring before birth.

DISABILITY (2). The loss of function resulting from the injury was mainly in motor coordination and hearing.

HANDICAP (3). The handicapping consequences resulting from the disability were slowness to develop coordination and balance in walking and slowness in developing speech. His speech, as it did develop, was difficult to understand. His physical movements appeared awkward because they included involuntary movements.

Therapeutic Procedures

INJURY (4). There was no treatment for the injury. It was considered permanent and not progressive.

DISABILITY (5). The cerebral-palsy clinic had treated George's disability with physiotherapy as part of the diagnostic procedure. This treatment reduced the tremor when he was under tension, but it was not recommended that it be continued. Medication to reduce or slow down his tremor was prescribed as part of the diagnostic procedure, and it was not determined whether he was being helped by it or not at the time of this study.

HANDICAP (6). There was no apparent long-term handicapping consequence of the treatment except that resulting from the time away from school. He had spent one-half day a week at the clinic for more than two months, and he was to continue until it was determined whether or not medication was beneficial. A short-term handicap resulted from George's overexpectation of the clinic. He felt that an effective treatment would follow the diagnosis.

Time Factors

INJURY (7). In terms of duration of the condition, the injury was permanent.

DISABILITY (8). George had been slow to walk and to develop motor coordination, although he had finally been able to develop control of his voluntary movements. He had also been very slow to learn expressive communication but had developed receptive communication through speechreading. In spite of his slowness of speech, he had shown considerable intellectual ability. In terms of time, George had taken longer to learn motor control and longer to learn to speak. He would never learn to perform these functions in a normal manner.

HANDICAP (9). George was making progress in the reduction of handicap. The more time he spent at developing manipulative skills, the more he learned how to integrate his voluntary and involuntary movements. It did not appear that he had the typical adolescent concerns about self at this time.

Social Conditions

INJURY (10). The diagnosis of George's brain injury changed the social condition for him in the home. The parents accepted the diagnosis. In the school and community it had been accepted that something was wrong with George before the diagnosis indicated the exact nature of his condition. This diagnosis did not appear to affect his social relationships outside of the home.

DISABILITY (11). The inability to communicate adequately was the main limitation, socially.

HANDICAP (12). The handicap, socially, was complex. Within the family his slowness had at first been regarded as dullness. His brothers treated him as though he were mentally subnormal and they expressed their embarrassment by making fun of him. There was evidence that the lack of an earlier diagnosis was the result of the mother's fear that the diagnosis would show George to be mentally defective. The family blamed George for their not being able to accept invitations to dine out because of their embarrassment at his awkwardness when eating. They expressed considerable anger toward him for knocking things over. Outside the family the social consequence of the communication difficulties was that people spent less time conversing with George. A sociometric study conducted within the hard-of-hearing class indicated that he had a high acceptability rating within that group. He participated in some activities at school, outside this class, with normal children.

The handicapping consequence personally was his impaired self-concept. At school he had seen success in terms of rather narrow conformity and had not made full use of his potential. He seemed to be unaware of his intellectual capacity.

SCHOOL VARIABLES

CONSISTENT APPROACH (A). The approach recommended was the one for children with neurotic conflicts. It was recommended that the teacher give additional encouragement and support for achievement and that he take the initiative in being actively friendly. The objective was to give George a better opportunity to see himself as an acceptable person and to learn to be realistic about his abilities.

TEACHING METHODS (B). The special methods employed in the hard-of-hearing class met most of George's special needs. Sentence construction, for example, was taught by a method which would appear quite formal for the hearing child. The suggestion was made that George could be assisted by more time on word stimulation to develop a vocabulary bank on which to base his lipreading.

SPECIFIC OBJECTIVES (C). George was able to make progress toward most of the objectives of education. His progress in music was so limited that it appeared unreasonable to consider that he could develop appreciation of music beyond some understanding of rhythm. Specific objectives, where fine coordination and speed of movement are required, were specified.

ANCILLARY SERVICES (D). Counseling was recommended as an additional support. This was not seen as intensive treatment but as occasional interviews of a supportive nature.

PLACEMENT AND PERSONNEL (E). George was placed at grade-five level in the class for hard-of-hearing located in a regular school. He was to be integrated with children about his age for industrial arts, art, and library to begin with, and in other subjects as his confidence improved. The teacher of the hard-of-hearing class was qualified in this branch of special education. The other teachers had no special qualifications for teaching the hard-of-hearing.

SUBJECT MATTER (F). The curriculum was modified consistent with George's handicap. He was to begin typewriting immediately because his slowness in handwriting was impeding his progress.

INSTRUCTIONAL MATERIALS (G). The extra graphic material used with the hard-of-hearing was the only recommended modification.

SPECIAL EQUIPMENT (H). The group hearing aid, charts and other visual aids, and a mirror for speech imitation are standard for the hard-of-hearing child. George also required an electric typewriter and an improved individual hearing aid. One of the type attached to his glasses seemed desirable, as the aid he was using picked up clothing noises made by his involuntary body and head movements.

SCHOOL PLANT (I). The room should be well lighted with shadow-free illumination to facilitate George's speechreading (lipreading). It should be large enough to accommodate the extra equipment required and should be acoustically treated to facilitate the use of group and individual hearing aids.

AUXILIARY AGENCIES (J). All the clinic services described in the section on assessment were available for George. The three specific services used at this time were (1) the social worker to help the family in their acceptance of George; (2) the medical doctor to explain the condition to the parents so they could realize that George could not control many of the awkward movements he made; (3) the hearing specialist to try a hearing aid where the whole apparatus was placed on the ear so that involuntary movements and noise of clothing would not cause distortions of sound.

SUMMARY

These cases illustrate different applications of prescriptive teaching utilizing the team approach. For Lily we employed a team of school-centered personnel. For Bobby we made use of the social, educational, and medical information that was available, and additional information was provided through psychological evaluation. For George we used a team of clinicians of which one member was primarily concerned with the educational implications of the handicap.

Lily's difficulty was considered essentially an emotional problem. The handicapping consequence of her illness was mainly the impairment of her self-concept resulting in underachievement. Teaching and learning were important factors in modifying Lily's self-concept and underachievement.

Bobby's difficulty was considered an emotional problem, and it was assumed that the causes were social. The handicapping consequence was primarily in his social interaction which resulted in some learning and behavior problems.

George's difficulty was considered essentially a physical problem with some emotional disturbance. The educational consequence of his disabilities was primarily the impairment of communication. The usual classification for George would be multiple handicapped. On the basis of the educational significance of his handicap he was able to function quite well in a class for the hard-of-hearing with some modifications for his coordination and emotional handicaps.

While the diagnosis and translation into a teaching prescription are important phases in the treatment of disturbed children, they are of value only to the extent that they are communicated to and implemented by the people responsible for action. With the diagnosis converted into a teaching prescription, we turn our attention to the implementation of these findings. The next three chapters deal with the communication of the prescription to the school personnel, teaching methods, and follow-up.

7

COMMUNICATION

Up to this point we have been dealing with the problem of how to promote the child's development through educational modifications. All this effort will come to naught unless the decisions regarding appropriate modifications are communicated to the personnel responsible for their implementation.

Communication is a subtle, complex, and perplexing process involved in all human relationships. Communication occurs through oral and written language, pictures and diagrams, gestures and facial expressions, actions and demonstrations, and human or emotional relationships. These means of communication are interrelated and important aspects of the total process, but this chapter deals primarily with meanings derived from words.

GENERAL SEMANTICS

General semantics is a recent movement which has given knowledge of and insight into the human evaluative processes and particularly the relationship between meaning and the symbols of language. General semantics is concerned with the study of communication for the purpose of improving verbalizations. In scientific fields, this problem has been largely resolved by using a unique word or symbol for each meaning. In mathematics, for example, language is extremely precise. As each science advances, its language becomes more specialized, enabling specialists to understand each other more precisely while at the same time preventing the uninitiated from understanding at all. Interdisciplinary communication, as required in prescriptive teaching, presents many problems which can be resolved by applying principles of semantics.

Words

A word is the smallest unit of language which has independent meaning. In using words we should be aware of their symbolic nature if we are to differentiate between the word and the thing which it represents. It is the thing represented, or the referent, which has real meaning, not the word or symbol. Thus one referent may be represented by many different words, some of which are charged with the user's feelings. The same behavior could be described as "predictable," "rigid," or "compulsive" and reflect the diagnostician's feelings. A child referred for evaluation may be called the "pupil," "student," "scholar," "child," "boy" or "girl," "youngster," "client," or by name—"Lily," "Bobby," or "George." Each of these correctly identifies the person referred to, but each has different meaning.

Several different referents may be represented by the same word. The term "discipline" is used in education to represent a branch of knowledge or learning, training that develops self-control and efficiency, orderly conduct, submission to authority, and punishment. The author was made aware of this problem when reviewing cases with the representative of a social agency. A number of children, known to the author, were classified by the agency as having "inadequate peer relationships." One, an autistic boy, was under psychiatric treatment and had been diagnosed as schizophrenic. Another was an intellectually gifted, creative girl who tended to follow her own special interests and who had friends older than herself. A third was a hostile, delinquent boy who did not integrate well in organized community activities but who had considerable influence in a subcultural gang. In this instance the same words, "inadequate peer relationships," were used to describe a wide variety of children. It is doubtful that the purposes of communication were served by these words even though technically they were correct. The referents of words are so important to the meaning to be conveyed that the search for the correct words for the correct referents is a major task of the effective communicator.

Two-way Communication

It is recognized that communication is most effective when it is two way and provides for clarification and restatement. This two-way communication takes place in discussions with teachers and others. The core of the concept is that by means of exchanging information, ideas, or viewpoints, people can develop common understandings and mutually agreeable working arrangements. In communication regarding the child's behavior in school, it is also neessary to communicate regarding the teacher's feelings and behavior or we have but half a process that is two-sided. For the teacher to be able to communicate his own anxiety, his own feelings about the pupil, and his own inadequacy in the teacher-child relationship, it is necessary that the teacher be comfortable with children, feel secure in his relationships with superiors and colleagues, and feel accepted as an equal by the consulting team members. Effective communication occurs as a result of continuous contact between staff and consultants.

The establishment of such meaningful communication depends upon the common objectives of team members. A mutual desire to meet the child's needs, a mutual sensitivity to him and his conflicts, and a mutual respect for one another in a situation where none feel threatened produce feelings of freedom which allow team members to express their anxiety and frustration without feeling on trial or needing to defend their positions.

Work with the child must be directed in an atmosphere where one discipline does not sit in judgment of the other, but where both are in a position to contribute their mutual skills to the benefit of the child. This situation requires that the coordinator be both a good listener and an effective speaker. Listening can be facilitated by an accepting permissive atmosphere in which the team members feel that they can speak freely. The coordinator can contribute to improved communication by attentive listening, by remaining relaxed, by focusing on total content, and by being alert to the values, motives, and referents of teachers and other personnel.

When two-way communication is effective, several problems are resolved. The school staff does not expect symptoms to disappear after the first consultation; the teacher becomes aware of numerous resources within his own capacities to deal with children's behavior; and the school is more able to develop consistently meaningful attitudes toward the child. The teacher and diagnostic team increasingly integrate their respective skills to the ultimate benefit of the child.

FOUR PHASES OF THE PRESCRIPTIVE TEACHING COMMUNICATION CIRCUIT

Any functioning communication system, from the simplest to the most complex, consists of a sender, a message, and a receiver. The effectiveness of communication depends upon all three. The system can fail because the sender is ineffective, the message is ambiguous, or the receiver fails to hear or comprehend the message or distorts its meaning. The communication system for prescriptive teaching consists of four principal phases—referral, report, implementation, and follow-up.

Referral

The first phase is communication from the area of the problem to the area of diagnosis. The teacher, aware of the child's difficulty, decides to refer the child to the diagnostic services within the school. His message may be communicated through a discussion with the school principal followed by a written description for the school psychologist. The data-gathering process of the case-study method adds to this phase so that the diagnostic team receives a more complete message regarding the problem area. Referral forms and interviews are used to clarify the message. The message in the referral phase is sent by the teacher, who is familiar with the child's behavior in the classroom, and is received by the school psychologist and other members of the diagnostic team.

Report

The second phase is communication from the area of diagnosis to the area of implementation. Through discussion at the case conference, the diagnostic findings and modifications of school variables are communicated to the teacher and to others responsible for implementing the recommendations. The communication is not completed when the group thinks its way through a case study and makes recommendations for action. There is still need to devise clear and understandable directions for carrying out adopted plans. This message is prepared by the coordinator of the program in the form of a written report and is received by the teacher and others responsible for taking the recommended action.

Implementation

The third phase is from the area of action to the area of the problem. Modification of school variables for the child is primarily the responsibility of the teacher with the assistance of various ancillary services. The consistent approach he uses, the things he says, the teaching methods he employs, constitute his message which presents to the child a new structure in his environmental stimuli. The child responds through modified behavior.

Follow-up

Communication from the area of the child's response back to either diagnosis or implementation is provided by the follow-up phase. Where the child's responses indicate progress toward the desired outcomes, feedback is directed to the area of diagnosis. Thus the flow of communication through the circuit is always supporting either the present implementation or is supporting diagnosis leading to further modification. This support, or reinforcement, always depends on the child's responses.

The balance of this chapter deals with the second phase of the communication system, the report.

THE REPORT

The purpose of the report is to facilitate the implementation of diagnostic findings. Hayakawa (1949) discusses attempts to control, direct, or influence the future actions of human beings by the use of words. He feels that the most interesting and perhaps least understood of the relations between words and things is the relation between words and future events. The directive use of language is a way of trying to make things happen. The effectiveness of the report writer depends upon how his words shape the future. Directive language symbolizes things to come and therefore influences a degree of control over future events.

While human learning experiments show that meaningfulness of a message, its vividness, and emphasis influence communication and recall of material, there are relatively few studies dealing with the effect of these factors at the level of complex prose material. Therefore, there is still a gap in the generalization of simple learning data to problems of communication of complex concepts and opinion (Hovland, 1953). The basic assumption is that the greater part of our influence upon each other is exercised by the use of symbols, although there is no exact method for assessing the extent to which communication is achieved. The communication of the report, therefore, must rely on the skill and art of the report writer as well as his knowledge of general semantics.

The acquisition and retention of information are paramount in any system of communication. Unless a message is structured appropriately to an individual's perceptual system, it must remain either unperceived, unintelligible, or misunderstood. In person-to-person interaction it is possible to perceive that messages have been misunderstood. Where reports are conveyed in writing, such detection of error is difficult.

The content of a message has a bearing on communication. If the content is unfamiliar or threatening to the teacher, communication is difficult. The author has found that the perceptual or phenomenological approach discussed in Chapter 2 can be communicated to the teacher with less effort than other psychological approaches. The view that the child's behavior is a consequence of how he sees himself and how he sees his world is acceptable to teachers because they are familiar with the child's individual perceptions (Combs and Snygg, 1959). The more creative activities carried out at school tend to encourage exploration of individual perceptions. Through these experiences the teacher becomes familiar with the individual child's responses. Children who apparently had the same experience will write about it or draw pictures which show individual differences. That the teacher values this phenomenon is borne out by the nature of many of the referrals. The teacher frequently shows the school psychologist a child's drawing or writing and says that it shows the way the child sees himself or his situation. A disturbed child may see everything as threatening or everything as dark and gloomy, and these perceptions influence his drawing and writing as well as other behavior.

Teachers tend to realize that a child does not respond to the external forces or stimuli as they are perceived by the teacher but only as they are perceived by the child. An understanding of personality theory, as such, is not required before the communication of the report is effective. The psychologist is able to start where the teacher is, base his communication on the teacher's experience with individual perception, and communicate quite directly regarding any distortions in the child's perceptual field. Because motivation and perception are an integral part of the learning process, the teacher can deal more directly with the problem when it is stated in these terms. The criteria of utility and economy have led the author to adopt this perceptual point of view when interpreting psychological findings to the teacher.

Psychologists must use understandable English. As part of their striving for invulnerability, they often resort to professional jargon which may be meaningful to them but is of little value to anyone else. The use of technical language in any given instance depends on who is to receive the message. The purpose of language is to clarify, not mystify. When professional people with advanced qualifications are communicating with one another, technical language is suitable as long as it really serves to communicate. This principle applies at all levels. The words used in messages to professional staff, nonprofessional staff, lay people, and children must be appropriate for each level. The only appropriate language is language which is understood.

The school psychologist responsible for coordination of the program should be able to communicate with members of the professions involved in diagnostic procedures. Each profession has its own language, and it may take considerable time and study before the coordinator can accomplish meaningful interdisciplinary communication. In some cases different theoretical frameworks exist which go beyond the mere terminology differences. This need not create a problem for the school psychologist using the prescriptive teaching method. The psychiatrist, the medical physician, and the social worker may be working from different theoretical bases, but the psychologist working for the school is concerned with the educational relevance of their evaluations. The school psychologist is interested in the psychiatrist's explanation of the child's problem but the school psychologist does not have to communicate the psychiatrist's theoretical framework to the teacher. The school psychologist wants to know from the psychiatrist how the child's cognition is affected, what results this factor has on social interaction, and how it effects sensation, memory, and physiological functioning. He wants to know if these are expressive or coping symptoms. With this information he can determine the procedures to be used in the school. It is not necessary to communicate to the teacher the personality theory the psychiatrist used as a basis for his explanation of the phenomena. Because these concepts are converted into learning terms before being presented as a teaching prescription, this communication helps establish the road back into the teaching area. Some teachers enjoy speculating in the realms of social and psychological theory, and nothing should be done to discourage this. In prescriptive teaching, though, communication is improved by the use of learning concepts and pedagogical terminology.

Research

The person responsible for coordination of the diagnostic efforts is usually responsible for report writing. The written report augments the oral communication by giving the teacher an opportunity to read over conclusions and recommendations at his convenience and by providing a record for succeeding teachers and other personnel.

The author (Peter, 1963) conducted research into the communication of written psychological reports. The development of the prescriptive teaching program, with its recommendations stated in terms of school variables, made possible more definitive follow-up studies. For two years the regular follow-up studies of referred children included questions regarding the reports. Modifications were made in the writing and terminology used as a result of these interviews. When the changes resulting from this system of feedback appeared to be complete, a more formal research project was conducted. The study was intended to determine if the written report contributed significantly to the communication of diagnostic findings and recommendations to teachers. It also investigated the report as a record for the school and as an instrument for the coordination of educational and health services.

The reports for 100 children referred during one school year were dealt with as follows. Fifty reports were communicated by means of a verbal report and fifty were communicated by a verbal and written report combined. Two weeks later the teachers were given a test which included questions about the recommendations in the reports. A further study compared verbal reports and written reports used alone.

The scores for the group receiving verbal reports and the group receiving written reports were tested to establish the statistical significance of the differences. Reactions of school principals and school nurses were surveyed by conducting individual interviews to assess the report as a record and its function in coordination.

The responses to the test by the teachers receiving written reports showed a significantly higher recall score for recommendations intended to modify the teachers' actions most directly, such as the consistent approach and teaching methods. The written report also resulted in improved acceptance of the recommendations and other content and was the communication method preferred by teachers. The written report was considered to be a useful record for the school administration and for the school nurse and doctor because it was available when the school psychologist was not present. The verbal report was a less valid communication medium than usually credited. The combination of the case conference with a verbal summary and statement of recommendation followed by a written report was considered to be the most effective communication and resulted in more complete acceptance of the teaching prescription.

The 100 cases reviewed for this study contained individual prescriptions which modified from one to ten elements. The prescriptions contained 396 recommendations regarding these school variables. The average prescriptions therefore involved about four modifications. The range was from one to ten recommendations.

REPORT WRITING

Hammond and Allen (1953) found that their study of the problem of improving psychological services indicated that since written reports were the medium most commonly employed by psychologists to transmit their ideas, the most expeditious solution would be to increase the effectiveness of the written psychological report. They dealt with the report's dual functions—the primary one of communicating information, and the secondary of providing a record.

To improve the implementation and acceptance of the teaching prescription by better communication, the report should consist of four sections: (1) identifying information, (2) statement of the problem, (3) brief summary of the background, test results, interviews, etc., and (4) school variables. A copy of the report written for Bobby, the second case discussed in Chapter 6, follows.

Identifying Information

School Psychologist's Report

Name: Bobby   Div.: Accelerated grades 4 & 5
Birth date:_____   School:_____
                                     Teacher:_____
                                     Date: _____

Statement of the Problem

REASON FOR REFERRAL. Robert was referred for psychological evaluation because of an emotional disturbance evidenced by lying, stealing, bullying, and rather consistent resistance to any emotional relationship, whether he is being praised or punished. He is also functioning below his intellectual level.

Summary

TESTS ADMINISTERED. Rorschach, Thematic Apperception Test, Machover Figure Drawing Test.

TEST BEHAVIOR. Bobby, a handsome, well-groomed boy, came willingly with the examiner for the tests. He was quiet and restrained. He was also slow to respond and answered most questions with one-word answers. Because he was verbally unresponsive, he was required to do only drawings at the first session. During the following five sessions of interviews and testing, he became only slightly more responsive.

TEST RESULTS. Bobby's intellectual efficiency is impaired by his lack of responsiveness. He perceives the world around him as threatening to his private world. This strong autistic defense reduces his responsiveness of expression, and as a result his thinking and conceptualization have become impoverished. He is untrusting of people and wants to keep them at a distance. He seems to identify with his mother and sees her opinion as more valuable than others. He shows suspicion and distrust of people in all his responses. His responses to the TAT showed him as feeling spied upon and not being able to trust the people close to him. He rejected some cards and on others gave only descriptive detail, but would not involve himself in a story.

Bobby is unresponsive in social situations because he is fearful that people will intrude upon and threaten his autistic or private world.

He functions better in social isolation. His maintenance of good achievement in arithmetic while responding poorly in the group work in the accelerated class is an example. Bobby was able to function better in the regular class where there was less group activity, less self-evaluation, and less emphasis on creativity. He perceives the world as threatening and therefore avoids activities which he sees as revealing.

He has had difficulty in athletic activities because he feels that everyone is out to get him, including his own teammates. He is very suspicious when challenged. When he is in difficulty and is requested to give an account of himself, he evades the issue by deception or refuses to talk. The tests and interviews support the proposition that this threat is very real to Bobby.

Little is known about the home background as the family has moved several times and the parents do not attend parent-teacher conferences. They have contacted the school twice. These were instances where the mother was suspicious of the school. Bobby seems to be particularly suspicious of males or father figures. He needs to learn how to trust people. He sees attempts to be friendly with him as threatening. Miss L. (school nurse) reports Mrs. R. (Bobby's mother) to be uncooperative and unwilling to discuss Bobby's problem.

School Variables

RECOMMENDATIONS.

1. The consistent approach recommended for you to use in working with Bobby is passive friendliness. This means that you are friendly with Bobby at all times without imposing your friendliness on him. You respond with warmth only to the extent that Bobby requests it. If Bobby is unfriendly, you show acceptance but not affection. In using this approach these are things you should do:

    a. Initiate no friendliness but wait for Bobby to reach out; then you accept his cue.

    b. Credit work to the degree that it is good but do not overcredit. If his work is poor, ignore it.

    c. Make no overtures toward him but do not ignore him. Be available if he reaches out for support.

    d. If Bobby's behavior is inappropriate, remain consistent with a passive-friendly reaction and redirect him to the task at hand.

    e. If disciplinary action is necessary, it should be handled
        by the principal using a matter-of-fact approach.

Bobby may try to test the sincerity of your friendship.
This is a necessary step in his improvement, and it may be
difficult to maintain the consistent approach prescribed.
However, if it is maintained, his suspicions will decrease.
This will be a difficult time for Bobby; he may always be of
a suspicious nature but will become more realistic about
what is really threatening and what he can trust.

2. For the balance of this term allow him to remain in his
present class and promote him to a regular grade-six class
for next term. (This report was written near the end of the
school term.)

3. Although it has failed in the past, if opportunities occur
for the school nurse to discuss the problem with the parents, a recommendation of referral to the mental-hygiene
clinic should be explored.

4. Have Bobby return to see the school psychologist on a continuing basis.

5. If Bobby is sent to the office regarding his behavior, the
principal should use the matter-of-fact approach. The
situation should be explained as clearly as possible with
little show of emotion. Bobby should be given many opportunities to express himself. If he declines to respond, no
action should be taken. If he expresses hostility, it should
not be reflected. Physical closeness or contact should be
avoided at these times unless he chooses to move closer.

DISCUSSION OF THE FOUR SECTIONS
OF THE REPORT

Identifying Information

Experience indicates the desirability of accurate identifying information at the beginning of the report. Reports which have to be read to
make sure they are for the right child are inefficient and annoying.
Names are changed through parents' remarriage and through changes
of foster parents. Children move from school to school. Identifying

information should include the child's name, birth date, school, class, teacher, date of the report, and any other data required.

Statement of the Problem

A statement of the problem or reason for referral is the first link in the communication system and is established by a request, usually from a teacher, for help with a child. As shown earlier, records and forms are used in gathering information about the referred child. The school psychologist can improve communication and clarify the statement of the problem by interviews with the teacher and by asking appropriate questions which will help him to arrive at a statement of the disability in terms of observable or measurable behavior. This is communication from the area of the problem to the area of the diagnostician's special competence. The objective is to state the problem briefly and meaningfully. When a teacher describes a child as naughty or lazy, the psychologist should help him explain, in terms of specific behavior, the manner in which the child's behavior is undesirable. This is then stated in the report as the reason for referral.

Summary

The summarized background of the problem includes statements about the mental, physical, emotional, and social factors involved in the disability and its handicapping consequence. This summary is not a full medical, psychological, educational, or social case history. It is not considered to be the purpose of the report to enlighten the teacher about the intricacies of psychological testing or to impress him with the complexity and difficulty of diagnosis and the erudition of the author of the report. Test results are given, and the teacher who is interested in their derivation is encouraged to discuss this with the psychologist. In cases where health problems are significant, a brief statement about the nature of the condition is made and it is suggested that the teacher wishing further details refer to the child's health record and to the medical staff. Where extensive social histories are available, teachers are referred to them. This method avoids much of the duplication of records and keeps the report brief and to the main points dealing with teaching.

School Variables

The teaching prescription is presented in the report in the form of recommendations.

CONSISTENT APPROACH (A). In Chapter 4 it was stated that while children differ greatly from one to another, there are groupings which respond favorably to similar treatment. The consistent approaches described here are based upon the attitude consistency program developed by Clarke (1958) and have been found suitable for working with children with a particular type of difficulty. Because each approach can be clearly described and because the six approaches form a continuum, the teacher is better able to identify the pattern of the approach he should adopt. The following examples illustrate the method used to communicate the consistent approach recommended for the teacher to use in working with the child.

Social Acceptance. Jean was not emotionally disturbed although her behavior appeared to the teachers to be similar to children who were. She came from a district characterized by social disintegration. Her parents were extremely hostile toward any kind of recognized authority. Jean was accepted in her neighborhood and had harmonious relationships with her parents. As she grew up, her set of values was in conflict with those of school and middle-class society. She opposed authority, and when she was punished for this, she felt justified in further retaliation. She was placed in a remedial class of underachieving children who had normal ability. The report recommended the approach as follows:

The social acceptance approach implies that you accept that Jean's behavior standards and values will differ from those of the school. For her to change significantly would make her a traitor to her own family and friends. This approach improves her opportunity for academic success which will result in some modification of her values through compartmentalization of what is required at home and at school. In using this approach here are some things you do:

    a. Strike a balance between sympathy and firmness. Jean would regard excessive sympathy as weakness and would feel that toughness would justify retaliation.

    b. Establish and hold limits without hostility.

    c. Do not moralize.

    d. Do not pay too much attention to the niceties of language.

    e. Provide Jean with opportunities to gain recognition.

    f. Give Jean practical experiences and concrete examples, avoiding the abstract aspects until she shows interest in them.

    g. Be patient and accepting; when Jean learns to like you, she will like what you stand for. Values are caught rather than taught.

    h. Express your hostility toward authority so that she can see that you can be angry with the government without wanting to overthrow it. You can be annoyed at getting a parking ticket without hostility toward the idea of law and order.

    i. Do not criticize her lower-class standards, her friends, or her home.

    j. Remember that your warmth, patience, acceptance, and respect for Jean will make her more responsive to your teaching and eventually to better citizenship.

Jean will not be able to express her appreciation of your respect for her and for the opportunities for recognition you provide. She may continue to be impulsive and hostile but should modify this sufficiently so that she will be able to handle the curriculum in this class. Jean's improvement at school and the reduction of complaints from the school may serve to reduce the parents' hostility toward this school.

Unsolicited Friendliness. Albert was diagnosed by the psychiatric clinic as psychotic. He was extremely withdrawn and had severe perceptual disturbances. He was placed in a special class and the following approach was recommended in the report:

Unsolicited friendliness implies that Albert receive affection and support at all times regardless of his reaction. This is a one-way process with the teacher always giving so that Albert can constantly absorb and therefore receive the maximum support to prevent further withdrawal or collapse. In using this approach here are some things you do:

a. Never reproach him.

b. Try to establish a close relationship when you are alone with him.

c. Help him feel that you are close to him and understand him.

d. Grant him special favors as rewards for good behavior.

e. Reward or reinforce any positive behavior, such as appropriate speech.

f. Hold no level of expectation over his head.

g. Place him at a desk close to you.

h. Protect him from the group and do not force him to go out at recess period.

i. Try to confront Albert with reality in a matter-of-fact way when he gives a bizarre or inappropriate interpretation of observations and experiences.

Albert will gain some feeling of worth and begin to come out of his shell, but do not try to integrate him into the group at this time. You can expect him to become suspicious of you and overdemanding or act out with other children for your attention. When this happens, you are reaching him, and soon he will begin to do some reality testing. At this point you will notice an improvement in his learning.

Active Friendliness. Lily, the girl whose problem was reviewed in Chapter 6, was insecure but fairly well adjusted. Her illness and some other contributing factors caused her to feel inadequate in spite of her actual adequacies or strengths. She was performing below her indicated capacities in academic subjects. The following approach was recommended in the report:

Active friendliness implies that you are friendly with Lily at all times. Your friendliness is actively presented to her. In this approach you give affection at a more mature level because Lily is not seriously maladjusted. In using this approach here are some things you do:

a. Take the initiative in being actively friendly with Lily.

b. Give her help and positive support. You need not go out of your way to apply this as long as Lily feels that you are available for encouragement and support.

c. Show feeling toward Lily and her best interests and comfort by your concern for some of the little things that interest her.

d. Use a positive voice tone.

e. Employ your most effective methods of motivation and encouragement.

f. Give criticism only to performance, never to Lily as a person.

g. When uncertain about crediting Lily's performance it is better to overcredit than to undercredit.

h. When you have to deal with acting-out incidents or testing of limits, use the matter-of-fact approach, which will help Lily learn to control herself. This should be explained so that she will realize that it is a direct aid to her and is not punitive.

i. Help her to realize her own resources.

j. When she encounters failure in her schoolwork redirect her to the assignment and show her how to correct it; then be quick to praise the improved result.

Lily will take more initiative in asking you for help. As self-confidence and assurance replace self-doubt, she will be more able to use her own resources. Also, her energies will be released for more constructive growth and a better organized attack on her problems. She may, at times, try out the sincerity of your affection and acceptance. Do not reinforce her doubt by rejecting her. Remain accepting of her but do not condone the oppositional behavior.

Passive Friendliness. The report for Bobby illustrates the passive friendliness approach recommended for the child with paranoid projections.

Firm Kindness. Tom was hyperactive, aggressive, and manipulative. His mother was severely disturbed and very inconsistent in her handling of Tom. He used smiles and tears, as well as flattery and temper tantrums, to manipulate adults. His mood changed rapidly from being gay to being suicidal. The psychiatric clinic performed its usual function of giving an accurate description of Tom and his mother but were unable to suggest anything that could be done other than to wait until something happened which warranted legal apprehension. This is of interest because the consistent application of the firm kindness approach resulted in improved behavior for Tom which eventually appeared to reduce his mother's anxiety. The report for Tom recommended the approach as follows:

Firm kindness implies that Tom is to be treated very firmly with definite limits established for his behavior. These limits are rigidly adhered to despite his reaction. He must not be allowed to manipulate adults as he has in the past. Definite tasks of a scheduled nature are used in conjunction with this approach. In applying this here is what you do:

a. Be very direct with Tom. Order him to do things. Do not ask him to do things.

b. Require production at his level. Make him stay in if necessary.

c. Give him extra work of a menial type, such as cleaning blackboards or desks and picking up stray articles around the room.

d. Give no extra privileges. Take away regular privileges if he gives no evidence of production.

e. Make him do his work over if it is not acceptable to you.

f. Allow little time for activities of his own choosing. Have his program well defined. Tom is expected to meet external demands, not his own demands.

g. Use stern language and positive voice tone.

h. Praise him for good production but do not overcredit his work.

i. Be kind to Tom but try to keep your feelings out of the relationship.

j. Do not show response to his flattery or tears. Direct him back to the job at hand.

Tom may seek punishment if you are not firm. He will become more hostile toward you at first. He will organize his defenses and become angry at you instead of at himself. When his aggression becomes externalized, you will be able to deal with him more productively. When he no longer sees himself as his own worst enemy, he will feel more useful and worthwhile. When he is producing satisfactory work and behavior, the consistent approach should be changed or modified through conferencing.

Matter-of-fact. This approach may be used interchangeably with any of the other five approaches, if the situation demands it at a given time, in order to control acting-out behavior. This does not interfere with the other approaches. The probability is that it will seldom be necessary to employ the matter-of-fact approach.

The author has prescribed the matter-of-fact approach only a few times as a consistent approach and only for long enough to establish some reasonable routines. It was then followed by the firm kindness approach.

Roy was diagnosed as having defective personality and as being an affectionless child. He indulged in delinquent acts which disrupted and demoralized the classroom. He argued with plausible logic in order to gain his own selfish ends. He lied for no apparent reason. He was very charming at times and could make a good impression and would promise anything but would seldom carry through. He appeared to have no loyalty to anyone. The following is the recommended consistent approach described in the report:

The matter-of-fact approach implies an objective attitude toward all his acts. It is used to establish limits and to enforce adherence to them. The limits need to be clearly understood by Roy. In applying this approach here is what you do:

a. Be very firm.

b. Try to keep your emotions out of your dealings with Roy. Avoid becoming involved emotionally in an incident and allowing these emotions to influence relationships with the child at other times.

e. Never go back on a statement or a demand. Do not relent. Only make demands you are prepared to carry out to the ultimate conclusion.

d. Use a show of force or actual force, if necessary, to enforce your demands.

c. Do not use threats, such as, "If you don't do this, I'll...." Tell and show him what to do and demand that he do it.

f. Be direct with a forceful show of confidence on your part. Let Roy know that there is no question about your demands or the demands of the situation.

g. Do not let Roy trap you into arguing the point with him.

Roy will conform enough to avoid punishment and loss of privileges. He will grudgingly accede to your demands as the only means to gain his ends. He may learn to consider the consequences to himself before following an impulse. This is a management device, and its main purpose is to incorporate some values in Roy, who has little conscience. It will be some time before Roy will be able to relate to anyone warmly or enduringly in class or at school, and he may never attain this.

TEACHING METHODS (B). Recommendations regarding teaching methods should be made in light of knowledge about the teacher. If he is familiar with a specific technique, the recommendation needs only to state the technique by name. In some cases the author started the remedial instruction during his interviews with the child. When the teacher wanted assistance with implementing the method in the classroom, he was invited to sit in on a session with the child and observe. This was followed by an interview in which the teacher's questions regarding sources of materials and references could be answered.

In cases when the teacher was a specialist in remedial education for the handicapped, the recommendation of method came from him. The report stated, "Mr. Jones suggested that George receive programmed instruction in vocabulary building to increase his word bank for lipreading." Although Mr. Jones made the suggestion and was responsible for implementation, it was stated in the report and as part of the record of discussions to support his decision.

For certain problems the author prepared or obtained separate mimeographed sheets of suggestions. The following examples illustrate what is important for the teacher to do in the classroom. It is not the purpose of these instruction sheets to enlighten the teacher about the etiology or symptomatology of the handicap. These factors are dealt with elsewhere.

SUGGESTIONS TO THE TEACHER OF A STUTTERER

These suggestions will help make the stutterer more comfortable in a classroom.

1. Get to know him by seeking opportunities to chat with him informally. This will develop a personal relationship and make him more comfortable in your class.
2. Give him the same opportunity to read or talk as everyone else in the class, because special consideration only amplifies his feeling of difference and inability.
3. Even though he may have a great deal of difficulty, encourage the stutterer to talk or read aloud as much as possible.
4. Give him a chance to finish his words, sentences, and ideas. If he stutters, do not let anyone answer or finish for him even though you know exactly what he is trying to say.
5. In cooperation with the speech therapist, help him admit he stutters because it is necessary to counteract his tendency to hide and avoid stuttering.
6. Help him discover and develop his special abilities.

Don't's

1. Don't tell him to slow down.
2. Don't tell him to stop and start over.
3. Don't tell him to think what he is going to say.
4. Don't tell him to take a deep breath before talking.
5. Don't tell him he talks faster than he thinks.
6. Don't look away or avoid his eyes when he stutters.
7. Don't fill in words for him to get him "off the spot."
8. Don't interrupt him until his sentence or thought is finished.
9. Don't let him feel he needs to hurry.
10. Don't feel sorry for him.
11. Don't let him think you wish he would talk better.

REMEDIAL READING: FERNALD–KELLER METHOD

To help children who have difficulty in reading (and spelling), stress is laid upon manual cues of writing and tracing and on articulatory impressions from saying the word as the children trace it.

Procedure

1. The child selects from context any word that he wishes to learn.
2. The teacher pronounces it and writes it on the chalkboard or, if preferred, on a strip of paper using a felt-nibbed pen or crayon.
3. The child then traces the word with direct finger contact, saying each syllable in the word as he traces. He repeats this process as many times as necessary to enable him to write the word without looking at the copy.
4. Words thus learned are used in writing his own stories and they become part of his own vocabulary, allowing him to experience new words in meaningful groups.
5. During the process of writing, the child is encouraged to ask for help with any word that gives him difficulty. The difficult word is written for his tracing.
6. To enable the child to recognize the new words in printed form, he is given the opportunity to read his own stories which are typed for him soon after he has written them.
7. If paper strips are used for tracing, they may be placed alphabetically in a word file box for future reference.

Many of Fernald's cases attained reasonable fluency after using this kinesthetic method for five or six months. The merit of the method is its emphasis on tracing and writing in order to particularize the observation of words. This method is appropriate for very backward readers in the initial stages of remediation. Other methods should be introduced later.

Reference

Fernald, Grace M.: *Remedial Techniques in Basic School Subjects*, McGraw-Hill Book Company, New York, 1943.

The written report generally states the recommended teaching method briefly. When necessary, demonstrations, reference books, or instruction sheets are employed to augment the report.

SPECIFIC OBJECTIVES (c). The aims of the individual program are stated in a direct manner in the written report.

ANCILLARY SERVICES (D). The supporting school services are represented at the case conference and the report merely states their involvement in treatment. For example, "It is recommended that Lily visit the counselor on a continuing basis."

PLACEMENT AND PERSONNEL (E). This recommendation must have administrative approval to be implemented. The principal should give his consent before the report is written; therefore, it is simply stated as a record of the decision.

SUBJECT MATTER (F). Special remedial programs are not explained in detail in the report. Reference is made to the appropriate sources of special curriculum.

INSTRUCTIONAL MATERIALS (G).

SPECIAL EQUIPMENT (H).

SCHOOL PLANT (I). Modification of these variables usually involves senior school administration staff and school-board officials. The recommendation is stated in the report, but other communication with the appropriate officials is also required.

AUXILIARY AGENCIES (J). Recommendations regarding referral to an agency outside of the school, recorded in a report for school personnel, contribute little to communication and coordination of services. The conference should decide who will be primarily responsible for liaison with the agency, and communication with the agency should be regular and continuing. The report simply states which agency is recommended and who is responsible for liaison.

SUMMARY

The success of the implementation of prescriptive teaching depends on the communication of recommendations to teachers, parents, administrators, consultants, nurses, doctors, social workers, and others. In school the teacher has the day-to-day contact with the child, is the greatest potential influence in modifying negative responses, and is the person most responsible for the area of implementation. The major emphasis, therefore, is on communication of diagnostic findings to the teacher. This is accomplished through case conferences and through written reports.

All the wisdom, knowledge, and special skill of the school psychologist will come to naught if he does not communicate adequately. The tools of his trade are mostly words. The success of the prescriptive

teaching program depends on the quality of the diagnostic decisions
and his ability to communicate with other human beings.

REFERENCES

Clarke, David L. "A New Approach to Classroom Guidance," *The Education Digest*, April, 1958, 23:34–36.

Combs, Arthur W., and Snygg, Donald. *Individual Behavior*. New York: Harper & Row, Publishers, Incorporated, 1959.

Hammond, Kenneth R., and Allen, Jeremiah M. *Writing Clinical Reports*. Englewood Cliffs, N.J.: Prentice-Hall, Inc., 1953.

Hayakawa, S. I. In E. J. McGrath (ed.). *Communication in General Education*. Dubuque, Iowa: William C. Brown Company, 1949.

Hovland, Carl J., Janis, Irving H., and Kelley, Harold H. *Communication and Persuasion*. New Haven, Conn.: Yale University Press, 1953.

Johnson, Roy Ivan, Schalekamp, Marie J., and Garrison, Lloyd A. *Communications: Handling Ideas Effectively*. New York: McGraw-Hill Book Company, 1956.

Keine, O. B., and Schmidt, L. G. "Guidance Implications of Psychological Reports in the Public Schools," *Journal of Educational Research*, April, 1958, 60:611–616.

Klopfer, Walter G. *The Psychological Report*. New York: Grune & Stratton, Inc., 1960.

Peter, Laurence Johnston. "An Evaluation of the Written Psychological Report in an Elementary School Guidance Program," unpublished doctoral dissertation, Pullman, Wash.: Washington State University, 1963.

8

TEACHING

It has been said that a good teacher is someone who can understand those not very good at explaining and explain something to those not very good at understanding. Although this saying would describe all good teachers, it is particularly true of the teacher of handicapped children. This simple description of the good teacher does not overlook but rather emphasizes the complexity and subtlety of the teaching art.

LIMITATIONS OF PRESENT KNOWLEDGE

The classroom has never been subjected to the kind of research which determines all the components of good teaching. The school program does not stand alone but is one of the social institutions in the community which shapes the child's learning. We are only beginning to understand the quadrangular interaction between social environment, family, school, and child. Scientific investigations of teaching have been faced with the dual problem of the complexity of teaching and the inability to control factors outside of the classroom which influence learning. Statistical methods have attempted to control these variables by sheer numbers. Scientific investigations have had to face the problem of the complicated and untidy nature of crude experience. Laboratory methods involve the isolation or abstraction of simple

210

elements from crude experience and the discovery of relationships between these elements. Both laboratory and statistical methods of studying teaching deal in abstractions or simplification and are thus in danger of missing significant factors.

This danger of course exists in all scientific effort. A classic illustration is Liebig's discovery of the functions of carbohydrates, fats, and proteins in his study of nutrition. In isolating these elements from the untidy complexity of our common everyday food, he did not realize that he had ignored very significant elements. In consequence, dieticians for many years concluded that fresh fruit and vegetables were only a luxury and that salads were merely a garnish adding a pleasant but unnecessary frill to our eating habits. Important as Liebig's discovery was, it did not focus attention on the totality or complexity of an adequate diet.

Our present knowledge of teaching is somewhat parallel. Some elements which apparently contribute to effective teaching have been isolated and studied, but when attempts have been made to teach by these elements singly, the results have been disappointing. Prescriptive teaching attempts to incorporate some of these known elements but does not presume to prescribe how to teach.

We cannot offer systematic proof that what is claimed for the school's influence is indeed true. Nor are we anywhere near being able to document that all the advice regarding a special educational program is in fact the preferable solution. Proof of this kind is hard to come by; obviously research is difficult because of the fact that the school's influence cannot be examined independently of a whole series of other variables (Gage, 1963).

Social influences affect the objectives of education and of diet. In the 1830s when Liebig made his discovery, the aim of most diets was to gain weight. In the 1960s the object of most diets is to lose weight. In education the objective of conformity has given way to the objective of democracy. In America styles of desirable behavior change, and therefore the aims of education also change. What is desirable teaching is determined in relation to the achievement of objectives. In diet, certain known variables can be manipulated in order to influence the achievement of specific results; so in teaching certain known variables may be manipulated to facilitate specific desired learning.

Prescriptive teaching is the manipulation of variables that experience and research indicate will influence learning in the desired direction. As new discoveries are made regarding teaching, greater control of outcomes will be possible. The present chapter deals with factors related to teachers and teaching which make the implementation of prescriptive teaching possible.

THE TEACHER

Nearly every child in our society spends an important part of twelve vital, developmental years in the classroom. The estimate is 14,000 hours. Many of these hours are spent in interpersonal transaction with a professional person trained in knowledge of children and their development, and whose professional goal is the actualization of each child's potentialities. Each classroom is a setting for a rich variety of personal transactions with peers in the presence of a trained teacher. These interactions take place under circumstances in which there is, on the average, one professional person for every thirty children. Supporting this basic functional unit is an elaborate and highly developed administrative structure and its ancillary services.

Of the many factors—curricula, methods, materials, buildings, etc.—that influence the kind of learning atmosphere prevailing in the classrooms, the most important is the teacher himself. Because the teacher's contact is continuous in its influence on the child's attitude and responses, it is the personality of the teacher as much as what he knows that determines the rate and direction of the pupil's growth. The teacher is a model for growth and maturity, for it is in the presence of other human beings that children learn to be the human beings they are. While the teacher does not have to be a specific personality type, he represents the adult world, the community, and the state and should be a healthy adult with a wholesome outlook on life.

Motivating a child to learn is not a superficial process. The compelling motivations lie within the child. Part of his motivation is his feeling of competence about himself, and part is his feeling that he is becoming like those he perceives as competent. Whatever he does is ultimately related to enhancing his self-perception or defending his self-concept. His perception of the teacher as a competent person who helps him satisfy his needs provides him with positive motivation. He will learn most from the teacher who gives him feelings of worth, acceptance, approval, and achievement. Much of the teaching-learning process is a human relationship, and while there are no magic formulas, there are factors within the process which are related to certain outcomes. We have no magic formula for health, but there are certain elements in diet which are related to health and illness.

The teacher can lead a child to become skilled, knowing, perceptive, and effective in his world; to master confusion; to reorder experience through his own invention; to communicate in the modes of his culture; to extend his interest to far places and times; to act, to organize, to accomplish, to reason, to reflect. He can be to the child a member of the adult community, one of the most important in the child's life, who can relate to him as a person respectful of his individuality, who understands his feelings as well as his capacities, and who is aware of the importance of his private world to him. There is no unitary good teacher; instead there is a broad range of ways of achieving good teaching. There are of course limits to this range that suggest themselves readily—chronically angry, rigid, withdrawn, or overly manipulative people are outside the limits of eligibility. The school's contribution to healthy personality will take a great step forward when teachers can be placed in jobs with intelligent consideration of their psychological suitability for working with children.

In-service Training

Many attempts at solutions to educational problems tend to oversimplify teaching. Teaching is a relationship, and an important and dynamic part of that relationship is the teacher's personality, which creates the learning situation. The teacher's effectiveness depends upon his creating an atmosphere in which the child can engage in the exploration of personal meanings and upon his setting limits which provide structure for the child's discoveries. Prescriptive teaching does not resolve the problems of the teacher with serious inadequacies. It supports the teacher's competency and brings improvement of interaction within the classroom. The author's experience indicates that teachers whose personalities differ widely can implement the approach that is prescribed. Teachers who have not previously been able to make modifications on the basis of clinical consultations have been able to implement prescriptive teaching. It provides a means of implementing a dynamic, ongoing, in-service program.

Prescriptive teaching avoids the circular confusion sometimes encountered in the casework approach. The social worker, concerned with the child's adjustment, says that learning will improve when the child's personality problems are resolved. The teacher says if the child was learning, he would feel better about himself, but he cannot get adjusted because he cannot learn. In prescriptive teaching, he gains adjustment through learning. This is primarily a teacher-centered guidance program which recognizes that the greatest opportunity for guidance is to be found in the daily pupil-teacher interaction. The objective is improvement in the quality of the educational experience in the classroom. This is a function which only the school can perform, and it is the function that the school with a prescriptive teaching program can perform very well.

The availability of special services does not ensure a successful school program. In fact, the proliferation of nonteaching specialists within the school may seriously limit the teacher's role and may succeed in taking some of the challenge out of teaching. It is the means whereby the services of the counselor, psychologist, visiting teacher, supervisor, speech therapist, consultant, etc., are brought to bear in the classroom that is the important link. When these services come between teacher and pupil, instead of supporting the teacher in meeting the needs of the pupil, the teacher's position is undermined.

There is a temperamental difference between persons who decide to engage in clinical work and those who choose teaching. The former feel more comfortable with individuals, the latter with a group. The teacher has special knowledge to offer the clinical staff, and the staff must understand the teacher's problems in the group relationship. The expert who requires that the teacher treat a child as an isolated individual, failing to see the teacher's function in the group setting, undermines his position and is unsuccessful in perceiving the real therapeutic potential of the school. Unless the members of the diagnostic team are aware that some of their training was lacking in knowledge of group psychology, they cannot function well in the school situation.

The teacher tends to be interested in the functioning of the child at a given moment, while the psychologist is more interested in unfolding the processes which led to, and account for, the functioning of the child. The teacher and psychologist supplement each other. The psychologist does not obtain enough material to evaluate the child; the teacher does not obtain enough material to evaluate the pathology and conflicts of the child. The beginning teacher may expect to refer all problem children to the psychologist or other clinician and have them return completely cured, docile, conforming, well-behaving children who gratefully absorb the knowledge that is presented to them.

Prescriptive teaching helps each member of the diagnostic team learn more about the complexity of the child. At the same time it helps each member limit himself to his own specific contribution. When the child has been receiving therapy, it helps the teacher understand his role in facilitating the results of therapy. He must recognize that the child has only succeeded in handling his problems on a symbolic level and that he has not been supplied with behavioral patterns consistent with the expectations of the school. Through the process of translation into learning terms, prescriptive teaching helps the teacher understand that the pupil returns to the classroom to have the opportunity to translate his symbolic handling of the problem into appropriate actions. Kelner (1958) presents practical methods for teaching the problem child and avoids suggestions which would make the teacher less like a teacher and more like a social worker or psychiatrist. The in-service aim of prescriptive teaching is to broaden the teacher's understanding of the child and the other professions concerned with his welfare and to help the teacher understand his role in terms of the unique contribution that teaching can make in the remediation of the child's handicap.

REMEDIAL TEACHING

Remediation begins with methods which bring immediate success. New work cannot be successfully introduced until the child has developed readiness for it. Diagnosis, fundamental to remedial teaching, begins with an analysis of the child's schoolwork to discover the hierarchy of his perceptual modes, perceptual inefficiencies within the modes, and specific weaknesses in basic skills. Teaching based upon this diagnosis may result in adequate progress. The follow-up may indicate that further diagnosis is required and a full case study should be undertaken. Diagnosis should be started by the teacher and should focus first upon the immediate problem. Evaluation of the learning problems in the classroom followed by corrective measures and follow-up not only leads to more direct educational treatment of the problem but also in cases requiring further diagnosis provides invaluable diagnostic data for the teacher and psychologist. Starting at his functioning level the child should move step by step through developmental tasks which promote learning in his areas of greatest inefficiency. Working with a skill that is well established has little positive value, and in remedial cases it may have a deadening effect, resulting in faulty attitudes toward instruction.

Motivation is not necessary in the usual sense since we cannot motivate a child to work at being unsuccessful. When we urge the child to greater effort by pleading with him to try hard, reminding him how much his success means or how important it is to his future or his family, his attention is directed to these emotionally loaded situations rather than to the things he needs to learn. The result is a decrease in learning. It is preferable to start him at a task at his level of perceptual development and reinforce his correct responses. He is then motivated by his competency and can move on to the next level. He should be provided with opportunities to feel successful in his work each period, every day. New learnings should be parceled out in small packages that he can cope with.

He should receive immediate feedback of the results of his learning. Individual help and examples with which he can check his work at each step help shape his pattern of response. He should be frequently informed of his progress through immediate reinforcement of correct responses, plus token rewards, charts, graphs, and records of improvement. His attention should be directed to his progress rather than to what he is unable to do. His present reading and writing should be compared with his own previous performance but not with that of other children. The Devereux Foundation (Smith, 1961) has conducted a number of experiments using reinforcement psychology in special education. Teaching machines were employed to provide massed practice in fundamentals and reinforcement through a variety of rewards. An experimental reading program assumed that reading provides its own reinforcement if it is taught at its proper level. Reading that is too easy is boring and reading that is too difficult is frustrating. Statistically significant differences were found in favor of the group where special efforts were made to give reading instruction at the appropriate individual level. It was concluded that when interest and difficulty of reading material are controlled, reading contains its own intrinsic reinforcing properties.

The child's needs must be met through the activities in which he is engaged. If he is sent back to regular instruction before remediation is completed, he finds himself failing again. The former negative emotional reaction is reestablished, and carries with it the additional difficulty of a negative conditioning of the new technique which apparently has failed to help him. In this situation it is difficult to reinstate the remedial methods he needs to use in order to learn.

The teacher will always ameliorate, when possible, the extenuating circumstances in the home and school environment. The task of correcting major social and personality defects in the home is beyond the usual scope of the classroom teacher. In the classroom, the fact that the teacher is doing something positive and taking an interest in the child will frequently alleviate his feelings of despair and inferiority. Often this results in a significantly positive effect on the parents. It may be that success in a school subject is the first step toward a more total personal-social adjustment. Success in one area can provide encouragement and fresh courage for him to tackle a new problem.

Definite feelings of satisfaction and accomplishment should accompany the child's efforts. Practice with satisfaction is the basis of rapid learning of basic skills, but this type of learning may require a period of special grouping or placement because the method which seems so effective in individual instruction may seem childish in the regular class. The very technique which gives positive results becomes negative in effect when the child does not want to use it in regular class.

For the child of normal ability who is not brain injured or hyperactive abundant and varied exercises and activities should be provided, because the desire for new experience is fundamental to the growth of the child. Materials and equipment for remedial teaching should be of the concrete-abstract type, such as the abacus, blocks, and Cuisenaire rods (Cuisenaire and Gattegno, 1959). Problems and illustrations using such things as cookies or candies for a party have social ramifications which may be confusing or threatening to the disturbed child. After the skill is developed, it can be transferred to a realistic problem.

Drill or practice after a basic skill is learned should take place in a variety of situations. Drill with the same materials in the same situations should be kept to the minimum to ensure learning. The teacher, by providing the child with a firm competency in various skills, gives him the tools necessary for increasing independence. A child gains in mental health, stability, and self-respect by doing the jobs he has to do. Not to meet his obligations results in loss of respect for self and in a generally deteriorated emotional condition.

Concentration is enhanced by reducing distractions to a minimum.

Loud noises, gaudy colors, and a multiplicity of stimuli not related to the immediate learning situation are distracting and reduce learning. Mechanical instructional devices often are effective in eliminating, to some extent, the external or distracting stimuli, an effect which may be partly due to the novelty of the situation. Procrastination and assumed disability are not supported by mechanical teaching devices, because they reinforce only correct responses and do not accept excuses.

Good teaching is the ability to challenge children without threatening them. Threatened children can learn, but their perception is narrowed or distorted so that the desired nature of learning is lost. Challenging children without threatening them involves acceptance, warmth, friendliness, willingness to withhold judgment, and ability to look at facts objectively. This openness of experience on the part of the teacher provides a basis for the child's progress.

Factors affecting learning continue to operate whether we take cognizance of them or not. The effective teacher has learned to use his personality to establish an atmosphere in which limits are clear, reasonable, and helpful in encouraging the child's exploration and discovery. A stable structure has important positive values in providing patterns against which the child evaluates his behavior. Structure which is neither threat nor coercion has important security values.

When a child can start on a new method of learning which does not produce his former negative emotional response, the method will benefit the child therapeutically as well as educationally. However when the subject matter appears to produce the negative emotional response, reconditioning is an appropriate technique. In cases where the child's problem results from unpleasant conditioning experiences, the symptoms may be inability to learn certain skills with resultant attempts to avoid the learning situation through daydreaming, antisocial behavior, dislike of school, or blocking. In such cases reconditioning in the particular subject is the first choice in treatment methods. When the diagnosis delimits the cause to a specific factor, reconditioning is an appropriate remedial technique. If the classroom experiences and diagnosis indicate that a specific stimulus causes the child to react negatively, reconditioning can be employed to modify the child's reaction. The subject, object, or task causing the block is avoided during the beginning phase of treatment and is replaced with some substitute stimulus which is connected with a positive emotion. When the second stimulus and positive response are well established, the orginal stimulus is introduced at the same time as the positive response occurs. When this process is repeated a sufficient number of times, the positive response will be produced along with the original stimulus. This method directs attention away from the undesirable emotional response.

SUMMARY

Prescriptive teaching attempts to place the school and the teacher in proper perspective in the total milieu affecting the child's learning. It recognizes that the teacher's personality provides, in large measure, the learning atmosphere for the child.

Teaching is a complex art with many variables which are not clearly understood and others which are difficult or impossible to control; prescriptive teaching modifies the controllable or independent variables in teaching. It has been established that there is a relationship between certain teaching variables and specific educational outcomes. Because the prediction of these outcomes is not absolute, prescriptive teaching constantly emphasizes the importance of validation through follow-up.

REFERENCES

Allinsmith, Wesley, and Goethals, George W. *The Role of Schools in Mental Health.* New York: Basic Books, Inc., Publishers, 1962.

Blair, Glenn Myers. *Diagnostic and Remedial Teaching.* New York: The Macmillan Company, 1956.

Cuisenaire, G., and Gattegno, C. *Numbers in Colour.* London: William Heinemann, Ltd., 1959.

Cutts, Norma E., and Moseley, Nicholas. *Providing for Individual Differences in the Elementary School.* Englewood Cliffs, N.J.: Prentice-Hall, Inc., 1960.

Devereux, George. *Therapeutic Education.* New York: Harper & Row, Publishers, Incorporated, 1956.

Dolch, Edward William. *Helping Handicapped Children in School.* Seattle, Wash.: Garrard Publishing Company, 1948.

Gage, N. L. (ed.). *Handbook of Research on Teaching.* Chicago: Rand McNally & Company, 1963.

Kelner, Bernard G. *How to Teach in the Elementary School.* New York: McGraw-Hill Book Company, 1958.

Miller, Marian B. *Guidance and Elementary School Children.* Dover, Del.: State Department of Public Instruction, 1961.

Redl, Fritz, and Wattenberg, William W. *Mental Hygiene in Teaching.* New York: Harcourt, Brace & World, Inc., 1951.

Smith, Edgar A. *Reinforcement Psychology in Special Education.* A Devereux Reprint. Devon, Pa.: Devereux Schools, 1961.

Tallman, Irving, and Levine, Samuel. "The Emotionally Disturbed Child in the Classroom Situation," *Exceptional Children,* October, 1960, 114–126.

9

FOLLOW–UP

Prescriptive teaching is a system wherein each phase prescribes the succeeding phase. It follows a sequence of (1) describing symptoms, (2) investigating etiology, (3) performing diagnosis, (4) making a prognosis, (5) prescribing treatment, (6) implementing, and (7) following up. This chapter completes the description of the circuit which was introduced and illustrated in Chapter 1.

Automation in industry has shown that electric circuits which provide feedback can improve the quality of production by reducing errors. Without automatic feedback a long production line may have one machine slightly out of adjustment with the result that the product is defective. This defect may not be discovered until final inspection of the product, and the whole production might have to be stopped to investigate the correction required. The rejection rate of finished products is high under this system. When the machinery in the production line is connected by a circuit which provides feedback, errors are corrected and the machinery adjusted so that the process is continuous and self-regulatory.

Although the processes of manufacturing and the processes of education are extremely different, the principle of feedback is appropriate for both. In the school we have a number of variables that are operating on the child. In prescriptive teaching these variables are connected by a regulatory circuit which adjusts them to the educational process. This circuit is used to achieve the individualization of education through processes that are not mechanistic but which contain many subjective elements.

An electrician builds an electric circuit step by step, but nothing electrical really happens until the circuit is complete and the electricity is flowing. Our prescriptive teaching circuit starts with the child in the classroom, in interaction with his social and physical environment. If he is unable to respond adequately, a referral is made to the school psychologist or coordinator of the diagnostic team. The diagnostic findings are translated into terms which can influence future events at school and are reported to the teacher and others responsible for implementation. The modification of school variables provides the child with new learning opportunities. When the modifications are appropriate, the child's behavior changes in the desired direction. The results of implementation are evaluated from time to time through follow-up studies conducted by the coordinator of the program and through the ongoing follow-up by the teacher. This sequence of follow-up validates the appropriateness of the modifications in terms of the child's responses.

FOLLOW-UP METHOD

If the child's responses to the modifications of his educational program indicate progress toward the desired outcomes, the feedback circuit supports continuation of the operating modifications. If the child's responses show the same limitations in his repertoire of responses as he had before his program was modified, the follow-up, or feedback, is directed to the area of diagnosis. The process of diagnosis is resumed, and new data are brought into focus. The circuit continues through the phases resulting in further prescribed modification, reporting, implementation, and follow-up.

When desirable progress has been maintained long enough for establishment of the new learning patterns, some of the variables may be modified in the direction of the standard practices for average children. Follow-up again provides the feedback which supports this modification. Because follow-up uses some of the same techniques employed in diagnosis, it is sometimes overlooked or is thought to be repetitious. This is a serious mistake. If any part of the circuit is missing, the system loses its dynamic function and its self-correcting or self-adjusting feature. It is only a prescriptive teaching circuit when it is complete with all phases operating.

The pupil personnel specialist responsible for coordination can encourage each person to do follow-up studies in his appropriate area. The criteria for evaluating progress are the same as those employed in diagnostic teaching. Progress is said to occur when (1) a remission of the symptom is evident, (2) the symptom has not returned, (3) no substitute symptom has been observed, and (4) there is no apparent long-term increase in anxiety. In some conditions a temporary increase in anxiety may be a phase in successful treatment. When Bobby responded to the consistent approach of passive friendliness, his anxiety increased and was shown in his testing behavior. Consistency resulted in differentiation which he resolved in his perceptual field by perceiving the person as trying to put something over on him or trying to get something from him. He tested this perception by acting against that person. His anxiety increased when the consistent approach was maintained. He then had to decide to try another test or accept that the person was somewhat reliable. This necessary process is anxiety-producing at this stage.

Follow-up Studies

Lily's problem was stated as underachievement. Her achievement was not consistent with her previous progress nor with her estimated capacity on the basis of an intelligence test. In the follow-up study conducted about five months from the implementation of the teaching prescription, Lily's teacher reported that her achievement had improved and that her grades were up to the level expected of her. She participated more fully in classroom activities including discussion and social activities. The principal reported that Lily had carried out the monitor duty well and had been dependable. Her attendance at school had improved, and she had missed no school for three months. The report of the school doctor and nurse stated they were working with the private physician and that the family members had resolved some of their attitudes toward the illness. Lily had no flare-ups of her arthritis for more than two months. The school psychologist who was conducting the counseling sessions used projective tests to determine changes in Lily's self-concept. She did not perceive of herself as so severely handicapped as she had earlier. On the basis of this information the teaching prescription was considered to be adequate. Underachievement had been reduced, her progress had been maintained, no new problems had arisen, and Lily's anxiety was not increased by this procedure. Further follow-up studies were conducted to evaluate progress and determine whether further modification would be made or when some of the special modifications should be discontinued. One year later she was maintaining normal progress with the only modification being in physical education.

Bobby was referred because of his hostile aggressive behavior, dishonesty, and refusal to speak under some circumstances. Follow-up studies six months from the time of implementation of prescriptive teaching showed that Bobby was making progress. The frequency of disciplinary visits to the office had decreased to the extent that he was no longer regarded as an exceptional problem. On some occasions when Bobby was asked questions about an incident, he explained his behavior. In the counseling sessions Bobby had trusted the counselor with some information about himself. He was learning to differentiate between those behaviors which were really harmful to him and those which were not. At this time personality tests yielded little new information.

Follow-up studies one year from the implementation of the teaching prescription showed further progress. From the principal's and the teacher's point of view, Bobby was no longer a problem child. His fighting and lying were not regarded as excessive. When he experienced difficulty, he was able to explain his situation to the teacher. The counselor found that Bobby was now able to make finer discrimination in his evaluation of people and social situations. Although still suspicious, he was seeing more people as trustworthy. He still felt that some of his classmates did things that were unfair to him. At this time he gave fuller responses both in interviews and in personality tests. He was still far from being an outgoing friendly boy, but he was no longer a major problem at school. The parents were still uncooperative with the school and the health services. On the basis of this evaluation of progress, the teaching prescription was considered to be adequate, and it was recommended that the approach be continued.

George had continued his good progress in academic subjects and appeared to be more creative in his approach to problems. In the industrial arts class he was learning to coordinate his involuntary movements with his voluntary movements and produce woodwork projects which were a source of satisfaction to him. He appeared to respond positively to the counseling interviews. He became more spon-

taneous and discussed his school p
the modification of school variable
significance than the modificatior
attitude, the total result was suc
toward actualizing his potentialiti

IMPROVEMENT O

Follow-up studies ar
procedure. The coordinator sho
ing the initial period of implei
to ascertain if any problems are encou
well under way, follow-up should occur when requested as wc..
certain specified times when reports can be gathered from each person
involved in implementation of the prescription. These cross-sectional
studies make it possible to look at the child's progress in terms of the
four criteria established for evaluation. The matter of substitute
symptoms requires that reports be received regarding the child in
different situations in the school, home, and community.

If the teaching prescription is effective, in time the child's need for
the prescription will be reduced. The follow-up will reveal when
modification of the prescription is required.

The follow-up study provides opportunities for in-service training
for teachers and other staff members. The teacher is helped to see the
contribution teaching makes as well as the limitations of the teaching
process. As the withdrawn child is observed learning to cope with
reality, the teacher may develop better understanding of his role in
helping the child deal with reality. As the overanxious or guilt-ridden
child is observed learning to have a more adequate self-concept, we
have opportunities of discovering those factors which support the
child's development of a better self-image. As the child with paranoid
projection is observed differentiating between what is truly threatening and what he only perceives as threatening, we have opportunities
of finding out how to assist him in learning how to be trusting. As the
hostile child is observed expressing himself through destructive aggressive behavior, we learn how to help him find more appropriate
means of expression. It is through the follow-up study that the prescriptive teaching program gains much of its support. When teachers
find that a method is effective in bringing about improvement for the

action in the classroom, succeeding cases receive
and the prescriptions are implemented more fully

that the school is an important influence in the child's
is logical to assume that a school program appropriate for
would facilitate overcoming individual handicaps. This
cal possibility has not been completely achieved in practice in
egular school system. Follow-up studies conducted in the pre-
iptive teaching program indicate that adequate, even if not ideal,
prescriptions can be implemented for most children. Implementation
of modifications such as placement and plant is frequently delayed
because of administrative, financial, and other difficulties. Consistent
approaches and special teaching methods may be delayed because the
teacher is incapable of implementation, and the modification of these
variables must wait until the child is moved to another classroom or is
promoted to the next grade. Only through follow-up can we determine
if the degree of implementation is adequate. The author's experience
suggests that nearly all teachers can implement the prescribed modifications to some degree and that follow-up, in most cases, supports or
reinforces the modifications. Through this experience the teachers improve their ability to teach children with a wider range of learning
problems.

If the prescriptions used to illustrate the program seem too simple or
too pat, it should be remembered that they were arrived at through the
process described above. Not all the appropriate answers are arrived
at the first time around the circuit. The cases used for illustration
were not intended to be ideal although the prescriptions were found to
be effective in terms of the follow-up criteria. The program appeared
to provide in-service training for all members of the team because the
results of implementation tended to indicate the validity of their
recommendations. Prescriptive teaching has provided the author with
the kind of in-service program wherein he can continue to improve the
quality of coordination, prescription, and communication toward the
objectives of the educational process.

The major contribution of prescriptive teaching is this dynamic
aspect which encourages, supports, and reinforces improvement in all
phases of the program from referral, through diagnosis and reporting,
to implementation and follow-up.

10

CONCLUSIONS

A large percentage of people now support the concept of equal educational opportunity for all children. Equality of educational opportunity is achieved through differentiation in programming enabling each pupil to develop to the maximum of his potentiality. Prescriptive teaching was designed to meet the challenge of deciding what can best be done for each child.

THE PROGRAM

Prescriptive teaching is a program for the utilization of diagnostic resources in an educational setting. It accomplishes this purpose through establishing a regulatory communication circuit which adjusts school variables to individual needs. There are four places in this circuit at which decisions are made that influence or prescribe the next phase. The first position in the circuit at which a decision must be made is in the classroom where the teacher decides that the child requires diagnostic services and prescribes the referral phase. The second position is diagnosis in which discussions, tests, and the case history prescribe the reporting phase. The third position on the circuit is the teacher and other school personnel who carry out the implementation phase. The fourth position is the child in the modified program resulting from implementation. The child's re-

227

sponses to the modifications provide the feedback which prescribes when and if further diagnosis, reporting, implementation, and follow-up are required.

Obviously there are very real problems of decision making at each of these four positions on the circuit. If the teacher is inappropriate in her referral, the diagnostician inaccurate in his assessment or uncommunicative in his reporting, or the school personnel ineffective in their implementation, the follow-up will indicate a need for continuation of the process to find more effective modifications. If follow-up is faulty or is not continuous, it may fail also.

Although diagnostic techniques are not absolute in their predictive validity, there are still two sound reasons for making modifications based upon what is available. The first is that the variables already exist in the child's educational program. If the validity of the diagnosis is adequate to improve the effectiveness of these variables, then the diagnosis is worthwhile. The second is that a system of feedback within the program provides schedules of reinforcement for those modifications which are effective; thus by a series of approximations the program comes closer and closer to being appropriate for the child.

Because there are subjective elements involved in each position on the circuit, faulty decisions can be made. For this reason prescriptive teaching places emphasis on the feedback system, which provides the means for correcting faulty decisions, within the circuit. Reliance on follow-up requires that the criteria for evaluating the child's responses be stated in terms of measurable or observable behavior. The criteria for evaluating improvement are related specifically to the disabilities stated as the basis for referral.

When the author was attempting to establish a program in which diagnostic services would result in improvement in educational practices, many of the techniques required were already available. Techniques of diagnosis and teaching had a degree of adequacy which made them acceptable. Means for referral to and evaluation by psychologists, psychiatrists, social workers, speech therapists, and medical practitioners had been developed. The major problem was the translation of diagnostic findings into educational implementation.

The rationale employed in solving this problem included the following ideas:

1. Learning impinges on factors which are broadly classified as mental, physical, social, and emotional. Therefore diag-

nosis of learning problems should be interdisciplinary and include investigation into these areas.

2. Children with serious injuries and disabilities may not be handicapped significantly in terms of their educational goals, while others with relatively minor injury or disability may be seriously handicapped educationally.

3. The educational relevance of the handicap is determined by the injury and disability in interaction with a number of situational factors.

4. Educational modifications are made on the basis of educational relevance and cannot logically be made on the basis of medical, psychological, or social-work relevance.

5. The prime responsibility in education of the handicapped child is for modification of variables within the school program. The implementation of these ideas was accomplished through the development of a model which provided a structure for the translation of interdisciplinary diagnosis into a prescription for teaching.

All problems are not solved when the translation of diagnostic findings is achieved. There is still much to be learned about diagnosis, communication, and teaching, but sufficient useful knowledge exists in these areas to justify implementation of the program. With establishment of the connecting link between diagnosis and teaching, improvement of all phases within the circuit is facilitated.

This book is a report of the program as it was developed by the author and is an outline of the procedures followed. It does not attempt to explain all the methods of teaching which can be employed within the program. Prescriptive teaching is not a system which limits teaching; it is an approach which embraces any constructive method or technique. As new methods develop, they can be prescribed where they are appropriate, and thus expansion and flexibility is encouraged.

Prescriptive teaching does not involve going back over the development of the maladjustment in order to correct it. It starts with the child in the classroom with the teacher. The teacher's regular contact with the child is modified, along with a number of other factors in the educational program, in a manner consistent with the child's special needs.

The school psychologist coordinated the team activities. It was assumed that because he was working with medical and social-work staff and with pupils, principals, teachers, and parents, he was best able to effect the collaboration desired for the team approach. All professions were not always represented for every case. The team structure was flexible and changing, offering services from the school or community which would aid in the specific diagnosis and treatment of an individual case.

Prescriptive teaching has been implemented in public schools for hundreds of problem children by regular classroom teachers who had no special training in this approach except through the in-service aspects of the program; it has also been used in special education classes.

Follow-up studies of individual students, conducted as a regular part of the program, indicated a high degree of success. This evaluation of the child's progress depended in large measure on the teacher's rating of the child in relation to the original referral and the follow-up criteria. Improvement was indicated in almost every case, and in most cases the improvement was regarded as substantial. It appeared that suitable teaching prescriptions could be devised covering a wide variety of handicaps and implemented in regular classrooms for most children.

A few children were so disturbed that they were placed in special classes or residential treatment centers. Segregation was a necessary phase of their treatment before integration could be effective. There were a few cases where the educational modifications did not result in significant improvement. These were cases of long-standing severe problems. An adolescent schizophrenic boy had been in and out of the mental hospital for several years, and modification of his educational program when he was attending school did not appear to have much relevance to his progress. A boy from an extremely disturbing home situation was able to make some progress with the prescriptive teaching program, but when the child-welfare authority removed him from his home for his protection and placed him in a foster home, his school progress improved greatly.

The traditional approach to mental-health problems places great emphasis on working with parents of disturbed children and predicts little hope for improvement where the parents are not amenable to help. Although prescriptive teaching does not detract from the importance of working with parents and makes every effort to provide or procure help for parents of disturbed children, some most encouraging results have been seen in the achievement of children from homes where the parents have not been able to involve themselves in therapeutic procedures. These families were variously classified by agencies as multi-problem, unreasonable, or hardcore; or the parents as psychotic, severely disturbed, distrustful, hostile, not subscribing to social norms, or incompetent. Some of these families had been approached by and involved with a number of agencies, but the agencies' efforts were apparently of little or no avail. Similarly the attempts of school personnel to work directly with the parents were frequently unproductive of beneficial results. Prescriptive teaching did not, in these cases, directly influence the nature of the social and cultural situation outside the school, but it did recognize the handicapping consequence of the child's social environment when modifying the factors involved in the teaching prescription. In other words, instead of resolving the child's emotional problems through modifying his parents, he was taught by methods which facilitated his learning.

When children from these distressing home situations were assisted in their school progress, two results were observed. The child achieved a more adequate self-concept, increased security, and more independence with which to cope with or withstand the home situation. A second, though less frequent result, was in the constructive change in the parents' approach to the child's difficulty. When the child was making better school progress, there was a concomitant beneficial effect on the parents' concept of the child and themselves, and as a result they were more willing to cooperate with the school. It is not intended that efforts to work more directly with home problems through counseling, social work, or psychiatry should be decreased. However, when a young child is responding negatively because of difficult relationships within the home, treatment which serves to focus his attention on the distressing situation has little chance of achieving positive results.

The prescriptive teaching approach, by providing the teacher with an effective means of teaching disturbed children, bolstered his feelings of competency. This increased confidence reduced his anxiety and contributed to improved interaction in the classroom.

Prescriptive teaching enhanced the teacher's role and gave it status with other professions. The author in his work with agencies outside the schools became aware of the improved status of the teachers in this program in the estimation of members of other professions. Similarly the teachers gained increased status with parents and in the community.

Prescriptive teaching provided an approach which differentiated between what was essentially an educational remedy and other forms of treatment. Differentiation was essential before integration of services could take place. A more satisfactory working relationship was established with the professions involved in the team approach to diagnosis and treatment.

The educational therapy of the prescriptive teaching program was not directed toward solving the underlying unconscious causes of the neurotic symptoms of these children. The aim was to make it possible for the child to tolerate emotional stress and live more comfortably even under difficult conditions. The results of reassessment at the mental-health clinic and psychological follow-up studies at school indicated in some cases that prescriptive teaching is effective in producing profound psychological or personality change but that these changes take considerable time. In most cases the change in behavior is greater than the change in personality, as evaluated by projective tests.

As teachers became aware of the successes achieved, they gave enthusiastic support to the program. Even when the prognosis, based on reports from psychiatric clinics, social agencies, and other schools, was poor, teachers were very willing to work with these children. In terms of acceptance by teachers and principals, the prescriptive teaching program appeared to be favored over other programs with which they had experience.

RECOMMENDATIONS

A system that insists upon all school-age children attending school should also insist that the attendance be profitable to the individual child and therefore to society. Insisting upon attendance of children who fail to learn and who eventually learn that they are incompetent, is insisting on crippling or handicapping children or insisting on mental or physical illness, delinquency, economic dependency, and probably another generation of parental ineptitude. If society insists that children go to school, then society must provide adequate education for every child or be prepared to deal with the consequences.

If schools and the society they serve accept the challenge of providing adequate education for all children, they will also have to accept more fully the concept of individual differences. They must not blame the parents, community, or the influence of peers for educational fail-ures but will instead have to devise a means of providing opportuni-ties for children with difficulties to become successful learners. This book was written for those who accept this challenge. It provides a structure within which this challenge can be accepted and the prob-lems resolved. It provides a system for resolution of problems and illustrates the processes with examples and case studies. These illus-trations are presented as examples and not as substitutes for more intensive study of the references cited.

Prescriptive teaching not only provides the framework for institut-ing a program but also provides examples based upon considerable experience with the program. This experience indicates that the pro-gram can be implemented by the regular staff found in a public school system.

It became apparent that most teachers could be of great help to the emotionally disturbed child if (1) they knew the appropriate ap-proach and methods to use, (2) they could be reasonably consistent, and (3) the other factors under control of the school were modified consistent with the educational relevance of the child's disability.

Prescriptive teaching provided a better opportunity for teachers to be creative in their own right. It helped the teacher to expand his perceptions of his role, as he explored his relationship with the child, through the adaptation of the school to individual differences. He was provided with the basis for a richer and an expanding relationship with the child.

Prescriptive teaching permitted the child to perceive new horizons for himself and aided the maximizing of his potentialities. Through the integrated modification of school variables, prescriptive teaching provided opportunities for the resolution of difficulties, for the re-moval of blocks, and for the perception of reality more fully and completely.

Implementation of a Program

A school psychologist or other guidance worker could begin the imple-mentation of a prescriptive teaching program with the next or any child referred to him. The person with responsibility for coordination of diagnostic resources for the individual child will already be doing many of the things required. A program can be implemented by the present personnel of a large or small school system. It can also be implemented with present resources existing in most school districts. All the possible modifications of the educational program do not have to be made at once. The approach can be adopted and the implementation of the program proceed dependent on the facilities available. The program helps determine needs more realistically. For example, it was found that many children with serious difficulties could benefit from regular class placement when integrated modification of the variables was achieved. The implementation helped determine, more realistically, the special-class needs of the school system.

Starting with the referred child, the coordinator adopting this approach must be determined to see that (1) diagnosis focuses attention on the educational relevance of the disability, (2) communication to the teacher describes the modification of school variables, and (3) the communication circuit is complete.

Prescriptive teaching does not require extensive retraining of personnel. It employs the established competencies of medical, social-work, psychological, and teaching personnel in both diagnosis and treatment. It requires of the coordinator of the program a working knowledge of the methods outlined in Chapter 4 for determining the educational relevance of handicap. It also requires the ability to translate and communicate this knowledge to the teacher, as outlined in Chapter 7. Through these abilities the coordinator can establish the phases of prescriptive teaching. These phases must form a loop wherein each step prescribes the succeeding step. The coordinator, starting with the referred child, must see that the phases of his program follow this loop so that implementation occurs in the classroom and through the other school variables. When this is achieved, he has a prescriptive teaching program for this child. With adequate feedback provided by follow-up, his program maintains its dynamic characteristics which result in progressively better teaching prescriptions.

Starting with this first child, the coordinator may spend considerable time studying the diagnostic findings and relating them to the principle of structure in the learning process so that he understands which modifications should be made. The skills required for this kind of coordination are achieved gradually through practice. It is recommended that the coordinator handle only a few cases to begin with and that they be studied intensively so that many educational possibilities are explored. As the coordinator explores the therapeutic and remedial potential of the school, he will become more proficient and will require less time for each child.

Coordination

A school psychologist, teacher, principal, or guidance counselor with an extensive knowledge of teaching techniques could coordinate the program. The school psychologist's task usually involves giving individual psychological examinations, holding conferences with teachers regarding individuals interviewed, contacting agencies outside of the school, and collaborating with general medical practitioners and psychiatrists. For prescriptive teaching he must be experienced in educational procedures in order to coordinate the planning of the remedial instruction of the child. The school psychologist with an assignment including these responsibilities and with this ability is in an excellent position to implement this approach. An important problem in implementation is the shortage of school psychologists with adequate qualifications in psychological diagnosis, interdisciplinary coordination, and educational practice. Where the school psychologist is not proficient in the area of educational practice, coordination of diagnosis and treatment should be a shared responsibility. The psychologist could coordinate the diagnostic resources in collaboration with the guidance counselor or other educator who would be responsible for coordinating the translation and reporting phase.

A school principal could be the coordinator of a program within his school. The author had experience in a school where this was effective. The principal had to be careful to avoid giving his opinion during the case study because of the influence of his position of authority. He became quite effective at bringing the information together, arranging conferences, and communicating results. In this case the author still did some psychological testing and assisted with translation of diagnosis into pedagogical terms. This increased involvement of the principal as coordinator resulted in more cases being handled in the school without increasing the time of the psychologist and other specialists.

The guidance counselor in a school is in an advantageous position to coordinate and implement a prescriptive teaching program. His training and assignment should be such that collaboration with other specialists within the school system and with community resources is facilitated. The guidance specialist attached to one school should be able to effect more implementation of recommendations than one who only visits the school. Recent development of elementary school guidance programs provides opportunities for wider application of this approach. The author has conducted workshops in this method for counselors in other school districts and was encouraged by the implementation they achieved. If school counselors are to be the coordinators of guidance services within the schools and if guidance is to be a dynamic part of the educational process, then prescriptive teaching methods should be part of counselor training. Recent extensions of guidance services and increased training facilities for counselors suggest increased opportunities for implementing prescriptive teaching.

A teacher who understands the prescriptive teaching approach could bring together the available information about a disturbed child and collaborate with the various diagnostic and treatment resources. With this information he could make a tentative decision regarding the prescription for teaching the child. Using the diagnostic teaching approaches outlined in Chapters 3 and 9, he can determine whether he should continue with the prescription or modify it. In a large urban community with many agencies in the field of child and family health and welfare, a teacher without special training and without time to explore community resources could overlook sources of information or help. In a small community the teacher is more able to know the available resources and coordinate these in the interest of the individual child.

The author has encouraged teachers to attempt diagnosis of learning problems using the diagnostic teaching method. He worked with them as a consultant and observed that they improved their ability to diagnose. Through this method it appeared that they also became more objective in their evaluations of other children. They also made better use of specialized services. It is not recommended that the teacher become the coordinator where a school psychologist or guidance specialist is available, but in some situations where the psychologist's visits are infrequent and where a teacher is motivated to try this method, he should be encouraged to do so. Clearly the teacher is going to do something about the problem child even if he merely attempts to ignore him. Through following the prescriptive teaching approach, he can arrive at a more effective way of promoting normal development.

THE FUTURE

The opportunities under school conditions for preventative and remedial work in mental hygiene are still largely unexplored. Prescriptive teaching offers opportunities for employment of known techniques in an integrated program. It offers opportunities for introduction of new techniques on the basis of a scientific rationale. It still has many subjective aspects which offer opportunities for research while providing a structure within which appropriate criteria can be derived.

Prescriptive teaching is a formulation that is explicit, teachable, and testable and which directs attention to what can be done rather than to the child's irreversible past.

Because outcomes are so dependent on uncontrolled variables, complete proof is not possible in most educational research. It appears, therefore, that in education we shall always find that we are somewhere between states of complete ignorance and complete proof. At some point between these two extremes the responsible person must take a calculated risk and decide to act. We reach a point in the research development of an idea when it becomes more unreasonable not to act than to act on incomplete evidence.

In recommending prescriptive teaching programs, the author is aware that many things have not been definitely proved. The recommendation is based upon experiments, experience, controlled comparisons, and intuitive judgment. It is recommended because it focuses both treatment and research efforts more realistically on the problem of educating the handicapped child. It is recommended because it offers the school psychologist and the teacher unique opportunities to devise, test, and evaluate techniques and to find their own destiny through experience and experiments. Prescriptive teaching is recommended because it is a system which brings about improvement in the treatment of the child, and the improvement in the treatment of the child brings about improvement in the program by providing reinforcements of appropriate modifications.

Because of this dynamic interaction within the prescriptive teaching circuit which brings about ongoing positive change, it is not suggested that the techniques used to illustrate the program are the best possible. The interaction within the program has resulted in discovery of improved techniques, and these techniques have improved the program so that growth is continuous. The wider implementation of prescriptive teaching programs holds the promise of continued improvement for the future.

INDEX

Accelerated class, 174
Acting-out child, 77
Adamson, G. T., 85
Adapted physical education, 83–86
Adaptive behavior, 108, 109
Adjustment through learning, 214
Administration, 88, 89
Advice to parents, 35, 36
Affectionless child, 78
Agencies, auxiliary, 99, 100
Ainsworth, S. H., 125
Allen, Jeremiah M., 194
American Association on Mental Deficiency, 108, 120
American Public Health Association, 48
Ancillary services, 88–91
Andres, Dean C., 3, 5
Aphasia, 135
Approach, consistent, 39, 40, 73–78
Arithmetic instruction, 83
Attitude-consistency study, 73
Automation in industry, 221
Auxiliary agencies, 99, 100

Baker, Harry J., 109
Baldwin, Willie K., 112
Baumgartner, Bernice B., 118
Behavior, adaptive, 108, 109
Bender-Gestalt test, 26
Bettelheim, Bruno, 73
Betts, Emmett A., 80
Big Brothers' Organization, 99
Birch, Jack W., 135
Blatt, B., 112
Bobby, illustrative case no. 2, 174–179
Bower, Eli M., 56, 147, 149, 152, 157
Brain-injured and hyperactive child, 134–140
  central nervous system function, 134–136
  counseling, 141
  cubicles, 145
  educational program, 138–146

Brain-injured and hyperactive child,
  educational therapy, 137
  etiology, 137
  extraneous stimuli, 140
  instruction for, 139
  integrated placement, 142
  perceptual tasks, 139
  physical movement, 136
  regular class, 142
  residential school, 142
  segregation, 142
  social problem, 138
  special class, 142
  special teacher for, 143
  teacher assistant, 143
  teacher directed approach, 139
Brain-injury, 69
Brereton, Beatrice, 87
Brinbrauer, J. S., 119

Cain, Leo F., 116
Carey, Charlotte C., 9
Carlson, Bernice Wells, 128
Carrier, Neil A., 108
Case-study method, 12, 43–45
  purpose of, 44, 45
  school, 45–48
  structure of, 43, 44
Cassidy, Viola M., 125
Causality, knowledge of, 42, 43
Centralization, 19
Cerebral palsy, 135, 179
Child development, 16–23
Child guidance clinic, 160
Children's Apperception Test, 26, 58
Circuit, described, 222
  prescriptive teaching, 12–14, 189, 190
Circuit training, 85
Clarke, D. H., 84
Clarke, David L., 73, 74, 199
Clarke, H. H., 84
Cleugh, M. F., 130
Closure in learning, 38